Managing China's Energy Sector

T0304004

Since China has now become the world's largest energy consumer, its energy sector has understandably huge implications for the global economy. This book examines the transformation of China's conventional and renewable energy sectors, with special attention to state-business relations. Two studies examine the development of China's energy profile, especially China's renewable energy. Two others explore governmental relations with state-owned enterprises (SOEs) and their reform. Despite drastic restructuring in the late 1990s, SOEs continue their oligopolistic control of the oil and gas sectors and even overshadow the stock market. Three studies investigate the factors that help propel the expansion of China's conventional energy firms, as well as those producing renewable energy (i.e. solar PV industry). An analysis of the 25 outward investment deals of China's two largest national oil companies (NOCs) during 2002–2010 suggested that a primarily upstream (exploration and extraction) NOC would seek natural resources in concluding these deals and that an NOC specialized in downstream business (distribution of processed oil products) would mainly go after strategic assets. A study of China's solar PV industry suggests that China's governmental support for it has evolved from subsidising production (a 'mercantile' stage aimed at expanding the industry's global production and export share) to subsidising the demand side (aiming at expanding domestic demand and absorbing redundant manufacture capacity). Another review of this industry finds that firms tend to pay heavy attention to extra-firm institutional network relationships both inside and outside China, and that buyer–supplier networks are influenced by extra-local managerial education. The final chapter compares China's provinces and their embedded carbon-footprints per capita in urban areas from a consumption perspective, using a self-organizing feature map (SOFM) model.

This book was originally published as a special issue of the *Asia Pacific Business Review*.

Hongyi Lai is Associate Professor at the School of Contemporary Chinese Studies, University of Nottingham, UK. His research and journal articles cover China's national and local reform strategies and regional development in China, as well as China's oil diplomacy and the internationalization of its energy firms. His books relate to China's political economy and include *Asian Energy Security: The Maritime Dimension* (2009) and *Reform and the Non-State Economy in China* (2006).

Malcolm Warner is Professor and Fellow Emeritus at Wolfson College and the Judge Business School, University of Cambridge, UK. He was the Editor-in-Chief of the *International Encyclopedia of Business and Management* (IEBM) (2002), and is the author/editor of many books and articles on China. His latest work is entitled *Understanding Management in China: Past, present and future* (2014). He is currently Co-Editor of the *Asia Pacific Business Review*.

Managing China's Energy Sector

Between the market and the state

Edited by
Hongyi Lai and Malcolm Warner

Routledge
Taylor & Francis Group

LONDON AND NEW YORK

First published 2016 by Routledge

2 Park Square, Milton Park, Abingdon, Oxon OX14 4RN
711 Third Avenue, New York, NY 10017, USA

Routledge is an imprint of the Taylor & Francis Group, an informa business

First issued in paperback 2017

Copyright © 2016 Taylor & Francis

British Library Cataloguing in Publication Data
A catalogue record for this book is available from the British Library

ISBN 13: 978-1-138-85828-2 (hbk)
ISBN 13: 978-1-138-08847-4 (pbk)

Typeset in Times New Roman
by RefineCatch Limited, Bungay, Suffolk

Publisher's Note
The publisher accepts responsibility for any inconsistencies that may have
arisen during the conversion of this book from journal articles to book chapters,
namely the possible inclusion of journal terminology.

Disclaimer
Every effort has been made to contact copyright holders for their permission to
reprint material in this book. The publishers would be grateful to hear from any
copyright holder who is not here acknowledged and will undertake to rectify
any errors or omissions in future editions of this book.

Contents

Citation Information

The chapters in this book were originally published in the *Asia Pacific Business Review*, volume 21, issue 1 (January 2015). When citing this material, please use the original page numbering for each article, as follows:

Chapter 1

Managing China's energy sector: between the market and the state
Hongyi Lai and Malcolm Warner
Asia Pacific Business Review, volume 21, issue 1 (January 2015) pp. 1–9

Chapter 2

The role of oil and gas in China's energy strategy: an overview
Elspeth Thomson and Augustin Boey
Asia Pacific Business Review, volume 21, issue 1 (January 2015) pp. 10–25

Chapter 3

China's renewable energy development: policy, industry and business perspectives
Christopher M. Dent
Asia Pacific Business Review, volume 21, issue 1 (January 2015) pp. 26–43

Chapter 4

The Chinese government and the national oil companies (NOCs): who is the principal?
Janet Xuanli Liao
Asia Pacific Business Review, volume 21, issue 1 (January 2015) pp. 44–59

Chapter 5

Corporate governance or governance by corporates? Testing governmentality in the context of China's national oil and petrochemical business groups
Tyler M. Rooker
Asia Pacific Business Review, volume 21, issue 1 (January 2015) pp. 60–76

Chapter 6

Rationale of internationalization of China's national oil companies: seeking natural resources, strategic assets or sectoral specialization?
Hongyi Lai, Sarah O'Hara and Karolina Wysoczanska
Asia Pacific Business Review, volume 21, issue 1 (January 2015) pp. 77–95

Chapter 7

From mercantile strategy to domestic demand stimulation: changes in China's solar PV subsidies
Gang Chen
Asia Pacific Business Review, volume 21, issue 1 (January 2015) pp. 96–112

Chapter 8

Enrolling in global networks and contingencies for China's solar PV industry
Douglas R. Gress
Asia Pacific Business Review, volume 21, issue 1 (January 2015) pp. 113–129

Chapter 9

Regional disparity of embedded carbon footprint and its sources in China: a consumption perspective
Jin Fan, Yanrui Wu, Xiumei Guo, Dingtao Zhao and Dora Marinova
Asia Pacific Business Review, volume 21, issue 1 (January 2015) pp. 130–146

Chapter 10

Conclusion – Transformation of China's energy sector: trends and challenges
Hongyi Lai and Malcolm Warner
Asia Pacific Business Review, volume 21, issue 1 (January 2015) pp. 147–153

Please direct any queries you may have about the citations to
clsuk.permissions@cengage.com

Notes on Contributors

Augustin Boey is an Energy Analyst at the Energy Studies Institute (ESI), National University of Singapore. His current research at ESI includes Asian energy security, transport sector energy efficiency and energy economy modelling. He is currently undertaking a Master of Social Science in Geography at NUS, where his thesis focuses on building efficiency certification schemes and the sustainability of the buildings sector in Singapore.

Gang Chen is a Research Fellow at the East Asian Institute, National University of Singapore. He has published extensively on China's environmental and energy policies. His is the author of *China's Climate Policy* (2012) and *Politics of China's Environmental Protection: Problems and Progress* (2009).

Christopher M. Dent is Professor of East Asia's International Political Economy at the University of Leeds, UK. His latest book, *Renewable Energy in East Asia: Towards a New Development*, was published by Routledge in December 2014. He has acted as a Consultant Advisor to the British, Australian, Chilean, German, Laos PDR and US Governments, as well as the Asian Development Bank, European Commission, ASEAN Secretariat, APEC Secretariat and Nike Inc.

Jin Fan is a Post-Doctoral Fellow at the School of Management in the University of Science and Technology of China, Hefei, China, and his primary research interests are environmental economics, and sustainable development in China.

Douglas R. Gress has lived and worked in Korea for over 20 years. He is currently Associate Professor of Economic Geography in the Department of Geography Education at Seoul National University, South Korea. His research is primarily concerned with the spaces and scales of change generated by globalization processes, particularly the impacts on multi-spatial and multi-actor firm network structures and the geography of innovation in East Asia.

Xiumei Guo is a Lecturer in Curtin University Sustainability Policy Institute, Perth, Australia. Her research covers China's environment, innovation and sustainable development.

Hongyi Lai is Associate Professor at the School of Contemporary Chinese Studies, University of Nottingham, UK. His research and multiple journal articles cover China's national and local reform strategies, regional development in China, as well as China's oil diplomacy and the internationalization of its energy firms. His books relating to China's political economy include *Asian Energy Security: The Maritime Dimension* (2009) and *Reform and the Non-State Economy in China* (2006).

Janet Xuanli Liao is Director of the PhD Programme and Senior Lecturer in International Relations and Energy Security, at the Centre for Energy, Petroleum and Mineral Law and Policy, University of Dundee, UK. Her current research interests include China's energy diplomacy (towards Central Asia, Africa and the Middle East), Sino-Japanese political/energy relations, China's climate change policy and global climate governance, subjects on which she has published widely.

Dora Marinova is Professor of Sustainability at Curtin University Sustainability Policy Institute, Perth, Australia. Her research interests include sustainability, environmental policy and economic development.

Sarah O'Hara is Professor of Geography and Pro-Vice-Chancellor of the University of Nottingham, UK.

Tyler M. Rooker is a Lecturer in Contemporary Chinese Studies at the University of Nottingham, UK, and has Postdoctoral status at the Institute of Sociology and Anthropology at Peking University, China. He has worked in both business and academic circles on China-related issues.

Elspeth Thomson is a Senior Fellow at the Energy Studies Institute, National University of Singapore. Her research interests span Asian energy security, Asian energy economics and energy and the environment. She has published extensively on the various types of energy consumed and traded in Southeast, North and South Asia.

Malcolm Warner is Professor and Fellow Emeritus at Wolfson College, and the Judge Business School, University of Cambridge, UK. He was the Editor-in-Chief of the *International Encyclopedia of Business and Management* (2002), and is the author/editor of many books and articles on China. His latest work is *Understanding Management in China: Past, Present and Future* (2014). He is currently Co-Editor of the *Asia Pacific Business Review*.

Yanrui Wu is Professor of Economics at the Business School, in the University of Western Australia, Perth, Australia. His research interests include Asian economies, environmental policy and economic growth.

Karolina Wysoczanska is a PhD Candidate in the School of Contemporary Chinese Studies, University of Nottingham, UK.

Dingtao Zhao is a Professor at the School of Management in the University of Science and Technology of China, Hefei, China, and his primary research interests are environmental economics, and pollution management in China.

INTRODUCTION

Managing China's energy sector: between the market and the state

Hongyi Lai[a] and Malcolm Warner[b]

[a]School of Contemporary Chinese Studies, University of Nottingham, Nottingham, UK; [b]Judge Business School, University of Cambridge, Cambridge, UK

As China has now become the largest energy consumer in the world, its energy sector has understandably huge domestic and global implications. In this *Special Issue*, which is an interdisciplinary one, comprising a set of eight in-depth empirical studies by leading international experts in the field, we set out to examine the management of the transformation of China's conventional and renewable energy sectors, with special attention to state–business relations and their link to the market.

Introduction

We will here attempt to place the theme of this *Special Issue* on *Managing China's Energy Sector* in its historical and contemporary context, as well as its economic, political and social importance, not only in the People's Republic of China (PRC) and the rest of Asia but also in the wider global economy. The Chinese economy has grown at a relentless rate, around 10% per annum, since the economic reforms were introduced by *Deng Xiaoping* in 1978 (see Warner 2014). As a result, it has become the number-two economic global superpower (see Aoki and Wu 2012). According to a recent World Bank study, China could surpass the USA to be the largest economy in the purchase power parity term in 2014 (*Financial Times*, 2014).

To sum up, as China has now become the largest energy consumer and is viewed by analysts as the largest carbon dioxide (CO_2) emitter and recently the largest net oil importer in the world, its energy sector has understandably huge domestic implications, as well as for the global economy. In this *Special Issue* comprising an introduction, eight empirical studies, all by leading international experts in the field, and a conclusion, we set out to examine the management and transformation of China's conventional and renewable energy (RE) sectors, with special attention to state–business relations and its links to the market. As a start, two studies examine the development of China's energy profile and especially China's RE. They highlight China's massive efforts to promote RE such as hydro, solar, wind and geo-thermal power, as well as cleaner conventional energy sources such as natural gas, in order to reduce pollution and CO_2 emissions. Meanwhile, the authors of these studies acknowledge the continuous predominance of conventional energy sources such as coal and oil in China. Another two studies are devoted to the governmental relations with state-owned enterprises (SOEs) and the reform of these SOEs. Despite drastic restructuring in the late 1990s, these firms continue their oligopolistic control of the oil and gas sectors and even overshadow the stock market. It is found that the government has even failed to act as a 'principal' and keep its 'agents', namely, largest oil and gas state firms, under its control. An analysis of the corporate performance of these firms suggests the limits of the improvement of corporate governance. For example, national oil and petrochemical companies were found to shun external financial markets and supervision and to rely more on ineffectual finance markets during 2007–2011. The next three studies investigate the factors that help propel the expansion of China's conventional energy firms (i.e. oil and gas firms) and firms producing RE technology [i.e. solar photovoltaic (PV) industry]. The analyses of the major international merger and acquisition deals of the two largest oil companies in China suggest that that these companies tend to choose the down-/up-stream sectors that they have specialized in inking of these deals and that strategic assets-seeking has gained increasing significance. A study of Chinese solar PV industry further suggests that China's governmental support for the industry has evolved from subsidizing the production side (a 'mercantile' stage aiming at expanding the industry's global share of production and exports) to subsiding the demand side (aiming at expanding domestic demand and absorbing redundant manufacture capacity). As a result, China could witness an exponential rapid growth in its PV installed capacity in the near future. Another study of Chinese solar PV industry finds that firms in this industry tend to pay high attention to extra-firm institutional network relationships, both within and outside of China and that buyer–supplier networks are spatially influenced by extra-local managerial education. Firms with internationally educated managers in turn tend to have more non-Mainland Chinese managers, circumventing traditional management practices at home. The last empirical study in this *Special Issue* examines the *per capita* embedded carbon footprints (ECFs) in urban China, among Chinese provinces from a consumption perspective, by resorting to a self-organizing feature map (SOFM) model. The research finds that the *per capita* ECF of the east coastal area reaches a high level and that per *capita* disposable income determines ECF.

Contributions

The contributors to this volume, a number of whom are originally of Chinese origin and affiliations, hail from a number of countries across the globe, including Australia, Singapore, South Korea, the UK and so on and from many universities and business schools. The authors are all leading international experts in their fields of study, as they relate to the energy sector policies of the 'Middle Kingdom'.

A set of summaries of the respective contributions to this *Special Issue* follows. They will be set out in the order in which they appear.

In Table 1, we list the titles of the contributions and the topics which will be covered by their respective authors.

The Editors first go on to outline the main topics in this *Special Issue* of the *APBR*. The studies contained all deal with the management of China's energy sector. They all focus on the main strategy in play but at the same time each take a different perspective from the view of the different disciplines or mix of such represented. Summaries of the contributions are presented in the order in which they appear in the Symposium.

Up-front is the contribution by Thomson and Boey (2014) dealing with the role of oil and gas in China's energy strategy. As a general overview, it sets the scene for the many themes raised in this *Special Issue*. These are of enormous importance in the international economy. Like all of the world's geographically large countries, it argues, China is clearly well endowed with energy resources. The Middle Kingdom has large quantities of coal, oil, gas and hydro-power, as well as significant solar, wind and biomass energy potential and even has its own uranium. To date, China has relied for the most part on coal and hydropower to generate its electricity, and on oil to power its transport. However, with

Table 1. Titles, topics and authors of the contributions in this *Special Issue*.

Contribution title	Topic	Authors
The role of oil and gas in China's energy strategy: an overview	Development and diversification of energy profile	Elspeth Thomson and Augustin Boey
China's renewable energy development: policy, industry and business perspectives	Development and pattern of China's RE	Christopher Dent
The Chinese government and the national oil companies (NOCs): who is the principal?	Reform of large national SOEs and SOEs–state relations	Janet Xuanli Liao
Corporate governance or governance by corporates? Testing governmentality in the context of China's national oil and petrochemical business groups	Reform and corporate governance of national SOEs	Tyler Rooker
Rationale of internationalization of China's NOCs: seeking natural resources, strategic assets, or sectoral specialization?	Pattern and rationale of overseas investment of China's major energy firms	Hongyi Lai, Sarah O'Hara, and Karolina Wysoczanska
From mercantile strategy to domestic demand stimulation: changes in China's solar PV subsidies	State subsidies and domestic and international markets of Chinese solar PV industry	Gang Chen
Enrolling in global networks and contingencies for China's solar PV industry	Global networks and expansion of Chinese solar PV industry	Douglas Gress
Regional disparity of embedded carbon footprint and its sources in China: a consumption perspective	Spatial differentiation of per capita ECF in urban China and key determinants	Jin Fan, Yanrui Wu, Xiumei Guo, Dingtao Zhao, and Dora Marinova

'climate change' and its accompanying rising sea levels, increased levels of drought, intense storms, increasing frequencies of heat waves and so on, China, having become the world's largest emitter of CO_2, is under increasing international pressure to re-examine its energy strategy and to find ways to cut its carbon emissions. Most recently, the Copenhagen conference renewed the pressure on it to revise its position. Thus, the government is planning to increase its utilization of natural gas in its power generation as gas emits less than half the CO_2 than coal. The authors argue here that over the next two decades, massive imports of gas via pipeline and LNG tankers, together with the development of unconventional gas reserves in the country, may in part substitute for the huge quantities of coal now being used to generate electricity, but will not likely completely replace them. All this will take time for the national configuration to adjust and change. As for transport-related fuels, China, like all other nations, has little choice but to keep on relying on oil no matter whether it is imported or the PRC builds up its own large-scale shale-oil operations. There appears to be, they continue, no alternative fuel of the same density available at the same or better price. The use of biofuels and electric/hybrid vehicles will not realistically supplant the use of gasoline or diesel. Thus, the role of oil and gas in China's energy strategy, they conclude, are set to remain very critical over the next couple of decades.

3

The insightful contribution by Dent (2014) that follows deals with China's RE development, in terms of policy, industry and business perspectives. It reveals how China has been at the forefront of the recent global expansion of RE activity, an enormous step for a country, which, although it has grown at a relentless pace economically, is still on the road to development. This study examines how the country has achieved its position as the world's largest producer and exporter of RE products, and biggest power generator from renewables. This holds out great prospect for future economic growth. Certainly, this represents a major achievement not only in East Asia but also globally. More specifically, the study explores the main motives pushing forward RE development in China, how this is embedded in broader new development thinking on realising 'ecological civilization' goals as they are described, evolving government policies on strategic planning on renewables, as well as the complex multi-layered landscape of Chinese RE business. Here, various categories of SOEs collaborate and compete among each other, alongside a large number of private companies, especially in equipment manufacturing. All in all, a fascinating complex set of economic and organizational possibilities.

Next, the highly relevant study by Liao (2014) deals with the relationship between the Chinese government and the national oil companies (NOCs) and asks 'who is the principal?'. It sets out to describe how China has conducted six major governmental reforms over the past three decades to separate government functions from the key industries, which brought a number of state-owned NOCs into being in the 1980s, and then listed in the international stock markets in a century after. *Prima facie*, this was a very significant policy initiative. However, due to the incomplete governmental and enterprise reforms, the author argues that the government has not been very successful as the 'principal' to make the NOCs an effective 'agent' to manage China's petroleum industry on its behalf. The study then goes into further detail about the notion of 'principal'. Since it seems unlikely for Beijing to change the ownership of the NOCs, there are two possible options to reinforce the 'principal–agent' relationship. One is to further remove the NOCs' political functions, and to boost China's energy market mechanism. Once there is a better environment for market competitions, she continues, it could be more sensible for the government to cut short its direct intervention in fuel price setting, and in market operations. The other alternative, she argues, is to set up an Energy Ministry that can assert absolute authority over the NOCs, and to manage the whole energy sector via a more coherent and effective incentive system. This incisive piece concludes after looking at these two possible remedies of the state–NOCs relations.

After this, the contribution by Rooker (2014) asks whether there is corporate governance or governance by corporates, testing the governmental logic in the context of China's national oil and petrochemical business groups. Like other industrial sectors with significant – 'pillar' – importance to China's overall economy and development, oil and petrochemicals are governed by state-owned business groups. In this context, 'corporate governance' of these groups is of fundamental interest. This study probes corporate governance of 31 national oil and petrochemical business groups in the PRC by examining their structure, development and business activities over the period from 2007 to 2011. The post-1998 restructuring of China's *qiye jituan* which are business groups like Korean *chaebols*, their related Party transactions and related Party corporate finance all yield insights into how property rights are critical in shaping how corporate governance based on 'governmentality' – or the interrelation of corporate, state and social relations – is effectively structured. This fascinating contribution sheds light on how China's big business policy and governance of the state–business interface works in a 'socialist market' economy. This contribution more broadly clearly has key implications for international trade and investment, as well as multinational corporations doing business with the PRC. It is a useful study for understanding the complexity of the relationships between the partners involved in the above linkages.

The next essay by Lai, O'Hara, and Wysoczanska (2014) on deciding between strategic assets or natural resources focuses on what has been dubbed the 'Going-Out' of China's oil and gas corporations. The bulk of the existing literature, it argues, has emphasized that Chinese companies seek strategic assets (technology, brands and access to markets) through internationalization, mainly in order to overcome late-comers' comparative disadvantage, while some studies they suggest that these firms sought natural resources to address China's rising oil imports. The third argument (which they coin the 'sectoral strength' hypothesis) suggested that the up-stream firms in extractive business would seek natural resources and good infrastructure, whereas down-stream firms would seek strategic assets and efficiency. In this article, the authors look in depth at the rationale of main overseas investment deals ('going out') of China's two largest NOCs during 2002–2010 which were also the top two non-financial outward investing Chinese firms in 2010. They conclude that these deals can be best explained by the 'sectoral specialization' hypothesis, supplemented with a consideration for strategic assets.

The study by Chen (2014) which follows looks at the switch from what the authors call the mercantile strategy to domestic demand stimulation, dealing with changes in China's solar PV subsidies. Through looking in depth at China's industrial subsidies towards its solar PV sector from a theoretical perspective constructed by the renowned Harvard-based strategic thinker, Michael Porter, on the government's role in forging national comparative advantages, this important contribution attempts to take a snapshot of the recent dynamics in China's state capitalism, which has been evolving from a mercantile stage in which most subsidies were designed to influence factor conditions and supporting industries, on to a new phase of domestic demand with more subsidies aimed at reshaping domestic demand conditions to absorb redundant manufacture capacity. China has lately emerged as the world's largest solar panel producer, but, compared to its fast-expanding wind power market that has many advantages in attracting policy support, China's domestic solar PV market has been underdeveloped and has been unable to absorb a sizeable element of its inflated production capacity. Empirical pieces of evidence have shown that, in sync with the state's recent policy shift to domestic demand from export-orientated mercantile strategy, the government's role in supporting the solar PV industry has been transforming from subsidizing the production side to subsiding the demand side. As solar PV power generation is fast coming to the breaking point of grid parity with existing subsidies and feed-in tariffs, China could soon see its PV installed capacity expand exponentially in the coming future. This is a useful piece which adds to knowledge in the field.

Next, the contribution by Gress (2014) deals with the issue of firms' 'enrolling' in global networks and how this may impact broader contingencies related to firm activity in the solar industry of the PRC. More specifically, this contribution tests the contention in the Asian business systems literature that interacting with global managers and increasing experience via international education are possible ways by which Asian firms enrol in global networks, thus potentially leading to changes in their broader network contingencies. Solar PV firms are examined in the study given the competitiveness of Chinese products in the global marketplace and the importance being placed on solar energy domestically as China confronts increasing pressure to better look after its environment and control pollution, whilst at the same time accommodating mounting energy needs. The upshot of the contribution suggests that an emphasis on extra-firm institutional network relationships, both within and outside of China, for all players is characteristic of a bourgeoning energy sector. A unique result, the research also finds, is that buyer–supplier networks are spatially influenced by extra-local managerial education. Enrolling in wider networks, Gress (2014) concludes, is also important in this context, as firms with internationally educated managers have more non-Mainland Chinese managers, which may mitigate traditional management practices at home. All in all, this proves to be a most insightful contribution.

The final empirical study by Fan et al. (Wu et al. 2014) examines in depth the theme of regional disparity of ECF and its sources in China from the consumption perspective. Carbon emission reduction could, the authors argue, be achieved through extensive cooperation between relevant groups such as businesses, governments and consumers. Overall, they continue, carbon emissions stem from consumer behaviour. To effectively deal with the increasingly serious energy crisis and climate change in China, it is thus critical to control carbon emissions generated by the country's urban consumers. From a consumption perspective, as the authors put it, they utilize a SOFM model to analyse the spatial differentiation of per capita ECF in urban China. The researchers found that the 'spatial differentiation' has been shown to be significant with the per capita ECF of the east coastal area at a high level and that per capita disposable income is the key factor affecting ECF. Based on these findings, they conclude, potential business opportunities to develop low-carbon products may be considered.

Last, the Editors of this *Special Issue* offer their concluding remarks concerning the upshot of the research published here. They then go on to evaluate the findings the authors have, respectively, put forward, in the light of the central themes of this Issue.

Discussion

The theme of 'global warming' is the most general of dimensions to take into account in concentrating one's mind of the issues we present here, as is also the growing pollution to be witnessed across the nation which has now become a 'negative' charge of China's growth. Since potential constraints on economic growth *per se* for China may occur when constraints on energy supplies occur, this aspect is another key one to emphasize in this review of the topic.

It will be seen that the above contributions each pinpoint relevant connections to the above generalities in this *Special Issue*, to focus it on the managing of China's energy sector. The studies look at, respectively, economic, political, strategic, as well as structural dimensions in particular detail, relating it to policy. They provide the much-needed insights on three topics, namely, the economic and corporate development of the energy sector, domestic energy policies and energy security in China.

There has been a limited yet growing literature on these three topics. Regarding the first aforementioned topic, namely, the development of the energy sector in China, several existing studies, which tend to be comprehensive and historically based, document the history of the reform of state energy firms, the growth of the energy sector in the pre-reform era, the transformation of the energy sector since 1978, the role of energy in economic growth, energy demand and supply, and profile of China's energy (IEA 2007; Andrews-Speed 2012). There was also an unusual but valuable study on the change in corporate governance of China's major energy firms compared to the major international counterparts (Zhang 2004). A second set of studies under this first category also take a closer look at the evolution, domestic reserves, geographic bases and import sources of oil and gas (Leung, Li, and Low 2011; O'Hara and Lai 2011) as well as the development and prospects of nuclear energy (Thomson 2011). A third set of studies, which are frequently conducted, tend to be econometric in nature and explore the factors that affect energy consumption, efficiency and structure in China's energy consumption (Kahrl and Roland-Holst 2009; Yuan et al. 2008; Ma, Oxley, and Gibson 2009).

Regarding the second aforementioned topic, i.e. energy policies, the existing literature surveys the governance of energy, including institutions, policy-making process, and regulation of the energy sector and the governmental reform of state energy firms in the recent decades (Kong 2010, 1–28; Andrews-Speed 2012; Andrews-Speed and Dannreuther 2011, 26–62, 97–112; Lin 2008). Studies on the third topic, namely, energy security in China, focus on oil and gas, the main energy resources that China heavily imports. These studies examine the formulation of China's international energy policy (Kong 2010, 29–60, 141–160; Andrews-Speed and Dannreuther 2011, 26–62, 97–112), China's energy diplomacy, strategic responses and international implications (Lai 2007; Kong 2010, 141–160; Zhao 2012), as well as specific issues such as overland and sea lane imports of Chinese energy sources and diplomatic and security implications (Downs 2006; Lai 2009). Though rich in empirical and historical analyses, there is an apparent lack of theoretical pursuit and tests in most of the existing literature.

The studies in this *Special Issue* make three following contributions to the existing literature. First, a number of these studies employ a hypothesis-testing approach and aim to provide rigorous analysis of the empirical data and evidence. In developing the hypotheses, relevant theories are examined and applied to the Chinese energy sector. This attempt to apply theories to Chinese energy sector is particularly evident in the studies by Lai, O'hara and Wysoczanska (2014), Rooker (2014), Gress (2014), as well as those by Chen (2014) and Liao (2014). Lai, O'Hara, and Wysoczanska (2014) scrutinize the validity of theories on internationalization of firms from developing countries and find that sectoral strengths and to a lesser extent strategic assets seeking best explain major overseas investment of Chinese oil and gas firms. Next, Liao (2014) applies the principal-agent model to the interaction between the government and national energy firms and argues that the government has yet to become an effective principal. Their analyses and findings help advance the knowledge on the relevance of business theories for the Chinese energy sector. Rooker (2014), who casts his study in the theoretical context of corporate governance and state–business relations, cautions us against a rushed declaration of either an outright victory of marketization or a simple continuation of the command economy in China. Chen (2014), who takes up again the topic of state capitalism covered by Rooker (2014), examines the role of the state in producing competitive advantage, a concept critical in business theories, for Chinese solar PV firms at different stages of the development of these firms. Gress (2014) turns our attention to the role of local and global networks, another important concept in business studies, in the expansion of Chinese solar PV firms.

Second, a number of these studies in this *Special Issue* take into account the rapidly changing dynamics of energy in China in light of the global concerns with carbon emission and pollution in the recent decade. They investigate the prospects and transformation of Chinese energy sector towards a sustainable path of development. Evident examples include studies by Dent (2014) and by Thomson and Boey (2014) which survey the rapid growth of RE and policy in this regard, by Wu et al. (2014), which examine carbon footprints across Chinese provinces and the underlying factors, as well as studies by Chen (2014) and Gress (2014), which examine the factors that contribute to the global ascent of Chinese solar industry.

Third, these studies try to capture recent developments in Chinese energy sector and important features of Chinese energy sector, mostly notably, the increasingly internationalization of the sector and growing linkages and networks of Chinese energy firms with global counterparts. Studies reflecting this last feature include Gress (2014), who studies the global networks of Chinese solar panel manufacturers, Lai, O'Hara, and Wysoczanska (2014), who shed light on the rationale of major overseas investment deals of the two largest Chinese oil and gas firms, and Chen (2014) who investigates the role of governmental subsidies in the evolution of Chinese solar PV industry.

Concluding remarks

It is therefore clear from the above discussion that China plays a pivotal role in the world global energy economy. As the implications of global warming sink in, the importance of what the PRC government does becomes more and more important. We hope that the readers of this *Special Issue* will find enough in the above-cited research to enhance their understanding of what is at stake.

References

Andrews-Speed, P. 2012. *The Governance of Energy in China: Transition to a Low-Carbon Economy*. Houndmills: Palgrave Macmillan.

Andrews-Speed, P., and R. Dannreuther. 2011. *China, Oil and Global Politics*. London: Routledge.

Aoki, M., and J. Wu. 2012. *The Chinese Economy: A New Transition*. London: Palgrave Macmillan.

Chen, G. 2014. "From Mercantile Strategy to Domestic Demand Stimulation: Changes in China's Solar PV Subsidies." *Asia-Pacific Business Review*.

Financial Times. 2014. "China Poised to Pass US as World's Leading Economic Power This Year." *Financial Times*. Accessed April 30. http://www.ft.com/cms/s/0/d79ffff8-cfb7-11e3-9b2b-00144feabdc0.html#ixzz34tjrqtYL

Dent, C. 2014. "China's Renewable Energy Development: Policy, Industry and Business Perspectives." *Asia-Pacific Business Review*.

Downs, E. 2006. *China's Quest for Energy Security*. Santa Monica, CA: Rank Corporation.

Fan, J., Y. Wu, X. Guo, D. Zhao, and D. Marinova. 2014. "Regional Disparity of Embedded Carbon Footprint and Its Sources in China: A Consumption Perspective." *Asia-Pacific Business Review*.

Gress, D. 2014. "Enrolling in Global Networks and Contingencies for China's Solar PV Industry." *Asia-Pacific Business Review*.

IEA (International Energy Agency). 2007. *World Energy Outlook 2007: China and India Insights*. Paris: OECD.

Kahrl, F., and D. Roland-Holst. 2009. "Growth and Structural Change in China's Energy Economy." *Energy* 34: 894–903.

Kong, B. 2010. *China's International Petroleum Policy*. Santa Barbara, CA: ABC-CLIO.

Lai, H. H. 2007. "China's Oil Diplomacy: Is It a Global Security Threat?" *Third World Quarterly* 28 (3): 519–538.

Lai, H. 2009. "Security of China's Energy Imports." In *Asian Energy Security: The Maritime Dimension*, edited by H. Lai, 49–77. New York: Palgrave Macmillan.

Lai, H., S. O'Hara, and K. Wysoczanska. 2014. "Rationale of internationalisation of China's NOCs: Seeking Natural Resources, Strategic Assets, or Sectoral Specialization?" *Asia-Pacific Business Review*.

Leung, G., R. Li, and M. Low. 2011. "Transitions in China's Oil Economy, 1990–2010." *Eurasian Geography and Economics* LII (4): 483–500.

Liao, J. X. 2014. "The Chinese Government and the National Oil Companies (NOCs): Who Is the Principal?" *Asia-Pacific Business Review*.

Lin, K. C. 2008. "Macroeconomic Disequilibria and Enterprise Reform: Restructuring the Chinese Oil and Petrochemical Industries in the 1990s." *The China Journal* 60: 49–79.

Ma, H., L. Oxley, and J. Gibson. 2009. "Substitution Possibilities and Determinants of Energy Intensity for China." *Energy Policy* 37: 1793–1804.

O'Hara, S., and H. Lai. 2011. "China's 'Dash for Gas': Challenges and Potential Impacts on Global Market." *Eurasian Geography and Economics* LII (4): 501–522.

Rooker, T. 2014. "Corporate Governance or Governance by Corporates? Testing Governmentality in the Context of China's National Oil and Petrochemical Business Groups." *Asia-Pacific Business Review*.

Thomson, E. 2011. "China's Nuclear Energy in Light of the Disaster in Japan." *Eurasian Geography and Economics* LII (4): 464–482.

Thomson, E., and A. Boey. 2014. "The Role of Oil and Gas in China's Energy Strategy: An Overview." *Asia-Pacific Business Review*.

Warner, M. 2014. *Understanding Management in China: Past, Present and Future*. London: Routledge.

Yuan, J.-H., J.-G. Kang, C.-H. Zhao, and Z.-G. Hu. 2008. "Energy Consumption and Economic Growth: Evidence from China at Both Aggregated and Disaggregated Levels." *Energy Economics* 30: 3077–3094.

Zhang, J. 2004. *Catch-up and Competitiveness in China: The Case of Large Firms in the Oil Industry*. London: Routledge.

Zhao, S., ed. 2012. *China's Search for Energy Security: Domestic Sources and International Implications*. London: Routledge.

The role of oil and gas in China's energy strategy: an overview

Elspeth Thomson and Augustin Boey

Energy Studies Institute, National University of Singapore

China is well endowed with energy resources, having large quantities of coal, oil, gas and hydropower, as well as tremendous solar, wind and biomass energy potential. It even has its own uranium. To date, the country has relied mainly on coal and hydropower to generate its electricity and on oil to power its vehicles. However, with climate change and consequent rising sea levels, increased incidence of drought, intense storms, etc., China, having become the world's largest emitter of CO_2, is under strong international pressure to re-examine its energy strategy and find ways to reduce its carbon emissions. Thus, the government plans to greatly increase its use of natural gas in power generation. Gas emits less than half the CO_2 that coal emits. It is argued here that over the next 20 years, massive imports of gas via pipeline and liquefied natural gas tankers, combined with the development of unconventional gas reserves in the country may partly substitute for the large quantities of coal currently being used to generate electricity, but will not likely completely replace them. As for transport fuels, China, like all other countries, has little choice but to continue relying on oil regardless of whether it is imported or China develops its own large-scale shale oil operations. There is no alternate fuel of the same density available at the same or better price. The use of biofuels and electric/hybrid vehicles will not supplant the use of gasoline or diesel in the near future. Thus, the role of oil and gas in China's energy strategy are set to remain very significant over the next 20 years.

Introduction

For decades, two factors have made the use of conventional oil and gas problematic for most countries. One is the fact that they are finite resources. The other is the fact that some of the largest deposits are found in parts of the world which are politically unstable. Government planners from around the world have long worried, in the short run, about supply disruptions, and in the long run, about what will eventually replace oil and gas when they become prohibitively expensive to extract either onshore or off.

Up to the early 1990s, China had prided itself on being self-sufficient in oil, but when it became a net importer in 1993, it began to share other countries' worries about security of supplies. As for natural gas, because the country was so well endowed with coal with which to generate electricity, the government did not initially agonize over gas imports. This changed, however in the early 2000s, when scientists seemed to become more certain about a connection between carbon emissions and climate change. As the world's largest consumer of coal, China came under immediate pressure to try to reduce its emissions. One way was to use more gas and less coal to generate electricity. Thus today, a third factor which makes the use of oil and gas problematic for most countries, especially China, is the increasing manifestations of climate change afflicting the Earth, and the belief that the emissions of carbon resulting from the use of fossil fuels are the main cause.

Research questions

In recent years, China's use of energy has received much worldwide attention. On the one hand, China's global pursuit of oil and gas supplies has been extensively discussed by economists and geopolitical analysts. On the other, the country's status as the world's largest carbon emitter has become a focal point in climate change mitigation debates. This overview asks the following research questions: Over the next 20 years, will the dominant role of oil in China's transportation fuel mix decrease? And in the country's electricity generation mix, will the rapid growth of the use of natural gas in recent years begin to falter over the next 20 years? The study begins by describing the current roles of oil and gas in the electron diet, then examines their outlook, relative to the other means of electricity generation, over the next approximately 20 years. The 'electron diet' refers to the provision of electricity for lighting, heating/cooling, running machines in homes, businesses and industry, etc. This is followed by an analysis of the mobility diet – the provision of fuels to power land, water and air transport – and the changing roles of oil and gas, vis-à-vis the other transport fuel options. Next, the over-riding concerns about the use of oil and gas – the security of supplies and delivery and climate change goals – are discussed. The conclusion is clear: the key role of oil and gas in China's energy strategy is not going to change a great deal in the near future.

Research method

The research draws on longitudinal academic studies of China's oil and gas sector, such as Tatsu Kambara and Christopher Howe's *China and the Global Energy Crisis: Development and Prospects for China's Oil and Natural Gas* (2008) and Philip Andrew-Speed's *China, Oil and Global Politics* (2011), as well as current reports written by professional analysts at think tanks such as the Lawrence Berkeley National Library, The Brookings Institution, Center for Strategic and International Studies, Oxford Institute for Energy Studies, IFP Energies nouvelles, Eidgenössische Technische Hochschule Zürich, etc. Most importantly, the authors examined the future energy mix scenario modelling of many organizations and scholars, including those of the International Energy Agency, Shell, Exxon, British Petroleum and dozens of academic researchers based not only in China but around the world.

Findings

Oil and gas in China's electricity generation mix today

China has made remarkable progress in providing electricity to its citizens since the reform and opening up programme in the late 1970s. Today, less than 1% of the country's 1.3 billion population, or about 8 million people, living mainly in very remote areas, still have no power. This is a tremendous achievement, considering that there are yet over 600 million people throughout the rest of Asia who still have no power (OECD iLibrary 2011). The main problem that China now faces in providing electricity is the very large carbon emissions that this sector generates. The country is making very impressive efforts to mitigate these, but the dominant role of coal will not change in the near future. Table 1 puts China's breakdown of electricity generation by source for 2009 into Asian perspective. Coal clearly dominates at 78.8% (whereas worldwide, the share of coal averages 40%). The next largest source is hydropower at 16.7%. The share of gas is a mere 1.4%.

Over the past decade, like most countries, China has been rapidly phasing out its use of oil in power generation. Its share in the electricity generation mix fell from 3.3% in

Table 1. China's Breakdown of Electricity Generation by Type in Perspective (2009)

	Coal and Peat	Oil	Gas	Biofuels	Waste	Nuclear	Hydro	Geo-thermal	Solar PV & Thermal	Wind & Tide	Other Sources
ASEAN	26.1	9.1	49.1	1.0	neg		11.4	3.2	neg	neg	neg
Brunei		1.0	99.0								
Cambodia		95.6		0.5			3.9				
Indonesia	41.8	22.8	22.1				7.3	6.0			
Malaysia	30.9	2.0	60.7				6.3				
Myanmar		8.9	19.6				71.5				
Philippines	26.6	8.7	32.1				15.8	16.7	neg	0.1	
Thailand	19.9	0.5	70.7	4.0			4.8	neg	neg	neg	
Singapore		18.8	81.0		0.2						
Vietnam	18.0	2.5	43.4				36.0				
Northeast Asia	64.9	2.5	8.3	0.3	0.2	9.9	13.1	0.1	0.1	0.6	neg
China	**78.8**	**0.4**	**1.4**	**0.1**		**1.9**	**16.7**	**neg**	**neg**	**0.7**	**neg**
South Korea	46.0	4.4	15.5	0.1		32.5	1.2	neg	0.1	0.2	neg
Japan (pre-Fukushima)	26.7	8.7	27.2	1.3	0.7	26.7	7.8	0.3	0.3	0.3	
Taiwan	53.9	3.8	19.3	0.2	1.3	18.1	3.1	0.3	neg	0.3	
Rest of World	36.5	5.7	22.4	1.3	0.4	14.8	16.8	0.3	0.1	1.6	0.1
OECD Americas	39.7	2.3	22.1	1.2	0.4	18.2	14.0	0.5	0.1	1.6	neg
EU-27	26.5	3.0	22.6	2.9	1.0	27.9	11.2	0.2	0.4	4.1	0.3
Latin America	2.0	12.5	13.6	3.1		2.1	66.2	0.3	neg	0.2	neg
Africa	39.5	12.5	29.3	0.1		2.0	16.0	0.2	neg	0.3	neg
Middle East	0.1	40.5	57.7	neg			1.8			neg	
World	40.3	5.1	21.4	1.1	0.4	13.4	16.5	0.3	0.1	1.4	0.1

Source: Calculated from International Energy Agency website: http://www.iea.org/stats/prodresult.asp?PRODUCT=Electricity/Heat;
Note: "neg" means negligible. Totals may not amount exactly to 100 due to rounding.

2000 to 0.4% in 2009 (OECD iLibrary 2011). In absolute terms, the amount of electricity produced from oil in China shrank from 46,280 GWh in 2000 to 1663 GWh in 2009. Oil costs more than coal or gas, and it has high carbon emissions. Moreover, as there are no substitutes for oil in the transport sector, almost all available oil is used in that sector instead. Of the oil which is still used in the power sector, most is in the form of diesel to fire generators. These play an indispensable role for some businesses and government services when power cuts occur. The country suffered massive power cuts in 2004 (Thomson 2005). Typically each year, there are rolling blackouts in various parts of the country, but their duration has been becoming much shorter. As a developing country, power outages are still a fact of life but compared to other countries, China's power infrastructure – plants, transmission and distribution – has been quite secure.[1]

Between 2000 and 2009, the share of natural gas in China's electricity generation mix held steady between one and two percent (OECD iLibrary 2011). While low in percentage terms, in absolute terms – from 17,997 GWh in 2000 to 62,005 GWh in 2009 – the reality is that in the space of just one decade, China's use of gas in the power sector almost trebled (see Figure 1). Imports of natural gas grew from 2450 ktoe in 2000 to 16250 ktoe in 2010, i.e. at a compound annual growth rate of 18.8%.

Oil and gas in China's electricity generation mix over the next two decades

The International Energy Agency (IEA) has formulated three energy scenarios: 'Current Policies', 'New Policies' and '450'.[2] The Current Policies Scenario assumes no changes in policies from the mid-point of the year of publication (previously called the Reference Scenario). The New Policies Scenario takes account of broad policy commitments and plans that have been announced by countries, including national pledges to reduce greenhouse gas emissions and plans to phase out fossil-energy subsidies, even if the measures to implement these commitments have yet to be identified or announced. The 450 Scenario sets out an energy pathway consistent with the goal of limiting the global increase in temperature to 2°C by limiting concentration of greenhouse gases in the atmosphere to around 450 parts per million of CO_2. The relative shares of coal, oil, gas,

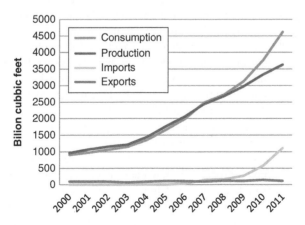

Figure 1. China's gas production, consumption, exports and imports, 2000–2011. *Source:* Drawn by the authors from EIA, n.d. International Energy Statistics [WWW Document]. URL http://www. eia.gov/countries/data.cfm (Accessed August 28, 2013).

Table 2. IEA Scenarios for China's Power Generation Mix to 2035 (%)

	2010	Current Policy Scenario	New Policies Scenario	450 Scenario
Coal	78	66	55	23
Oil	0	0	0	0
Gas	2	6	8	12
Nuclear	2	8	10	20
Hydro	17	11	14	18
Biomass and waste	0	2	3	6
Other renewables	1	6	11	21

Source: IEA, World Energy Outlook 2012 (Paris: OECD/IEA), pp. 620–1.
Note: See the text for explication of the scenarios.

nuclear, hydro, biomass and waste and other renewables used for electricity generation in China under these three scenarios up to the year 2035 are presented in Table 2.

Over the next two decades, no matter which scenario, apart from the continued use of back-up generators, the use of oil in China's power sector will be eliminated completely. Coal will by far remain the main fuel used. In the Current Policies Scenario, the share of coal will be 66% in 2035. In the New Policies Scenario, it will be 55% and in the 450 Scenario, 23%. China has no option but to rely heavily on coal. It is the cheapest, most available and easiest option. The main drawback of China's heavy dependence on coal is the heavy emissions of carbon and sulphur and nitrogen oxides. The country's coal consumption and use of outdated power plant technologies has contributed to China's becoming the world's largest emitter of CO_2 and also the world's leading emitter of coalmine methane (Yang 2009). Another serious disadvantage of relying so heavily on coal is the number of deaths in the mines. Between 2000 and 2010, more than 47,000 miners died in coal mining accidents(Moore 2011).

According to all three scenarios, the next largest source of electricity will be nuclear. In the Current Policies Scenario, the share of nuclear will be 8% in 2035. In the New Policies Scenario, it will be 10% and in the 450 Scenario, 20%. The increasing role of nuclear power in China's electricity generation supply can be attributed to a few factors. Amongst them is the need to mitigate greenhouse gas emissions. China aims to reduce its ratio of GDP from carbon dioxide emissions by 40–45% between 2005 and 2020. Energy security also plays an important role in the government's quest for nuclear power. China has made it a long-term energy policy objective to use domestic resources and generating capacity to meet 90% of its energy demand (Yun 2010). Nuclear power contributes towards building a more diversified energy base and also slows the depletion rate of indigenous non-renewable fossil fuels. Ambitious nuclear expansion goals are underway, with 25 reactors under construction in 2011, or half of the new projects worldwide, to fulfil the energy targets in China's latest (12th) Five-Year Plan.

China's nuclear expansion programme was temporarily put on hold after the 2011 Fukushima disaster in Japan so that that Chinese reactor construction and operation, as well as nuclear safety standards and emergency procedures could be reviewed. This moratorium on the approval process for new nuclear projects was removed in June 2012 after the review was completed and the Chinese cabinet approved a new 2020 Nuclear Safety Strategy (AFP 2012). The country is now aiming to have 60 GW of nuclear capacity in 2020, down from the previous target of 86 GW by 2020. The authorities have indicated that some of the country's reactors require upgrades to meet the new safety standards, including the need for flood-safety and seismic-related retrofits (Hook 2012).

China's nuclear power programme also faces some fundamental long-term issues. There is a labour shortage constraining China's nuclear power programme, specifically a lack of trained nuclear technicians to support its growth (Xu 2014). Globally, the issue of spent fuel disposal also remains to be resolved. It is estimated that China's nuclear power industry produced about 600 tons of used fuel in 2010 and will produce 1000 tons in 2020 (World Nuclear Association 2011). As in most other countries with nuclear power plants, the used fuel at China's nuclear power plants is stored at the reactor sites and/or permanent, deep geological storage sites.

As a percentage share of total electricity generated, the future role of gas looks rather limited. But in actual terms, the planned increases are staggering. According to one estimate, China will import 66 mtoe of natural gas in 2030 (Rout et al. 2011), which is more than four times the amount imported in 2010. Thereafter, the imports are forecast to more than double from 166 mtoe in 2050 to 207 mtoe in 2100. In the IEA's Current Policies Scenario, the share of gas in total electricity generation will be 6% in 2035. In the New Policies Scenario, it will be 8% and in the 450 Scenario, 12%. Gas is relatively cheap and it is also relatively easy to build gas-fired plants. Most importantly, gas emits a quarter to half the amount of carbon dioxide that coal does. In the 1980s and 1990s, after extensive exploration, it was determined that China's reserves of conventional natural gas are small, falling way short of demand. Thus, the government embarked on the construction of pipelines to bring in imports from the west (Central Asia), the south (Myanmar) and the north (Russia). China is also building several liquefied natural gas (LNG) terminals. From an energy security point of view, these rate highly because there are many places from which the gas can be shipped apart from the Middle East. Also, the cost of building these terminals has dropped sharply in recent years.

Also, quite recently, with the remarkable success of hydraulic fracturing, or 'fracking', in the United States, the Chinese government has similarly launched ambitious plans to develop its shale gas reserves. According to the First Five-Year Plan for Shale Gas Development, released in 2012, unconventional gas is targeted to contribute 6.5 billion cubic meters to the country's annual gas production by 2015, which is around 2–3% of the projected national gas production in 2015 (Hook 2012) and 60 billion cubic meters by 2020 (China's Shale Gas Subsidies Underpin Expansion of Gas Generation). It is believed that China has the largest shale gas reserves in the world, although commercial production has yet to commence due to the challenges presented by China's unique geology and water shortages. Fracking is associated in some places with water contamination and subsidence.

The next largest source of electricity will be hydropower. In the IEA's Current Policies Scenario, the share of hydro will be 11% in 2035. In the New Policies Scenario, it will be 14% and in the 450 Scenario, 18%. China has the world's largest hydropower potential, but only approximately 40% of this, or around 400 GW, is currently economically exploitable (Crompton and Wu 2005). Also, the main sources of hydropower are in the country's western areas, too distant from where the power is needed. The reliability of hydroelectricity is also dependant on normal precipitation patterns. However, in recent years, likely related to global warming, the country has suffered from severe droughts. In 2011, a drought caused power shortages in central and eastern China when the water levels at several hydropower dams, including the Three Gorges Dam, fell below the threshold for full power generation (Qiu 2011). The Three Gorges Dam was also blamed for exacerbating water supply problems downstream during the 2011 drought.

While hydropower is usually considered a clean energy source, dam construction projects can cause ecological and social damage. For instance, the construction of the Three Gorges Dam entailed the creation of a 1080-km^2 reservoir that displaced over a million people and submerged around 500 urban settlements (Stone 2011). The construction of the dam also had negative impacts on the local ecosystems. Most obviously, the previously terrestrial ecosystems were entirely converted to aquatic ones, causing a loss of terrestrial biodiversity through the flooding and fragmentation of ecosystems. The biodiversity of aquatic species has also been affected by the inundation, especially fish species, such as the Chinese sturgeon and Chinese river dolphin, due to the disruption of their migratory paths and loss of spawning grounds due to the damming (Zhang and Lou 2011).

Over the next two decades, China will use more renewable energy. Obviously, it is in the IEA's 450 Scenario that the various forms of renewable energy have the greatest representation, 6% from 'biomass and waste' and 21% from 'other renewable'. In the Current Scenario, these are 2% and 6%, respectively, while in the New Policies Scenario, they are 3% and 11%. China has large amounts of wind power potential, particularly in the coastal southern regions and the western regions. In these windy areas, wind power has become economically competitive and has received significant investment. Strong policy and financial incentives have been successful in spurring this sector's development. However, the entrepreneurial land-grab by wind farm companies for sites with abundant wind resources has often outstripped the pace of the government's provision of energy distribution infrastructure and associated regulatory and support systems (Yu and Qu 2010). Therefore, many wind farms have yet to be connected to the main grid and are becoming economically unviable due the fact that proper feasibility studies were not conducted before they were constructed.

Due to the large size of the country, China receives a substantial amount of solar energy, but its development is somewhat constrained by technical and economic barriers (Dinçer 2011). Solar PV is currently an expensive means of producing electricity in China in relation to the cost of electricity produced from coal. In 2010, the cost of solar power was about ten times as much (Liu et al. 2011), but the difference is narrowing and the Chinese government has announced plans to have 1.8 GW by 2020 and 1000 GW by 2050 (Dinçer 2011). The Chinese Electric Power Research Institute has forecast that solar PV will account for 5% of the total electricity generation capacity by 2050. The solar PV manufacturing industry has been developing rapidly over the past decade, and turned out more than 1200 MW of solar PV in 2007, making China the largest producer in the world (Dinçer 2011).

Oil and gas in China's transport fuel mix today

Like almost everywhere else in the world, oil, or more precisely, oil products, account for almost all the fuel used in China's transport sector. The reason is that to date there is no alternative fuel of the same density, available at the same price or at a lower price. Over the past 20 years, governments around the world have been trying to develop superior biofuels and also electric/hybrid cars, but there are yet many problems to be overcome before large numbers of consumers will want to buy them.

China's demand for oil has been growing very rapidly over the past decade. In 2010, China consumed 9.2 million barrels of oil per day (mb/d), a 400% increase from the 2.3 mb/d in 1990. The country is still a major producer of oil, but became a net importer in 1993. Demand far outstrips supply (see Figure 2) and China now imports about 50% of its oil requirements.

At present, relatively small amounts of natural gas are used in China's transport sector. The main problems are the higher cost of vehicles designed to run on gas, and the dearth of refuelling stations. A large number of taxis operate on gas, but most private vehicles do not. At the end of 2010, there were only about 1000 stations in some 80 cities across China that offered compressed natural gas (CNG) or LNG (Perkowski 2012). Most of these are concentrated in Shanghai, Chengdu, Xi'an, Chongqing Xinjiang and Hebei. In 2010, about

60 natural gas vehicle manufacturers produced over 150,000 natural gas-powered vehicles, and the production capacity of some 20 engine manufacturers was 1.0 million units per year.

Oil and gas in China's transport fuel mix over the next two decades

Oil

The demand for energy in China's transport sector is expected to soar over the next two decades. It is estimated that the country's vehicle population will rise from 16 vehicles per 1000 population in 2002 to 269 vehicles per 1000 population in 2030. For perspective, the world average is expected to be 254 vehicles per 1000 population by 2030 (Dargay, Gately, and Sommer 2007). China's transport sector will remain almost completely dependent on oil products. Widespread use of biofuels and electric/hybrid vehicles is not expected. Table 3 delineates the IEA's three scenarios for the transport sector. Under the Current Scenario, oil will account for 91% of all the transport fuels used in 2035. Under the New Policies Scenario it will account for 89% and in the 450 Scenario, 82%.

Table 3.   IEA Scenarios for China's Transport Fuel Mix to 2035 (%)

	2010	Current Policy Scenario	New Policies Scenario	450 Scenario
Oil	92	91	89	82
Electricity	2	3	4	7
Biofuels	1	3	4	9
Other Fuels	6	3	3	3

Source: IEA, World Energy Outlook 2012 (Paris: OECD/IEA), pp. 618–9.
Note: See the text for explication of the scenarios.

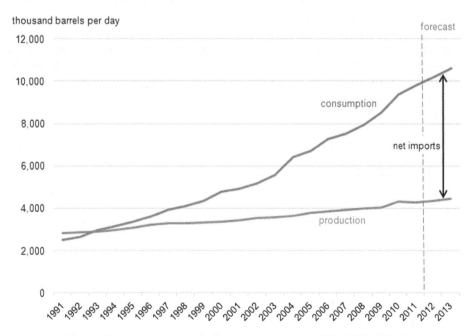

Figure 2.   Chinese oil consumption, production and net imports, 1990–2013 (EIA 2013). *Source:* Drawn by the authors from EIA, n.d. International Energy Statistics [WWW Document]. URL http://www.eia.gov/countries/data.cfm (Accessed December 24, 2013).

In the 1970s and 1980s, China prided itself on its self-sufficiency in oil. However, as mentioned, it must now import over half of the oil it uses. According to the IEA, China will consume 15.3 mb/d by 2035, overtaking the US as the largest oil consumer in the world (IEA 2011). An energy and emissions outlook for China produced by the Lawrence Berkeley National Laboratory predicted in its baseline scenario that China's transport sector would consume 566.48 million tons of oil equivalent (mtoe) of energy by 2030 and 708.02 mtoe by 2050 (Nan et al. 2011).[3] This is 2–3 times what was consumed in 2010. In their projections, diesel is expected to retain its position as the predominant fuel in China's transportation energy mix while the use of electricity and heavy oil will continue to rise.

Natural gas

China's use of natural gas in the transport sector is expected to increase slightly in the coming years. The government hopes that the country's natural gas vehicle ownership will reach 1.0 million in 2012, 1.5 million in 2015 and 3.0 million in 2020 (Perkowski 2012). These are modest gains considering there are currently over 114 million registered motor vehicles on China's roads (Chinese Auto Ownership). However, if the country succeeds in developing its unconventional gas reserves, the use of gas to fuel cars, buses and trucks could potentially become far more widespread.

Biofuels

The National Reform and Development Commissions set a target for domestic biofuels production to increase from 1 million [metric] tons (mt) in 2005 to 12 mt in 2020. If these targets are met, domestic biofuel production could provide up to 15% of China's transportation needs (Zhong et al. 2010). In February 2004, China made 10% ethanol blending with petrol mandatory in 27 cities in nine provinces. By 2007, ethanol production stood at 1.35 mt with ethanol gasoline accounting for 20% of national gasoline consumption that year. By 2009, eight ethanol plants with a total capacity of 2.2 mt had been built. China now has the third largest bioethanol industry in the world after the US and Brazil (Platts 2011). Corn and cassava are used as the main raw materials for bioethanol production in China, with 80% of fuel grade ethanol being produced from corn.

However, increasing demand for corn caused corn prices to increase by 23% in 2006 and in 2010, China became a net corn importer, indicating that the use of corn as bioethanol feedstock may have negative implications on food security. As a result, China has been making an effort to move into alternative feedstock. In 2008, grain-based ethanol subsidies were eliminated (Platts 2011). Alternatives to corn as a feedstock include sugarcane, sugar beet, sweet sorghum and lignocellulosic material. Sugarcane and sugar beet are the preferred feedstock for bioethanol because they do not require costly pre-treatment. However, this is not feasible in China because sugar production from sugarcane and sugar beet is more profitable than using them to produce bioethanol. Sweet sorghum and lignocellulosic material are particularly attractive because they do not compete with other food crops and reduce food security. Bioethanol production from these feedstocks is still in the research and development phase (Zhong et al. 2010).

The government is promoting biodiesel production using a variety of feedstocks. Currently, most biodiesel plants utilize industrial waste oil and waste cooking oil. Industrial production of biodiesel began in 2004 (Wang, Xiong and Liu 2009) and by the end of 2007, 10 biodiesel plants were in operation. By 2009, China had 2.6 mt of biodiesel producing capacity (Platts 2011). In 2010, the State Taxation Administration announced consumer tax exemption for pure biodiesel produced from waste animal and plant oils

(Zhong et al. 2010). There are two major barriers to biodiesel production in China, namely a stable supply of cheap feedstock and the high production cost. The components of waste oil are complex and inconsistent; this can cause variation in the quality of biodiesel. Potential alternative feedstocks include rapeseed and woody oil plants like jatropha which can be grown on marginal land and do not compete with food crops. Further research is required to determine their long term viability (Zhong et al. 2010).

Electricity

The government has set ambitious targets for electric vehicle (EV) penetration: 0.5 million EVs on the road by 2015 and 5 million by 2020. In October 2010, China's Science and Technology Minister announced an output goal of 1 million EVs by 2020. Aside from subsidies for private car owners, Beijing also pledged to invest 100 billion yuan to support the fledgling industry by 2020 (Fang and Willis 2012). The government is also building charging stations and battery-swapping networks for alternative vehicles, with a goal of installing 75 charging stations and 6000 charging poles in 27 cities by the end of 2010 and 10,000 charging stations by 2016 (General Motors 2010). Provincial and local governments and power companies are also collaborating to build charging networks in major cities in order to establish a nationwide charging network by 2020 (Bonnefont 2011).

Although subsidies have been generous, they have not been sufficient to make EVs cost competitive with conventional vehicles running on gasoline and petrol. In Shenzhen, even after generous subsidies, the Shenzhen e-taxi costs 80% more than the incumbent Volkswagen Santana. The scarcity of charging stations and repair shops has resulted in slow uptake of EVs. Drivers fear that their batteries will run out before they reach their destinations, a phenomenon referred to as 'distance anxiety'. In Shanghai and Hangzhou, sales were only in double digits as of June 2011(Yan and Durfee 2011). In 2009, China launched the 'Ten Cities, Thousand Vehicles' New Energy Vehicles Programme, where each selected city should employ 1000 new vehicles in municipal fleets. In late 2010, the list was expanded to cover 25 cities. However, results have fallen short, with many cities having less than 100 EVs as of the end of 2011 (Zhang 2012).

The output of hybrids and EVs for the whole of 2011 stood at 8368 vehicles, of which 8159 were sold. This pales significantly in relation to the 14.6 million cars sold throughout the country in 2011. Consumers are less concerned about government interests and the environment than the economics and practical aspects of owning a vehicle. The popularity of EVs has not been helped by negative publicity regarding the safety of this new technology. The pilot programme in Hangzhou was temporarily halted from January to June 2011 when one cab's engine compartment caught fire. Assuming EVs are adopted as an appreciable proportion of China's vehicle fleet in the medium to longer term, their ability to mitigate oil and gas import dependence will ultimately depend on the electricity generation structure. Because China's electricity generation mix in the foreseeable future will continue to be dominated by coal-fired power, this might well mean substituting the energy security problem of import dependence with the environmental problem of increasing emissions of carbon dioxide and other atmospheric pollutants.

Discussion

China is still a very large producer of oil. However, demand has far exceeded domestic supply for some time. Using conventional technologies, most of China's large oil fields have reached peak production and the smaller ones will be quickly depleted. Extensive surveying has not resulted in the discovery of further large deposits in China, but worldwide it is expected that there is considerable oil left. Indeed, in November 2012, the IEA predicted that the United States would become the largest oil producing country in the world, surpassing Saudi Arabia. Completely unimaginable only a few years ago, the situation has completely changed with the advent of new technologies enabling extraction of oil from shales. In future, the US may not need to import any oil at all.

As with tight gas, the Chinese government is likewise hoping that China may have similar shale oil reserves. At the time of writing, the government was in the very early stages of inviting large surveying companies to assess the potential of the country's known shale oil formations. If both China and the US become major producers of "unconventional" gas and oil, and no longer need to import them, it is an understatement to say that global energy trading markets will be entirely different. As mentioned, China is currently importing over 50% of its oil requirements. Until recently, most analysts were forecasting that in two or three decades' time, the county would need to import 80% of its oil imports. However, depending on the scale and geological complexity of the shale oil resources found in China, the rapidly increasing dependence on imports could be slowed over the next 20 years.

In 2011, it imported 51% from the Middle East, 24% from Africa, and 25% from elsewhere (Wu 2014). The Middle East has long been a troubled region, vulnerable to upheavals stemming from historical and socio-political differences within and among the various countries. At present, the main problem relating to oil exports from the Middle East is Iran's alleged covert programme to acquire nuclear weapon capability. To prevent Iran from going ahead, the United States and European Union agreed to place sanctions on imports of oil from Iran and to freeze the assets of the Iranian Central Bank. They have also put considerable pressure on Asian countries to reduce their imports of oil from Iran in order to try to starve it of revenue for its nuclear programme.

China had been buying the largest share of Iran's oil exports, followed by India and Japan. Together, China, Japan and Korea had been buying nearly half of Iran's oil. Now they are all looking to rely more on supplies from US allies, notably the Gulf Cooperation Council countries. Saudi Arabia, Kuwait and the United Arab Emirates have all increased their output but some analysts believe these countries do not have enough spare capacity to make up the difference.

In addition to the political instability in the Middle East region itself, the transport of the oil from the region is complicated by the need for the thousands of tankers to pass through two strategic chokepoints: the Straits of Hormuz and the Straits of Malacca and Singapore. If sanctions prevent it from selling oil, Tehran has threatened to block the Strait of Hormuz, which is the only egress from the region. There are no pipelines that could bring the oil out. China may need to work alongside the US and other navies to ensure the area is not blocked. As for the Straits of Malacca and Singapore, some analysts regard this area as one of the most critical geo-political chokepoints in the world. Some 70% of Northeast Asia's oil imports pass through these straits each year. The aperture south of Singapore is only 2.5 km and there are many shallow reefs and small islands. Some governments fear that traffic could be halted by a '9-11'–type air crash, a tanker collision, blockage or other by means.

In an attempt to provide a supply/price buffer in the event of some major disruption in oil supplies, the Chinese government has constructed some strategic petroleum reserves (SPRs) and is building more (Thomson and Boey 2013). It initiated its strategic oil reserve plan in 2003 and is developing the largest SPR outside of the OECD. Four SPRs with a combined capacity of over 100 million barrels of storage have been completed on the eastern coast and SPR capacity is planned to increase to 500 million barrels by 2020 (IEA 2012).

As for natural gas, over the past decade, the government decided to build many new pipelines from the west, south and north to bring in as much gas as possible from the neighbouring regions. While these are being built, during the coming months and years, the government will learn more about the potential scale of the unconventional gas reserves within the country. Over the next 20 years, China's large reserves of shale gas could enhance the country's energy security but they will not likely obviate the need for huge imports of gas. It is possible that some of this unconventional gas could be used in the transport sector, but it is more likely that it will be used to generate electricity.

Now the world's largest carbon emitter, China is under intense international pressure to reduce its carbon footprint. In 2005, the government pledged to reduce its energy intensity by 20% from 2005 levels by 2010, and in 2009, it promised to cut the amount of carbon emissions per dollar of economic output by 40–45% by 2020 compared with 2005 levels (Wall Street Journal 2010). Table 4 shows the energy efficiency and climate change goals outlined in China's 12th Five-Year Plan (2011–2015).

In order to meet these targets, the Chinese government has adopted a multi-pronged approach. This involves optimizing industrial structure, promoting energy conservation, developing low carbon technologies and promoting technology innovation. Table 5 gives an overview of these measures.

Table 4. Energy and climate change goals in China's 12th Five-Year Plan (Liao 2012).

Indicator	Target
Total energy consumption	Control absolute consumption
Energy intensity	Reduce by 16% from 2011 to 2015
Energy savings	Achieve savings of 670 mtce
Carbon intensity	Reduce by 17% from 2011 to 2015
Non-fossil fuel sources	Account for over 11.4% in 2015 and over 15% in 2020

Source: Liao (2012).

Table 5. Overview of China's measures to reduce energy and carbon intensity (Wang 2007).

Approach	Key measures
Optimizing industrial structure	• Use command and control methods to restrain the development of energy intensive sectors • Developing emerging strategic* and service industries
Promoting energy conservation	• Assign energy saving targets to specific regions • Carrying out energy conservation projects such as the 'Ten Key Energy Conservation Projects'**
Developing low carbon technologies	• Develop non-fossil fuel energy sources such as wind, solar and coalbed methane • Institute financial subsidies, tax incentives and subsidies for electricity generation
Promoting technology innovation	• Increase research funding to 2% of GDP by 2010 and 2.2% by 2015

Notes: *The emerging strategic industries comprise the biological, new-generation IT, new energy, new materials, high-end equipment manufacturing and new energy vehicles industries. ** The 'Ten Key Energy Conservation Projects' is a billion-dollar programme that provides financial support for energy saving projects ranging from the power sector to construction. *Source*: Drawn up by authors based on information compiled by Wang (2007).

China is trying hard to meet the 16% energy intensity reduction target stated in the 12th Five-Year Plan whilst witnessing the fastest growth in energy use in four years. China's carbon emissions are largely attributed to its heavy dependence on conventional coal-fired generation. Of all the fossil fuels, coal has by far the highest emissions per unit of energy. Most of China's thousands of coal-fired plants do not have the most efficient emission-capturing technologies available, though China has become the world leader in super-critical power plant technologies which are able to capture almost all of the nitrogen and sulphur oxides, as well as much of the carbon emissions.

The Chinese government is contributing a great deal of investment and other resources into carbon capture and storage (CCS).[4] Many countries are hoping this technology will enable them to continue using large amounts of fossil fuels. There are some 160 planned or commissioned CCS projects in the world today. Nine of these are in China (Thomson and Boey, 2014). Actually however, it is in fact the transport sector which has the fastest growth rate in terms of greenhouse gas emissions and these are far more difficult to capture. Over the next two decades, as noted above, the number of cars on China's roads will increase several fold. In an attempt to reduce these emissions, Chinese car manufacturers are aiming to produce cars with exceptionally high emission standards.

Policy implications

In terms of global energy security and finance, a key implication of this research is that China will continue to import enormous quantities of oil and gas and thus could strongly influence global oil and gas supplies and prices. Producers of oil and gas will continue to survey for and prepare as of yet untouched oil and gas reserves in the hopes of securing and/or maintaining large, long-term contracts with the world's largest consumer.

From an environmental perspective, though the Chinese government is devoting a great deal of attention to carbon mitigation, as well as nuclear power and renewable forms of energy which emit little if any carbon, the country's total CO_2 emissions will continue for many years to soar far above those of any other country. While per capita energy consumption in China is still way below that of the developed world, many scientists believe that if China continues to consume fossil fuels at the current rate, the incidence of intense storms resulting from climate change will steadily increase and put millions of people living in coastal communities around the world in great risk. Global food production could also be jeopardized. Despite the fact, as argued here, that China has little alternative but to continue using vast amounts of fossil fuels, China may be singled out by some observers as being the root cause of multiple calamitous weather events in the twenty-first century.

Conclusion

In terms of the 'electron diet', China's use of oil over the next two decades will soon be phased out entirely. The role of gas, however, will increase greatly. The main reason is the international pressure that China is under to reduce its carbon emissions. Natural gas emits less than half the amount of CO_2 per unit of energy that coal does. As for the mobility diet, like every other country in the world, China will necessarily continue to rely almost exclusively on oil products. Over the next two decades, biofuels may be blended with gasoline and diesel in larger amounts, but they will not completely substitute for them. Electric and hybrid vehicles may become more popular, but at present, their costs, drivers' distance anxiety and lack of plug-in infrastructure mean that there are relatively few on China's roads at this time.

In order to meet the burgeoning demand for gas and oil, over the past decade, the government has done all it can to arrange as large as possible imports of these commodities, by all possible means. At the time of writing, the various gas pipeline and LNG terminal projects were advancing as planned, as were the contracts for oil shipments. However, the advent of hydraulic fracking may drastically change China's use of oil and gas over the next 20 years. Preliminary estimates indicate potentially very large amounts of trapped gas being available, as well as oil. However, it will take some time before the true feasibility of harnessing these will be apparent. Thus, the country will continue to import huge quantities of oil for the transport sector.

While China's carbon emissions may be mitigated somewhat by the central government's ambitious renewable energy targets, it is not possible over the next 20 years for the various forms of renewable energy to completely substitute for the use of fossil fuels in electricity generation and the use of oil in the transport sector.

Notes

1. In July 2012, India experienced major power failures. Some 680 million people across nine northern states were without electricity for many hours. There were several factors involved: some states drawing more electricity than authorized, old and deteriorating power plants and grid infrastructure, less hydropower being generated due to weak monsoon, etc.
2. See: IEA website: http://www.iea.org/publications/scenariosandprojections/ [Sept 2012].
3. The authors of the outlook made a number of assumptions in producing their baseline scenario energy projections, key amongst which are the assumptions that the Chinese economy will continue reducing its energy intensity as a function of GDP and will achieve efficiency levels common in industrialized countries.
4. CCS is considered the most feasible approach to reduce CO_2 from large emission sources. The International Energy Agency has identified it as being critical in stabilizing global atmospheric CO_2 emissions at 450 parts per million by 2050.

References

Agence France-Presse (AFP). 2012. "China Could Restart Nuclear Power Programme, June 2." channelnewsasia.com.

Andrews-Speed, C. P. 2011. *China, Oil and Global Politics*. New York: Routledge.

Bonnefont, Y. 2011. *Electric Vehicles—International Initiatives and Best Practices*. Presented at the VBO-FEB Colloquium, Brussels EXPO.

Chinese Auto Ownership Rose to 114 Million. 21 July 2012. Available at: http://chinaautoweb.com/2012/07/chinese-auto-ownership-rose-to-114-million/

China's Shale Gas Subsidies Underpin Expansion of Gas Generation. December 2012/January 2013. Available at: www.gastopowerjournal.com

Crompton, P., and Y. Wu. 2005. "Energy Consumption in China: Past Trends and Future Directions." *Energy Economics* 27: 195–208.

Dargay, J., D. Gately, and M. Sommer. 2007. "Vehicle Ownership and Income Growth, Worldwide: 1960–2030." *The Energy Journal* 28: 143–170.

Dinçer, F. 2011. "The Analysis on Photovoltaic Electricity Generation Status, Potential and Policies of the Leading Countries in Solar Energy." *Renewable and Sustainable Energy Reviews* 15: 713–720.

Energy Information Administration (EIA). 2013. Independent Statistics and Analysis: China.

Fang, Y., and K. Willis. 18 April 2012. Reuters "China Wants 5 mln Hybrids on the Road by 2020."

General Motors. 2010. Roadmap to 2030 (GM Sustainable Urban Mobility Blue Paper).

Hook, L. 2012. "China sets target for shale gas development." *Financial Times* March 16.

International Energy Agency (IEA). 2011. *Overseas Investments by Chinese National Oil Companies – Assessing the Drivers and Impacts*. Paris: International Energy Agency.

International Energy Agency (IEA). 2012. *Oil and Gas Security: Emergency Response of IEA Countries, People's Republic of China*. Paris: International Energy Agency.

Kambara, T, and Howe Christopher. 2008. *China and the Global Energy Crisis: Development and Prospects for China's Oil and Natural Gas*. Cheltenham: Edward Elgar.

Liao, H. 2012. "Energy Conservation Strategies in China." Paper presented at China Energy Issues in the 12th Five Year Plan and Beyond Conference, organised by the Energy Studies Institute, Singapore 24 February 2012.

Liu, T., G. Xu, P. Cai, L. Tian, and Q. Huang. 2011. "Development Forecast of Renewable Energy Power Generation in China and its Influence on the GHG Control Strategy of the Country." *Renewable Energy* 36: 1284–1292.

Moore, M. 2011. "20 Chinese Coal Miners Killed in Latest Accident." *The Telegraph*.

Nan, Z., D. Fridley, M. McNeil, N. Zheng, K. Jing, and M. Levine. 2011. *China's Energy and Carbon Emissions Outlook to 2050*. Berkeley, CA: Lawrence Berkeley National Laboratory.

OECD iLibrary. 2011. "IEA World Energy Statistics and Balances. [WWW Document]." URL http://stats.oecd.org.libproxy1.nus.edu.sg/BrandedView.aspx?oecd_bv_id=enestats-data-en&doi=data-00510-en

Perkowski, J. 2012. "Natural Gas Vehicles in China." *Forbes*. [WWW Document] URL http://www.forbes.com/sites/jackperkowski/2012/04/13/natural-gas-vehicles-in-china/

Platts. 2011. "China Biofuel Policy May be in Conflict With Food Security Objectives." *Platts*, September 7.

Qiu, J. 2011. "China Admits Problems With Three Gorges Dam." *Nature News*.

Rout, U. K., A. Voβ, A. Singh, U. Fahl, M. Blesl, and B. P. Ó Gallachóir. 2011. "Energy and Emissions Forecast of China Over a Long-Time Horizon." *Energy* 36: 1–11.

Stone, R. 2011. "The Legacy of the Three Gorges Dam." *Science* 333: 817.

Thomson, E. 2005. "Power Shortages in China: why?" *China: An International Journal* 3: 155–171.

Thomson, E., and A. Boey. 2013. "Securing Energy Supply: Strategic Reserves." In *International Handbook of Energy Security*, edited by Hugh Dyer and Maria J. Trombetta. Cheltenham: Edward Elgar.

Thomson, E. and A. Boey, 2014. "China's Coal Consumption and Use of CCS", ESI Working Paper ESI/WP-05/2014-07.

Wang, B. 2007. "An Imbalanced Development of Coal and Electricity Industries in China." *Energy Policy* 35: 4959–4968.

Wang, F., X. R. Xiong, and C. Z. Liu. 2009. "Biofuels in China: Opportunities and Challenges." *In Vitro Cellular & Developmental Biology-Plant* 45: 342–349.

World Energy Outlook. 2012. *Organisation for Economic Co-operation and Development*. Paris: OECD/IEA.

World Nuclear Association. 2011. "China' s Nuclear Fuel Cycle [WWW Document]." URL http://www.world-nuclear.org/info/inf63b_china_nuclearfuelcycle.html

Wu, K. 2014. "China's Energy Security: Oil and Gas", *Energy Policy* 73: 4–11.

Xu, Y.C. 2014. "The Struggle for Safe Nuclear Expansion in China", *Energy Policy* 73: 21–29.

Yan, F., and D. Durfee. 2011. "Analysis: Chinese Electric Taxis Struggle to Win Mass Appeal." Reuters.

Yang, M. 2009. "Climate Change and Energy Policies, Coal and Coalmine Methane in China." *Energy Policy* 37: 2858–2869.

Yu, X., and H. Qu. 2010. "Wind Power in China—Opportunity Goes With Challenge." *Renewable and Sustainable Energy Reviews* 14: 2232–2237.

Yun, Z. 2010. "Why is China Going Nuclear?" *Energy Policy* 38: 3755–3762.

Zhang, Y. 2012. "Bumpy Road Ahead for Electric Autos." *China Daily*, April 23.

Zhang, Q., and Z. Lou. 2011. "The Environmental Changes and Mitigation Actions in the Three Gorges Reservoir Region, China." *Environmental Science & Policy* 14: 1132–1138.

Zhong, C., Y. X. Cao, B. Z. Li, and Y. J. Yuan. 2010. "Biofuels in China: Past, Present and Future." *Biofuels, Bioproducts and Biorefining* 4: 326–342.

China's renewable energy development: policy, industry and business perspectives

Christopher M. Dent

East Asian Studies, University of Leeds, Leeds, UK

China has been at the forefront of the recent global expansion of renewable energy (RE) activity. This study examines how the country has achieved its position as the world's largest producer and exporter of RE products, and biggest power generator from renewables. More specifically, it explores the main motives driving RE development in China, how this is embedded in broader new development thinking on realising 'ecological civilization' goals, evolving government policies on strategic planning on renewables and the complex multi-layered landscape of China's RE business where various types of state-owned enterprises collaborate and compete among each other alongside a now large number of private companies, especially in equipment manufacturing.

1. Introduction

1.1. Background

The rapid expansion of renewable energy (RE) in China since over the last decade is of some considerable significance for understanding current and possible future thinking on the country's economic, social and business development. Over time the Chinese government has afforded greater strategic priority to developing renewables as an energy sector and industry for three main reasons. First, China faces serious energy security challenges, as burgeoning industrial-based development and rising material demands of business and society have intensified pressures on domestic energy reserves and raised dependency on foreign energy sources. China is now consequently one of the world's largest energy importers. Second, RE technologies are being promoted for important environmental and welfare imperatives. High carbon economic activity is causing acute pollution and other environmental problems in the country, correspondingly leading to adverse social welfare effects. The ability of renewables to produce cleaner energy makes them a vital part of the solution to this problem and addressing climate change risk. Third, RE sectors such as solar and wind are viewed as important emerging strategic industries by the Chinese government, forming part of its push to make the country an 'innovation hub' economy as envisioned in the 12th Five-Year Plan (FYP) (2011–2015). Relatedly, RE is a core element of the country's new low(er) carbon development strategies and efforts on sustainable development generally.

RE development in China should thus not be considered in isolation of broader development processes, strategies and contexts in which it is embedded. Thinking on

China's RE development also combines ideas from ecological modernization theory (EMT) and strategic industry theory. This applies to both government policy and business practice. The landscape of China's RE business across different industry value-chains is characterized by dynamic entrepreneurism, inter-sectoral connections, a dense mix of state-owned enterprises (SOEs) and private sector companies, intensifying competition and fast expanding production capacity. The relationship between government and business here is a complex and complicated one, yet this is to be expected in a large fast-growing economy where the state is proactively supporting the development of dynamic industries such as wind and solar energy.

1.2. Research methods and questions

Research undertaken for this work is of a qualitative political economy nature, drawing upon various types of analytical and information sources over a 2-year period from October 2011 to November 2013. The empirical work is set within a theoretical–conceptual framework later defined in this study that helps provide deeper explanations on both the causes and consequences of China's RE development. The analysis addresses a number of research questions. It begins by asking what RE is and why is it so important? These are the main research questions we have chosen, rather than straight hypotheses. Theoretical explanations for the rise of RE are considered, and also what have been the main motives behind China's RE development. It also explores whether the Chinese government is pursuing a unique RE policy and strategy, and how this may be different to other countries. In addition, what different patterns of Chinese business development have occurred in the country's RE industries and what are the key issues arising in state–business relationships here? Furthermore, what are some of the impacts that China is making globally on RE business and industries?

2. China and the global development of RE

2.1. What is RE and why is it important?

RE is derived from replenishable natural processes, sources or phenomena, such as wind, solar, geothermal, hydropower, tidal and biological matter. They are 'renewable' because in actual or theoretical terms they can provide inexhaustible supplies of energy to meet the needs of humankind. In contrast, fossil fuels (coal, oil and natural gas) and nuclear (based on uranium) are non-renewable because their energy sources are ultimately exhaustible. Today, we often refer to renewables in terms of their technological applications, among the most common being wind turbines, solar photovoltaic (PV) modules or panels, tidal barrages, biofuels and so on. These can vary enormously in terms of scale, for example from small solar PV cells that generate a few watts of electricity to power electronic devices such as calculators to huge hydropower plants such as China's 22.5 GW capacity Three Gorges Dam, the world's largest power station. RE is arguably the main element of a broader green energy cluster of technologies that additionally includes energy efficiency and saving, electric vehicles, fuel cells and other eco-industry sectors.

RE technologies provide critically important options for China in meeting various development challenges that lie ahead but nevertheless come with their own environmental and socio-economic costs. The most controversial of all has been the construction of numerous large hydroelectric dams that have caused destruction to local eco-systems and the relocation of millions of Chinese from their homes. The future development of large-scale tidal barrages could have similar adverse effects. More generally, RE systems are in some way materially based, and require industrial processes to produce installation equipment. Consequently, no RE technology is completely carbon neutral, or in an absolute pure sense completely 'renewable' as most of the materials on which they depend are depletable. Emissions from biomass and biofuel combustion can cause their own environmental problems. Some RE installations also require large areas of uninhabited space, such as wind farms and solar parks, presenting certain environmental, economic and spatial constraints. Notwithstanding these points, the ability of renewables to produce much cleaner and safer energy than fossil fuels or nuclear makes them essential to decarbonizing economic activity, securing long-term energy futures, achieving sustainable development and tackling climate change. This is especially relevant to China given the country's closely related economic, energy and environmental challenges it faces domestically and its impacts in these areas globally.

2.2. The global rise of renewables

RE technologies have long been used by societies and civilizations around the world. In the modern era, hydroelectric dams have long been the dominant form of RE installations generating utility-scale electricity, these dating back to the late nineteenth and early twentieth centuries. Although the inclusion of hydropower in the renewables category remains controversial due to the adverse ecological and socio-economic effects caused by large-scale dams locally, most analysts still consider it as a valid RE sector, not least because of the recent growth of small-scale hydropower which is far less impactful. Other types of modern RE technology have been developed, many of which have been scaled up into mainstream industries (e.g. wind and solar) while others have remained low-level power producers such as geothermal, tidal and concentrating solar power, with some still largely experimental, such as wave energy.

It was not until the early 2000s that significant growth and development in renewables generally began as new RE technologies became gradually scaled up and approached commercialization. Wind, solar and bioenergy deserve special mention here, and electricity generation is arguably where renewables have made the biggest impact on global energy systems. Worldwide RE power capacity has risen from 931 GW in 2005 to 1473 GW by 2012, which represents 26.0% of global total, leading in addition to a rising share of global electricity generation output from 15.6% to 21.7%. As Table 1 indicates, hydropower accounted for 16.5% of global electricity generation in 2012, this being around three-quarters of the total renewables contribution. From 2005 to 2012, wind power installed capacity has increased from 59.0 to 282.6 GW, and solar PV from 5.4 to 102.1 GW, the two fastest growing RE sectors. In terms of global primary energy demand, renewables accounted for 19.0% of the total in 2011, with traditional biomass being the most prominent RE sector (9.3%) and primarily related to cooking and heating in remote areas of developing countries.

China has been at the forefront of this global expansion of RE. For a number of years, its power generation capacity has been far greater than any other nation, having almost tripled from 122 GW in 2005 to reach 341 GW by 2012: the next ranked countries that year were the USA (164 GW), Germany (76 GW), India (67 GW) and Japan (59 GW). Admittedly, China's dominant position owes much to a large and still expanding hydropower programme, yet even if this sector was excluded, China would still be ranked first globally with 92 GW and the USA second with 86 GW (REN21 2013). Furthermore, China has been responsible for adding around 40% of new additions to global RE capacity since the late 2000s (REN21 2006, 2013).

Table 1. China's RE profile.

Power generation[a]	Installed capacity, MW								Global installed capacity, MW (2012)	China % share of global total	Sector targets
	2005	2006	2007	2008	2009	2010	2011	2012			
Power generation											
Hydropower[a]	117,390	130,290	148,230	172,600	196,290	216,060	232,980	248,900	990,000	25.1	325 GW, inc. 41 GW pumped storage (2015); 430 GW (2020)
Wind	1060	2599	5912	12,210	25,810	44,733	62,634	75,374	282,587	26.7	100 GW, inc. 5 GW offshore (2015); 200 GW[b], inc. 30 GW offshore (2020)
Solar PV	0	80	100	145	373	893	3093	8300	102,156	8.1	39 GW (2015); 47 GW (2020)
Biomass	2000	2500	3000	3270	4600	5500	7000	8000	83,000	9.6	13 GW (2015); 30 GW (2020)
Geothermal	24	24	24	24	24	24	24	24	11,700	0.2	110–120 MW (2015) geothermal and tidal; 50 MW ocean (2015)
Ocean (tidal and wave)	3	3	3	3	3	3	3	3	527	0.6	
Concentrating solar power (CSP)	0	0	0	0	0	0	0	0	2550	0.0	1 GW (2015); 3 GW (2020)
RE total	120,477	135,496	157,269	188,252	227,100	267,213	305,734	340,601	1,472,520	23.1	Non-fossil fuel (inc. nuclear): primary energy 11.4% (2015), 15% (2020); electricity generation capacity 30% (2015)

(*Continued*)

Table 1 – continued

	Installed capacity, MW								Global installed capacity, MW (2012)	China % share of global total	Sector targets
	2005	2006	2007	2008	2009	2010	2011	2012			
% share total installed capacity	23.0	22.0	22.0	23.0	25.0	26.0	28.5	29.6			
% share total power output generated	16.0	15.0	15.0	17.0	17.0	18.0	16.0	20.0			
Nuclear	6850	6850	8850	8850	9080	10,820	12,570	13,800	364,078	3.8	40 GW (2015); 58 GW (2020)
% share total installed capacity	1.3	1.1	1.2	1.1	1.0	1.1	1.2	1.2			
Other energy production											
Solar water heaters (million m^2)	80.0	90.0	108.0	136.0	160.0	185.0	217.4	257.7			400 million m^2 (2015)
Biogas users (million households)	18.1	21.8	26.2	30.5	35.1	39.0	43.0	–			50 million households (2015)
Solid biomass (1000 tonnes)	0	0	30	1000	2000	3000	3500	6000			10 million tonnes (2011–2015)
Bioethanol (1000 tonnes)	1020	1020	1290	1580	1720	1860	1900	2000			4 million tonnes (2011–2015)
Biodiesel (1000 tonnes)	50	50	100	300	500	500	400	500			1 million tonnes (2011–2015)

Sources: BP (2013), CNREC (2013), EPIA (2013), GWEC (2013), REN21 (2013).
[a] Includes pumped storage. General: data source figures differ for China's installed wind, solar PV and geothermal energy capacity. The author has chosen to use international sourced data from international sectoral and other organizations (GWEC, EPIA, REN21, BP) for these sectors for international comparative reasons over Chinese national data, which is generally believed to under-estimate capacity levels
[b] Unofficial government target.

2.3. Theoretical explanations

Much of the academic literature examining the recent growth of renewables is located in energy science–engineering fields where development is studied from primarily a technical perspective and focused on new technological advances. Social science explanations on the subject from the relevant disciplines of political economy, business studies and sociology have tended to explain the rise of renewables from one of two main theoretical approaches, both of which situate RE development in broader development contexts.

The first of these is EMT, which first emerged in the early 1980s (Huber 1982; Jänicke 1984). This essentially is premised on the idea that sustainable development can be achieved through continual reform, modification and adaptation of existing economic and business structures. As York and Rosa (2003) succinctly summarize: 'Central to [ecological modernization theory] EMT is the view that … industrialization, technological development, economic growth, and capitalism are not only potentially compatible with ecological sustainability but also may be key drivers of environmental reform' (p. 274). From this perspective, RE is viewed as providing *technical* solutions to sustainable development challenges facing humanity. Despite criticisms made of EMT for prescribing incremental rather than revolutionary change, it remains the dominant discourse among key decision-makers in both government and business circles regarding environment-related policies. An important reason for this is the appealing economic case it makes on how companies can increase profitability by pursuing green corporate strategies, through for instance improving material efficiency and waste management, and exploiting the emerging market potential of environmentally friendly products such as renewables (Christoff 1996; Jänicke 1988). EMT postulates that economic and business growth is reconcilable with resolving environmental problems, and firms can generate financial gains through adopting new environmental technologies and practices (Langhelle 2000; Weale 1992).

Founded on closely related theories of industrial policy, strategic trade and state capacity, *strategic industry theory* is the second broad social sciences approach that can explain RE development. It essentially concerns the state's promotion of industries deemed essential to the nation's long-term economic security, welfare and prosperity. The theory's main premises are based on public good and externality arguments. While the market mechanism can account for the 'private' and purely price-determined costs and benefits arising from economic transactions, it can fail to capture their external 'social' costs and benefits. Public actions undertaken by the state are thus required in such circumstances to both minimize negative externalities and properly capture or optimize positive externalities. Thus, state policies and investments in RE installations and technologies will reduce carbon emissions, lead to cleaner air and mitigate society's supply risk dependency on exhaustible fossil fuel resources. These state actions constitute the provision of public goods where the market (i.e. private enterprise) alone is unable to independently and sufficiently deliver these welfare-enhancing outcomes, and more broadly placing the economy and society on track to a lower carbon future. Left purely to the market, many RE sectors would not become technologically developed enough or adequately commercialized to compete on price with fossil fuel-generated energy.

Strategic industry theory further makes a case for state support towards covering the proportionately high initial capital costs (e.g. infrastructure and new technology research) arising at the early development stage of emerging strategic industries with significant futures based on the expectation of substantial long-term returns on this state investment for the economy and public welfare (Lall 2003; Rodrik 2004, 2007; Schmitz 2007). The theory has had a particularly strong influence on development thinking in China and other East Asian states, as clearly demonstrated in their macro-development plans in which fostering emerging strategic industries constitutes a core programmatic element. Where the government seeks more direct involvement in strategic industry development, it will form new or encourage existing SOEs to play an active part in meeting plan objectives. In addition, the government will look to develop close relationships with business enterprises generally through using a comprehensive range of policy mechanisms. Ecological modernization also highlights the importance of state policies and institutions in helping markets and paths of economic development evolve towards more environmentally friendly outcomes.

2.4. China's RE development

2.4.1. Power generation and energy production overview

As Table 1 shows, hydropower has clearly dominated China's RE development over time, this being broadly consistent though with international norms. The government has targets to increase power capacity levels in this essentially state-run industry to 325 GW by 2015 under the 12th FYP, and then to 430 GW by 2020 under its medium to long-term RE strategy. This is primarily based on the further construction of large hydroelectric dams, the country's programme for which is the world's largest (IHA 2013). Meanwhile, China's installed wind energy capacity industry has expanded dramatically since the mid-2000s to reach 75.4 GW by 2012, and further rapid growth is planned in accordance with government targets. The country's fastest growing sector, however, is solar PV, increasing over 100-fold since 2006 to reach 8.3 GW by 2012. China's biomass power generation sector has meanwhile experienced steady growth, rising to 8.0 GW installed capacity by the same year. These four sectors – hydropower, wind, solar PV and biomass – are responsible for virtually all the country's power generation from renewables. A further four sectors make an extremely minor contribution: geothermal is a relatively mature technology industry that has grown very slowly worldwide. Tidal energy and concentrating solar power are both still infant micro-sectors but with considerable potential for future market and industry growth. As indicated earlier, wave energy technology remains at the experimental stage with no installed capacity yet worldwide. Even in these very small sectors the Chinese government has set relatively ambitious targets for future development, as it has for all RE sectors (Table 1). Together, all RE sectors accounted for 29.6% of China's electricity generation capacity by 2012, a share of the total that has gradually risen since the late 2000s.

National power generation capacity in total has increased almost 10-fold over the last two decades or so, from 126.6 GW in 1990 to 1150.5 GW by 2012, and most of this can be attributed to a rapidly growing coal power sector. This contributed to 758.0 GW (66.0%) of total generation capacity in 2012, three times that of hydropower, while the fast growing gas sector had reached 38.1 GW. Under the 12th FYP period (2011–2015) there is a programme to develop 16 large coal-power bases in the north and north-west provinces, where the bulk of China's coal deposits are situated, which will increase coal power capacity by 33% by 2015 (Yang and Cui 2012).

2.4.2. Main motive factors for China

There have been three main motives that have driven the expansion of RE in China, the first being important *environmental and welfare imperatives*. High carbon economic activity is causing acute pollution and other environmental problems in the country, correspondingly leading to adverse social welfare effects. China overtook the USA in 2006 as the world's biggest carbon dioxide (CO_2) emitter. Latest available figures show that by 2009 China's annual CO_2 emissions level was estimated at 7687 million tonnes, around a quarter of the global total. This has been principally driven by the country's burgeoning demand for fossil fuel energy that is thought to have increased between five and sixfold since 1990 (Zhao and Yin 2011). Two key points should be made here. A significant degree of China's energy demand derives from the carbon-intensive manufacturing operations of foreign investor firms that have been relocated from their originating countries (mainly from Europe, Japan and North America), thus helping them reduce their own carbon emissions. This carbon-intensive activity hosted by China serves the world market: foreign-invested enterprises account for around 60–70% of the country's exports. One could therefore argue that China's high carbon emission levels are as much a product of global capitalism as national economic development. Furthermore, China's energy demand is in a functional relationship with realising important domestic policy goals. Many communities in the nation's more remote interior provinces either have inadequate electricity supply or none at all. Strengthening the national grid in these areas is integral to achieving the Chinese government's overarching twin socio-economic objectives of closing income gaps within the country and lifting further hundreds of millions of its people out of poverty. The provision of key welfare services (health, education and utilities such as freshwater supply) all depend on electricity supply, whether grid-connected or off-grid generated. In sum, China's power needs over the next few decades will be far greater than any other nation.

Rising fossil fuel consumption is nevertheless causing significant environmental and welfare degradation in China. The government's ambitious strategy for expanding coal-power capacity locks the country into a high emissions trajectory for decades to come, unless both clean coal and carbon capture and storage technologies make considerable advances in the future. Chinese cities are already among the world's most polluted. The China Council for International Cooperation on Environment and Development (2012) reported that in the year 2000 almost 300 people per million population were dying in China due to high emission particulate levels, the world's highest rate, and this was expected to rise to almost 900 per million by 2030, placing the country even further ahead of other parts of the world. Many parts of China are also highly vulnerable to the climate change risks of extreme weather and rising sea levels. The nation's burgeoning middle class is correspondingly becoming more politically vocal about quality of life issues, such as pollution abatement.

The second main motive behind China's push for renewables is *energy security*, which can be understood generally as addressing supply risk, price risk and environmental risk, this last aspect has already been discussed above. In relation to the first two risk types, sustained high growth rates in energy demand are rapidly depleting China's own fossil fuel deposits. It is the world's second largest oil and coal importer, and the fourth largest importer of liquefied natural gas (BP 2013; Yang and Cui 2012). Concerning nuclear, the country possesses only an estimated 1% of global uranium reserves, currently maintains a 65% import dependency on the mineral and has seen its uranium import levels triple from 2009 to 2011. Analysts expect China to overtake the USA as the world's largest uranium importer by 2020 (Massot and Chen 2013). Although its energy import dependency ratio overall is not high by most international comparisons (9% in 2010), this is set to rise inexorably in the future, consequently making China more susceptible to the vicissitudes of foreign supply sources (Dent 2013). This is potentially further compounded by volatility in international prices for oil, gas and coal. Renewables have the advantage of being inherently indigenous energy sources, thus providing a long-term solution to foreign energy supply risk. Although some RE sectors are prone to occasional spikes in commodity price levels (e.g. polysilicon and solar PV cell manufacturing), they have been historically less exposed to price risk than fossil fuel sectors. The third main motive can be linked directly to strategic industry theory. Renewables are seen by China and most other countries as *emerging strategic industries.* The rationale for government support of their development was previously made.

3. China's RE policies and strategies

3.1. Renewables as part of a new development approach

RE development in China cannot be considered in isolation of the broader development processes, strategies and contexts in which it is embedded. The government's more substantial promotion of RE and national business growth of RE sectors over the last decade or so has occurred during a phase when China's leaders have adopted new approaches and thinking on national economic and social development generally (CCICED 2009a, 2009b, 2010, 2011, 2012; NDRC 2006, 2007, 2011). Soon after assuming power, President Hu Jintao proclaimed that the 'scientific development concept' would form the new ideological basis for China's future economic and social development, formally ratified into the national constitution at the 17th Party Congress in October 2007. One of its core aims was to foster a resource-saving and environment-friendly 'harmonious society', and 'developing the economy in a more balanced manner, paying less attention to gross domestic product (GDP) growth *per se* and more attention to such things as the ecological costs of the headlong rush for development' (Fewsmith 2008, 88). This new vision for China's development connected especially with the first identified motive (environmental and sustainable development imperatives) driving the promotion of RE, and the government's FYPs and associated strategic development programmes reflected this shift towards more qualitative development objectives.

The 11th FYP (2006–2010) was the first to do so, and it was also during this time that ideas on ecological modernization were beginning to influence Chinese policy-makers. In the year 2007, three key inter-related events reflected new development thinking in China: the Chinese Academy of Sciences published its inaugural *China Modernization Report 2007: Study on Ecological Modernization* and the government launched its first National Climate Change Strategy as well as its Medium and Long-Term Development Plan for Renewable Energy, also the first of its kind and that introduced a substantive strategic industry development programme for renewables. The convergence of ecological modernization and strategic industry thinking was even more clearly evident in the overarching aims of the current 12th FYP (2011–2015). As well as aiming to achieve more equitable income growth, promote domestic consumption, improve social infrastructures and strengthen China's innovatory capabilities, a prime focus of the 12th FYP was to promote lower carbon development (NDRC 2011). The stronger ecological modernization approach to China's future development was re-affirmed at the 18th Party Congress held in November 2012 when Hu Jintao announced the goal of building an 'ecological civilization' and 'achieve lasting and sustainable development of the Chinese nation' (address to the 18th Party Congress, 8 November 2012).

3.2. Is China's approach to RE development different?

By early 2013, 127 countries worldwide had introduced RE policy support mechanisms (up from just 55 countries in 2005), and 138 countries had set defined RE targets. RE policy instruments come in various forms but may be generally categorized as follows:

- *Regulatory mandates*: establishing legally binding requirements on firms to undertake particular action, such as renewable portfolio standards (RPSs).
- *Direct financial support*: such as state subsidies, grants, loans and capital investment in RE sector plants and infrastructure.
- *Market-based instruments*: adapting or using the market mechanism to provide a variety of different financial incentive measures, for example tax incentives, feed-in tariff (FiT) systems, competitive bidding and tradable permits.

Considerable convergence has occurred internationally around the utilization of similar policy instruments, such as FiTs where the government offers price-based incentives to individuals and companies to install and operate RE equipment. By early 2013, 71 countries and 28 sub-national states around the world had enacted FiT legislation, where in China it has proved a significant spur to business growth and investment in renewables from small to larger scale installations. China is also among the 22 countries to have introduced RPSs that mandate energy suppliers to source minimum quota levels of electricity generation from RE systems.

Developed economies and larger emerging economies, such as China, tend to have comprehensive RE policies that include a mix of regulatory mandate, direct financial support and market-based mechanisms. The application and balance of these will depend on the development stage of the RE sector in question and the prevailing political economy of the country. Generally speaking, market-liberal country governments unsurprisingly have a special predilection for market-based instruments, whereas more state-directed economy governments have more frequently deployed direct financial support policies. The latter is not just relevant to China but also to many other East Asian economies with strong state capacity traditions (e.g. South Korea and Malaysia) and where SOEs play an important role in the energy sector. East Asian states have additionally demonstrated a proclivity for substantive strategic long-term planning on RE development, this being arguably more evident in the region than any other (Dent 2012). What makes China most notably different, though, from all other countries is the absolute scale on which its policies, strategies and investment (both public and private) are facilitating RE development, particularly regarding installed capacity and equipment manufacture, and in the prospective future on efficiency performance and techno-innovation. The relationship between government and business in China's RE industries is also rather uniquely complex due to the sheer density of state and corporate actors, the burgeoning expansion of business activity and issues of policy co-ordination involving multiple state agencies.

China's hydropower policies date back many decades but it was not until the 1990s that the government started to pursue a multi-sector RE policy. The 1995 China Electric Power Act was the country's first legislation to call for the promotion of renewables generally. This was soon followed by the first specific RE policy landmark with full legal status, the 1996 brightness programme, located in the 9th FYP (1996–2000) and based on approximately US$1.2 billion public investment to install hydropower, solar PV and wind energy facilities in over 1000 townships and villages in rural communities. Soon thereafter, a series of direct financial support measures were introduced in the 10th FYP (2001–2005) period. The 10th FYP proclaimed that production capacities in the wind, solar and geothermal energy sectors should be increased but did not set specific development targets (NDRC 2001; NREL 2004). These came later when renewables became priority emerging strategic industries. The 2003 Wind Power Concession Programme included plans to create up 20 large wind farms of 100–200 MW capacity and the National Development and Reform Commission (NDRC) correspondingly set China's first national target of reaching 20 GW of wind energy capacity by 2020.

The introduction of the renewable energy law in 2006 at the eve of the 11th FYP proved critical to expanding and diversifying renewables development. It created a far more robust legislative basis for business investment and established national standards for RE technologies and production (NEB 2008). This was complemented by the medium and long-term development plan for RE, implemented from September 2007. The plan set out China's ambitious targets for multi-sector RE development to 2020 and backed up with US$263 billion of public investment. Even greater government stimulus was provided in the 12th FYP (2011–2015) that included a RMB4 trillion (US$610 billion)-funded programme to promote seven strategic emerging industries (SEIs) for 'clean' development and a 'new industry base', namely: new energy, new generation information and communications technology, energy-saving and environment protection, biotechnology, high-end equipment, new materials and alternative energy cars. Renewables are specified as a key component of the 'new energy' SEI sector that in addition included nuclear power. Under the SEI programme, China plans to enhance its new technological and innovation capabilities in wind energy and solar PV as part of a broader strategy of transforming China from a 'world factory' into an 'innovative hub' economy. The 2012 energy policy white paper reaffirmed the government's commitment to vigorously develop renewables as 'a key strategic measure for promoting the multiple and clean development of energy, and fostering emerging industries of strategic importance' (State Council of China 2012, 11).

In the 12th FYP period to date, China's RE policy has intensified with an increasing number of initiatives and regulations introduced in order to keep pace with business and industry growth, and deal with challenges arising from it (CNREC 2013). These include problems arising with gaps in grid connectivity and other infrastructural bottlenecks, establishing up-to-date technical standards, co-ordinating central and local government policies concerning regional RE business development, and establishing clearer demarcations of responsibility among various actors in different RE systems. It is beyond the scope of this study to explore these issues in great detail but some will be examined in the discussions that follow on state-business relationships in China's RE industries.

4. Discussion

4.1. Overview

From the early 2000s to early 2010s, China has made the transition from being a net importer of RE products to the world's largest manufacturer and exporter of them, and the largest investor in RE plant development. In addition to its dominant position in the global hydropower industry, the country now produces around two-thirds of solar PV equipment (up from just 5% in 2004), four-fifths of solar water heaters and almost half of wind turbines worldwide (EPIA 2013; REN21 2013; GWEC 2013). The burgeoning growth of national RE production and installed generation capacity has been driven by rising public and private sector investment. In 2005, China invested US$5.8 billion in RE rising to US$66.6 billion by 2012, almost twice that for the USA (US$36.4 billion) and not far behind Europe's combined figure of US$79.9 billion (REN21 2013).

China's SOEs play a very active role in national RE development. These can be generally categorized as large-scale central government-administered corporations or smaller local government-owned companies serving the energy needs of city municipalities and individual provinces. Examples of the former include the two state-owned grid companies that monopolize China's electricity grids, the government's five power generation companies (e.g. Guodian, Huadian) and national energy companies, e.g. Sinopec and SinoHydro. Naturally, both SOE types have close relationships with governing state agencies responsible for central and local government RE policy, although they can exercise high degrees of corporate autonomy and moreover compete among each other. Just as RE sectors vary significantly from each other, so there are many differences in the types of enterprises and markets that exist across them. Broadly speaking, an energy industry value-chain can be divided into the following elements, upstream to downstream:

- Fuel source explorers or surveyors
- Equipment manufacturers (including upstream suppliers)
- Source or plant developers
- Energy infrastructure providers
- Plant or system maintainers
- Retail market suppliers

Table 2 provides a comparative overview of how these differ across fossil fuel, nuclear and RE sectors, also indicating the mix of Chinese public and private sector enterprises that exist in each part of the matrix. As indicated, SOEs dominate along the whole value-chain of China's 'incumbent' fossil fuel, nuclear and hydropower sectors and many RE industry aspects. Li (2013) reports that by 2011 there were some 700 SOEs involved, for example in wind farm plant development. The country's five government power generation companies alone were responsible for installing 57.0% of wind energy generation and local SOEs another 22.4%. This contrasted with just 4.6% for China's private wind farm developers, 1.3% for foreign firms and 14.7% for foreign joint venture projects. A similar situation exists at the plant development level in the biomass power generation industry. However, the solar PV industry is different due to its highly 'distributed' nature (i.e. multitudinous building-integrated installations) that has allowed a growing number of private sector firms over time to enter various aspects of the value-chain. The wider deployment of micro-scale RE technology applications generally – roof-top PV, small wind turbines, biomass boilers, pico-hydro devices, etc – has created 'prosumer' individuals and organizations (including firms) that both produce and consume their own generated electricity and thermal power by and large independently, thus diminishing the need for energy supply companies. However, despite the rapid growth of PV prosumers in China, utility-scale solar park capacity has grown even faster and is now presenting opportunities for energy SOEs to become market players here also (IEA 2013). In general, the country's established energy SOEs with roots in fossil fuels, nuclear and hydropower have simply diversified into wind, solar, biomass and other renewables by applying their economies of scope advantages of existing technical expertise and assets to these new emerging power sectors. China's public and private sector enterprises have in addition become more vertically integrated up and down industry value-chains. Some illustrative examples of the above points are as follows:

- Deploying its marine engineering expertise, national oil company CNOOC has developed offshore wind projects, as well on onshore wind farms, biomass generation plants and biofuel production. Other major state-owned oil companies, Sinopec and CNPC, have too become scaled up biofuel producers.
- Hydropower SOEs SinoHydro Group, and HydroChina Corporation and China Three Gorges Corporation have engaged in wind farm development, the latter two

Table 2. Energy enterprises in power generation (public/private sector mix in China).

	Coal, oil, gas	Nuclear	Hydropower	Wind	Solar PV	Biomass
Fuel source explorers or surveyors	Public	Public	Public	Public/private	Public/private	Public/private
Equipment manufacturers (plus upstream suppliers)	Public/private	Public/private	Public/private	Private	Private	Private
Source or plant developers	Public	Public	Public	Public	Public/private	Public
Energy infrastructure providers	Public	Public	Public	Public	Public	Public
Plant or system maintainers	Public	Public	Public	Public	Public/private	Public/private
Retail market suppliers	Public	Public	Public	Public	Public, n/a prosumers	Public

Source: Authors research.

Notes: For the public/private sector mix in China status for each segment, 'Public/Private' indicates a situation where neither sector dominates. 'Public' or 'Private' indicates a situation where either correspondingly dominates. Private can also include foreign firms, such as hydropower turbine manufacturers.

enterprises in overseas projects, e.g. in Pakistan. Shenhua Group, the world's largest coal company, and China Guangdong Nuclear Power are also among China's major wind farm developers.

- China's largest wind farm developer is Longyuan Power Group, a subsidiary of power generation SOE China Guodian Corporation. Longyuan is also involved in developing solar, biomass, geothermal and tidal energy projects.
- Sinovel, originally an SOE then turned private enterprise from 2011, is China's largest wind turbine manufacturer and additionally has operations in wind-field design and planning, equipment transportation and installation, plant maintenance and remote data analysis services.
- In June 2013, private wind turbine manufacturer Mingyang Wind Power formed a joint venture with state-owned China National Nuclear Corporation to develop wind farm projects in Henan province.
- Hong Kong-based GCL Poly, the world's largest producer of polysilicon, the base material for mainstream solar PV cells, has recently ventured downstream into wafer manufacture, and is also developing the 300 MW Datong solar park that when constructed will be the world's largest.

In many other countries, fossil fuel companies are also major players in developing clean energy systems. However, it is the scale on which this business diversification is occurring in China's energy companies that is somewhat exceptional. Their evolutionary transformation into eventually green energy businesses, if this indeed transpires, is likely to prove a very slow process through gradual adaptations in response to changing technological, market and policy conditions. Yet this is consistent with the ecological modernization approach. Government regulatory mandates will in the meantime require Chinese companies to source more power generation from renewables. In general the country's larger incumbent, and mainly SOE companies have most successfully diversified and thrived in most aspects of China's RE industry, primarily due to economies of scale and scope advantages, and being well positioned to benefit from state support due to close connections with government ministries. There are additionally some interesting market dynamics at play. For instance, wind power generators rarely compete against coal-power generators as they are invariably the same companies. There exists intra-company competition between old and new energy divisions, China's hydropower companies may take a competitive position against their fossil fuel rivals and the country's five large state-owned power-generating companies compete against their local-level counterparts, but as they are all SOEs this may be considered an intra-state competition of sorts.

Indeed, intra-state competition and tensions have had a profound impact on China's RE business on various levels, this proceeding from governance and co-ordination challenges involving central government, local government, SOEs and private companies. On the retail side, competing SOEs provide the main bulk of electricity sold to consumers (Table 2) at prices regulated locally but in accordance with centralized NDRC guidelines, yet a significant lack of transparency persists on both price formulation and the allocation of retail market contracts among enterprises (Lin and Purra 2012). Furthermore, as Shi (2013, 8) observed that local governments in China were often encouraging the development of RE plants to help meet their economic growth targets, more specifically arguing that 'The construction of power plants is mainly for increasing GDP rather than meeting the demands for electrical power, leading to serious blind construction of power plants in various areas'. Applying this to the wind energy industry, plant developer companies such as Longyuan have built numerous wind farms that may take a considerably long time before they are connected to the grid, explaining why by the early 2010s an estimated one-fifth of China's wind power installations were in effect dormant. Contestations over grid connectivity and market demarcations among mainly power generation SOEs, grid infrastructure SOEs, local energy SOEs, local government and central government have created a difficult business environment in many aspects of this industry (GWEC 2013; Li 2013), and to some extent in the smaller solar PV power generation sector (CPIA 2013). Notwithstanding these problems, these industries continue to demonstrate robust growth.

Table 2 shows that the only element of the value-chain where the private sector dominates in China's RE industries (except hydropower) is in equipment manufacture. Wind energy companies such as Goldwind, Sinovel, Mingyang, United Power and Dongfang have all become key global players in their industry, as have Yingli, JA Solar, Suntech and Trina in the PV sector. Although some of these firms once had SOE origins (e. g. Sinovel and Goldwind), the rapid expansion of this value-chain element is a critically important part of China's RE development story. In 2004, the country had just 6 wind turbine firms, rising to 40 by 2007 and to around 90 by 2011 (Li 2013). Best estimates suggest over 400 solar PV manufacturers now operate in China (IEA 2013). There has been a dynamic entrepreneurial response generally from the nation's public and private business sectors to the government's strengthening policy support and ambitious strategic planning on renewables. However, the rapidly increasing number of RE equipment producers has created overcapacity problems in wind and solar PV most notably, this also having a significant global impact. Despite that in 2012 alone around 50 solar PV manufacturers filed for bankruptcy in China – five times the number of their European rivals – the country continued to expand PV production capacity (9.5% growth in module output in 2012) as surviving companies take a positive view on long-term market growth and strong government support for the sector (CPIA 2013).

Most recently, the government has incentivized the growth of domestic PV installations after the sharp fall in Western market demand, and state-owned banks have also provided assistance during these upheavals, for instance lending the nation's top 10 PV firms a combined US$20 billion in 2012 (REN21 2013). Current structural changes are likely to make China's solar PV manufacturing industry far more concentrated, as small-scale producers either go bust or are taken over, and SOEs also extend their interests into this value-chain element (Solidiance 2013). We may additionally expect greater further vertical integration in China's wind and solar PV sectors as enterprises seek to diversify and consolidate their competitive positions. Here we see a convergence of interest between the Chinese government and energy companies towards achieving yet greater scale advantages in both power generation and equipment manufacture, making China even more price competitive in international markets.

Western criticism of the Chinese government's strategic industry support of its RE enterprises has led to intensifying trade disputes over solar PV equipment and wind turbines in particular. On the other hand, downstream firms in these industries worldwide (e.g. installation and maintenance companies) have welcomed China's mass production of affordable RE goods, and have lobbied against the application of US and EU trade restrictions on Chinese imports. Whatever transpires on the trade diplomacy front, Chinese government and companies share a similar strategic vision of strengthening domestic techno-innovatory capacity in RE industries. This is consistent with the 12th FYP's core development objective of transforming the country into an 'innovative hub' economy, and Chinese company strategies of competing increasingly on technological terms and not just price.

5. Conclusions

The environmental and welfare costs of China's high carbon activity are mounting. In acknowledgement of this, the government has endeavoured to establish a new development approach influenced by ecological modernization thinking that seeks to reconcile these core objectives. This has combined with strategic industry theory ideas on state proactivity on supporting the development of renewables as key emerging industries of the future. Over time, the Chinese government has gradually strengthened its RE policies and strategies that are in turn embedded in larger policies and strategies that aim to foster greener, cleaner economic and business development. It has been shown how various types of SOEs still dominate most aspects of China's RE industries. This has made it often difficult to identify where the demarcations of state and business lie. One could make a case for considering SOEs themselves as a form of policy instrument, or at least an extension of China's RE policy. Yet intense business competition also exists among these public enterprises. Overall, China's RE business landscape is highly complex, and can be generally characterized by dynamic public and private sector entrepreneurism, strong inter-sectoral connections that extend to fossil fuel and nuclear power industries, a dense mix of SOEs and private companies, intensifying business competition at multiple levels, and fast expanding production capacity based on optimistic expectations on future industry growth.

Notwithstanding the country's notable achievements on RE development to date, both the Chinese government and business face some difficult challenges ahead. We have only been able to touch upon those facing policy-makers in particular, namely grid connectivity problems and other infrastructural bottlenecks, establishing up-to-date technical standards, co-ordinating central and local government policy concerning regional RE business development, and establishing clearer demarcations of responsibility among various actors in different RE systems. The government's future targets on renewables development may look impressive in absolute terms (e.g. 430 GW hydropower and 200 GW wind by 2020) by direct international comparison. However, given that the country's energy system is growing fast on most fronts, the real challenge will be to raise renewables' relative share of national energy generation and consumption. Many nations have set the goal of renewables contributing around 15–30% of the nation's total electricity generation or total energy mix by 2020 (REN21 2013). China's present targets on electricity generation from non-hydro renewables especially are not that remarkable by comparison. For Chinese business in the international market context, the two main challenges will be how to address the protectionism of foreign trade partners and to improve domestic techno-innovatory capacity. The first of these challenges will naturally depend largely on factors beyond Chinese company control, specifically how foreign firms and governments respond to the perceived competitive threats China's RE industries pose. Regarding the second, with strong state support aimed at transforming the country into an 'innovation hub' economy – for example through the 12th FYP's SEIs programme – backed by considerable levels of domestic business investment, Chinese companies are already making significant advances on techno-innovation in wind, solar and other RE sectors. This represents another area where China can make increasingly important contributions to global RE development in the future.

References

BP. 2013. *Statistical Review of World Energy 2012*. London: BP.
CCICED (China Council for International Cooperation on Environment and Development). 2009a. *China's Pathway towards a Low Carbon Economy*. Beijing: CCICED.
CCICED (China Council for International Cooperation on Environment and Development). 2009b. *China's Green Prosperity Future: Environment, Energy and Economy*. Beijing: CCICED.
CCICED (China Council for International Cooperation on Environment and Development). 2010. *Annual Policy Report 2009*. Beijing: CCICED.
CCICED (China Council for International Cooperation on Environment and Development). 2011. *China's Low Carbon Industrialization Strategy*. Beijing: CCICED.
CCICED (China Council for International Cooperation on Environment and Development). 2012. *Annual Policy Report 2011*. Beijing: CCICED.
Christoff, P. 1996. "Ecological Modernisation, Ecological Modernities." *Environmental Politics* 5 (3): 476–500.
CNREC (China National Renewable Energy Centre). 2013. *Renewable Energy in China Database*. Beijing: CNREC.
CPIA (China Photovoltaic Industry Alliance). 2013. *Annual Report of China PV Industry 2012*. Beijing: CPIA.
Dent, C. M. 2012. "Renewable Energy and East Asia's New Developmentalism: Towards a Low Carbon Future?" *The Pacific Review* 25 (5): 561–587.
Dent, C. M. 2013. "Understanding the Energy Diplomacies of East Asian States." *Modern Asian Studies* 47 (3): 935–967.
EPIA (European Photovoltaic Industry Association). 2013. *Global Market Outlook for Photovoltaics 2013–2017*. Brussels: EPIA.
Fewsmith, J. 2008. "China in 2007: The Politics of Leadership Transition." *Asian Survey* 48 (1): 82–96.
GWEC (Global Wind Energy Council). 2013. *Global Wind Report: Annual Market Update 2012*. Brussels: GWEC Secretariat.
Huber, J. 1982. *Die Verlorene Unschuld der Okologie* [The Lost Innocence of Ecology]. Frankfurt am Main: Fischer Verlag.
IEA (International Energy Agency). 2013. *National Survey Report of PV Power Applications in China, 2012*. Paris: IEA.
IHA (International Hydropower Association). 2013. *IHA Hydropower Report 2013*. London: IHA.
Jänicke, M. 1984. *Umweltpolitische Pravention als Okologische Modernisierung und Strukturpolitik* [Ecological Modernization: Options and Restrictions for Preventative Environmental Policy]. Berlin: Wissenschaftszentrum.
Jänicke, M. 1988. "Okologische Modernisierung: Optionen und Restriktionen Praventiver Umweltpolitik [Ecological Modernization: Options and Restrictions Preventative Environmental Policy]." In *Preventive Umweltpolitik* [Preventative Environmental policy], edited by U. Simonis. Frankfurt am Main: Campus Verlag.
Lall, S. 2003. *Reinventing Industrial Strategy: The Role of Government Policy in Building Industrial Competitiveness*. QEH Working Paper Series, No. 111. Oxford: Queen Elizabeth House.
Langhelle, O. 2000. "Why Ecological Modernization and Sustainable Development Should not be Conflated." *Journal of Environmental Policy and Planning* 2 (4): 303–322.
Li, J. 2013. *China's Wind Energy Outlook 2012*. Brussels: Global Wind Energy Council.
Lin, K. C., and M. M. Purra. 2012. *Transforming China's Electricity Sector: Institutional Change and Regulation in the Reform Era*. Centre for Rising Powers Working Paper Series, No. 8. Cambridge: CRP.
Massot, P., and Z. M. Chen. 2013. "China and the Global Uranium Market: Prospects for Peaceful Coexistence." *The Scientific World Journal*. doi:10.1155/2013/672060
NDRC (National Development and Reform Commission). 2001. *China's 10th Five-Year Plan for Economic and Social Development*. Beijing: NDRC.
NDRC (National Development and Reform Commission). 2006. *China's 11th Five-Year Plan for Economic and Social Development*. Beijing: NDRC.

NDRC (National Development and Reform Commission). 2007. *China's National Climate Change Programme*. Beijing: NDRC.

NDRC (National Development and Reform Commission). 2011. *China's 12th Five-Year Plan for Economic and Social Development*. Beijing: NDRC.

NEB (National Energy Bureau). 2008. *China's Renewable Energy: Development Overview 2008*. Beijing: NEB.

NREL (National Renewable Energy Laboratory). 2004. *Renewable Energy in China*. Washington, DC: NREL.

REN21. 2006. *Renewables 2005 Global Status Report*. Paris: REN21 Secretariat.

REN21. 2013. *Renewables 2012 Global Status Report*. Paris: REN21 Secretariat.

Rodrik, D. 2004. *Industrial Policy for the Twenty-First Century*. KSG Working Paper Series, No. RWP04-047. Cambridge, MA: Kennedy School of Government.

Rodrik, D. 2007. "Normalizing Industrial Policy." Paper prepared for the Commission on Growth and Development, Harvard University, Cambridge, MA, September 2007.

Schmitz, H. 2007. "Reducing Complexity in the Industrial Policy Debate." *Development Policy Review* 25 (4): 417–428.

Shi, L. 2013. "Removing System Barriers, Ensuring the Large Scale Wind Energy Development." *China Renewable Energy* 2 (1): 4–9.

Solidiance. 2013. *China's Renewable Energy Sector: An Overview of Key Growth Sectors*. Shanghai: Solidiance.

State Council, China. 2012. *China's Energy Policy White Paper 2012*. Beijing: State Council.

Weale, A. 1992. *The New Politics of Pollution*. Manchester: Manchester University Press.

Yang, A., and Y. Cui. 2012. *Global Coal Risk Assessment: Data Analysis and Market Research*. Washington, DC: World Resources Institute.

York, R., and E. Rosa. 2003. "Key Challenges to Ecological Modernization Theory." *Organization and Environment* 16 (3): 273–287.

Zhao, X., and H. Yin. 2011. "Industrial Relocation and Energy Consumption: Evidence from China." *Energy Policy* 39: 2944–2956.

The Chinese government and the national oil companies (NOCs): who is the principal?

Janet Xuanli Liao

Centre for Energy, Petroleum and Mineral Law and Policy, University of Dundee, Scotland, UK

China has conducted six government reforms over the past three decades to separate government functions from the major industries. These reforms enabled a number of national oil companies (NOCs) to be established in the 1980s, and the NOCs were further listed in the international stock markets in the new century. However, due to the incomplete government and enterprise reforms, the government has not been very successful in playing a role as the 'principal' to make the NOCs as an 'agent' to manage China's petroleum industry on its behalf. A sensible government–NOCs relationship may be created by either further removing the NOCs' political functions, and strengthening China's energy market mechanism, or by establishing a Super-Energy Ministry that can assert fundamental authority over the NOCs, and manage the energy sector.

Introduction

China surpassed the USA in 2012 to be the top energy consumer (*BP* 2013, 40), and a year later became the world's number one oil importer (Crooks 2013), making energy security one of the greatest challenges to the Chinese government. By far, Beijing has relied on its major national oil companies (NOCs) to ensure the country's energy supply, by enhancing domestic oil production and overseas oil exploration. The government has also taken measures to boost NOCs' efficiency and productivity through government reforms and NOCs restructuring, which have allowed the NOCs to be listed at the international stock markets and obtained top ranks worldwide as well. In 2013, the China Petrochemical Corporation (Sinopec) and the China National Petroleum Corporation (CNPC) were ranked as the world's fourth and fifth largest enterprises respectively, followed by the China National Offshore Oil Corporation (CNOOC) at 93th (Fortune Global 500 2013). Despite their seemingly impressive potential, however, the Chinese NOCs have faced an identity problem in their development. As internationally listed companies, they are supposed to be business-oriented entities focusing on profitability. However, as the Chinese NOCs enjoy many privileges that are unavailable to private companies (similar to their foreign counterparts), such as monopoly power in China's oil market and special influence in China's political system, the western oil majors have not viewed Chinese NOCs as fair partner for competition. Inside China, the NOCs' monopoly and ineffectiveness have also encountered severe criticism, and further market reforms were urged by scholars to limit NOCs' privileges (Sheng 2013).

This study intends to examine the relationship between the Chinese government and the NOCs, applying the Principal–Agent (P–A) theory, in order to reveal the reasons behind NOCs' special status in Chinese politics. The discussion below comprises five sections. The first reviews literature on NOCs and presents the P–A theory as the analytical framework. The two sections followed examine China's government and corporate reforms since the 1980s, respectively, to identify the problems that prevented the Chinese government from acting as a 'principal' against the NOCs. A case study of fuel-price reform in China will then be conducted to provide evidence for NOCs' political influence and market monopoly, and the conclusion will look at theoretical implications and prospects for future reforms in China's petroleum sector.

Literature review

NOCs were first emerged in the early twentieth century, in those states that had strong corporatist traditions, such as Austria, France and Italy. They became a popular phenomenon in the 1960s–1970s with the rise of resource nationalism, mainly in resource-rich countries in the Middle East and Africa. By the 1980s, the highly industrialized countries privatized the bulk of their state-owned enterprises (SOEs), which was followed by developing countries in the 1990s; yet privatization did not happen to NOCs the same way, due to its capacity to generate huge profits (Victor, Hults, and Thurber 2012). In contrast, NOCs from the former communist countries, such as Russia, China and Central Asian countries, were established as the main pillar in their economies, although they varied considerably from the above mentioned due to their inherent political influence. Starting from the 1970s, research on NOCs has been a significant focus for academics, and various theories were applied to the analysis of NOCs, centring on the necessity of NOCs existence, the governance of NOCs and the problems between NOCs and the government. Those who supported NOCs (Griffin and Steele 1980) held that, 'a NOC increases a government's ability to implement a more effective energy policy and environmental protection' (quoted from Stevens 2003, 8). Some others argued that the purpose for governments to create SOEs (such as NOCs) was to marshalling popular support, while 'profitability was one, but often not the most important, goal behind their creation' (Smith and Trebilcock 2001, 218). A third rationale claimed that governments found it harder to control foreign oil firms as their agents for developing the country's natural resources, and NOCs were, therefore, created as agents to serve the purpose of the principal – the government (Victor, Hults, and Thurber 2012). Critics of NOCs warned that NOCs could become too powerful in the context of domestic politics, and Pemex from Mexico in the 1970s, and Russia's Gazprom in the 1990s were often cited to illustrate the point (Victor, Hults, and Thurber 2012, 10).

The emergence of the Chinese NOCs was in the 1980s resulted by the government reforms of separating the government from the industries. Heavily influenced by the former Soviet Union, the Chinese economic system was established as a socialist planned economy in 1956, after a transitional period since the establishment of the People's Republic in 1949. Under which the Chinese economic development was directly commanded by politics and central planning, with all industrial sectors highly integrated with the government. Until the mid-1980s, there was no modern sense enterprises existed in China. The so-called state-run enterprises (*guoying qiye*), particularly in resources and power sectors, were under direct administration by government ministries. For instance, China's petroleum sector between the 1950s and 1978 was directly controlled by two government ministries: the Petroleum Ministry (for upstream) and the Petrochemical Ministry (for downstream), though the ministerial structures varied at different times. China's major oil fields, such as Daqing, Shengli and Keramai, were all managed by their respective Oilfield Management Bureaus, and their development was directly instructed by the Petroleum Ministers, Yu Qiuli (1958–65) and Kang Shi'en (1975–78, 1981–82).

Most of the literature on Chinese SOEs/NOCs has been published since the new century. Some focused on personnel reshuffle of the NOCs or the government–NOCs interactions (Downs 2006; Downs and Meidan 2012). Some others investigated NOCs' reform on efficiency and concluded that the government's preferential treatment had undermined NOCs' efficiency and fair competition (Yang 2003; Han 2006; Guo 2007; Eller et al. 2011; Zhao 2011). Yet Jiang (2012) disagreed, arguing that CNPC's inefficiency was due to China's incomplete transition from a planned economy to a market one. In terms of the theoretical approach, most of the research applied the corporate governance theory, focusing on the ownership and efficiency of the SOEs (Xu and Wang 1999; Ewing 2005; Aivazian, Ge, and Qiu 2005; Huyhebaert and Quan 2011; Lin 2012). Ewing (2005, 322), for instance, held that the 'dominant state ownership' was 'the single most important problem confronting proper governance among Chinese corporations'. He mentioned the P–A problem in the context of corporate governance but did not apply the theory in his analysis. Lin (2012) contended that the SOEs' inefficiency and corruption was not due to the ownership, but was rooted in their monopoly in the markets. The consensus seems to be that the state-ownership was liable for NOCs' inefficiency, but most scholars did not see privatization as the solution, not least for the time being. To date, few scholars have applied the P–A theory to analysing Chinese government and NOCs, probably because that it cannot offer sufficient explanation for such a relationship. Nevertheless, this research intends to reveal the nature of the government–NOCs relationship via the lens of the P–A theory, which may not be fully applicable but could at least provide a good basis for the analysis.

The research question and methodology

The research question for this study is that *have the government reforms in China enabled NOCs to be an agent to help secure energy supply?* The hypothesis is that the Chinese government has not managed to make the NOCs as its agent, due to NOCs' remaining political influence on China's energy policy-making and their market monopoly in China's petroleum sector. As having mentioned above, the study will apply the P–A theory as the analytical framework, via linking the key assumptions of the P–A theory with the Chinese practice, followed by reviews of government reforms and a case study on fuel price setting and the conclusions.

The P–A theory

Emerged in the 1970s, the P–A theory has been applied, mostly by economists, to analysing the relationship between a principal and an agent via a contractual agreement, 'under which one or more persons (the principal(s)) engage another person (the agent), to perform some service on their behalf which involves delegating some decision making to the agent' (Jensen and Meckling 1976, 308). Many of the ideas in this model motivated policymakers to establish NOCs in the 1970s. The state, acting as *principal*, relies on its governance system to direct the NOC, serving as *agent*, to fulfil state objectives or 'national missions' (generating profits, securing employment, etc.) (Marcel and Mitchell 2006). The model has also been, increasingly, used by political scientists to study accountability in hierarchical relationship where monitoring costs make direct control infeasible (Miller and Whitford 2002, 232).

The P–A theory makes three assumptions in a P–A relationship: informational asymmetries, goal conflicts and different risk preferences (Saam 2007). The theory views information asymmetry as a challenge to the principal who cannot monitor the agent properly, the main task for the principal is, then, about how to design a proper incentive structure to discourage opportunistic behaviour by the agent (Kassim and Menon 2003). Deriving from the issue of lack of monitory, the P–A theory argues that it is difficult or expensive for the principal to verify the efforts made by the agent, outcomes are thus often the only factor that matters to the principal, assuming greater effort by the agent results in great outcome (Miller and Whitford 2002). Yet as greater efforts may require greater disutility on the side of agents, the issue of goal conflicts arises. Finally, the principal and agents are supposedly different toward risks: while 'the principal is assumed to be risk neutral', agents would be 'risk averse' due to their preferences over different compensation schemes (outcome-based vs. effort-based) (Saam 2007, 827). Miller and Whitford (2002, 237) held that a risk-averse agent can be motivated via providing extra bonus, but it 'is costly to both agent *and* principal' (emphasis original), because the real cost is efficiency loss.

While applying the P–A theory to the Chinese context, three issues deserve special attention. First of all, asymmetry of information does affect the government–NOCs relationship, but it does not fully explain such a relationship. Unlike the cases in most oil-rich countries, where the NOCs were set up through nationalization of private companies, NOCs emerged in China through the separation of the government and the SOEs. The remaining personnel interchange between the NOCs and the government has enabled the NOCs to enjoy considerable political power and they are thus not simply an agent. Second, there is a conflict of the goals between the two parties but is not triggered by information asymmetry. Instead, the central government has set twofold of goals for NOCs: to help ensure China's oil supply security, and to enhance efficiency and profitability (Shi 2007). But the NOCs have often given priority to profitability through their monopoly, while energy supply and efficiency enhancement are only their secondary concerns. Finally, the risk factor has little relevance in Chinese circumstances, as the NOCs could always bargain for preferential policies from the government to offset the likely risks. Beijing has attempted to keep the agent under control through appointment/dismissal of the Chief Executive Officers (CEOs), taxation and price-setting power, but such efforts have constantly been undermined by NOCs' political power and monopoly status.

The sections below review China's political and corporate reforms since the open-door era, and the main issues to be addressed include the motivations and objectives of the government reforms, the interests and ambitions of the NOCs' development and the effectiveness of the government control over the NOCs.

Government reforms and emergence of the Chinese NOCs

The Chinese government has carried out six government reforms since 1982, aimed to streamline and restructure the government and to separate the ministries from industrial functions. As previously mentioned, under the pre-reform Chinese economy, the key state enterprises were owned and directly managed by the government ministries. The initial government reform was thus focused on separating the ownership from administration, and on delegating responsibilities and power of management to SOEs to enhance their efficiency, thus the emergence of Chinese NOCs (Yao and Zhang 2013). The objective of the reform was to make the NOCs as an 'agent' and operate under the laws of the market, and the role of the government also changed to indirect management of the NOCs, through ownership and personnel appointment (Ewing 2005; Mattlin 2009).

After the first two government reforms in 1982 and 1988, a number of NOCs emerged for the first time in Chinese history. The first was the China National Offshore Oil Corporation (CNOOC 2008 Report), incorporated in January 1982 and was authorized by the State Council to assume the overall responsibilities for the exploitation of oil and gas resources offshore China in cooperation with foreign partners. With four regional branches (the Bohai Sea, the East China Sea, the South China Sea Eastern and the SCS Western), CNOOC headquartered in Beijing and enjoyed monopoly in China's offshore petroleum exploration; it was also the first Chinese NOC that cooperated with foreign oil companies ('95 Energy Report of China). In February 1983, the State Council decided to set up the China Petrochemical Corporation (Sinopec, formally launched in July 1983), and the Ministry of Petro-Chemistry was dissolved accordingly (Sinopec website, *PD* 2008). In 1988, the Ministry of Energy was established to replace the Ministries of Coal, Petroleum and Nuclear, and the Ministry of Water Resources and Power was replaced by the Ministry of Water Resources. The industries that embedded in the ministries all became SOEs, including the CNPC. Nevertheless, at the early transitional stage from planning to marketization, the industry sectors were not completely separated from the government: in February 1988, a government decision requested that Sinopec should still be under the control of the State Council (Sinopec website). Moreover, due to the vested interests of other stakeholders, the Ministry of Energy was dismantled during the 1993 government reform, while the Ministry of Coal Industry and the Ministry of Power Industry were resumed (*PD* 2008; Downs 2006). The government reforms also failed to prevent CNPC and Sinopec from playing administrative functions of the ministries, including to help formulate environmental protection policy and to coordinate the development of the oil industry (Shi 2007, 116 and 117).

In 1998 at another governmental reshuffle under Premier Zhu Rongji, 10 government ministries directly linked with industries, such as the Ministries of Coal, Chemistry and Metallurgy, were all downgraded to vice-ministerial level Bureaus (including the State Bureau of Petroleum and Chemical Industry) and were put under the administration of the State Economic and Trade Commission (SETC). The Ministry of Power Industry was replaced by the State Power Company and was no longer a government agency (baidu.com). The Ministry of Land and Resources (MLR) was established by merging the Ministry of Geology and Mineral Resources, the State Land Administration, the State Oceanic Administration and the State Bureau of Surveying and Mapping. The MLR was given responsibilities 'for the planning, administration, protection and rational utilization of such natural resources as land, mineral and marine resources' (mlr.gov.cn). This reform helped reduce the Ministries from 40 to 29, making it possible for the government to focus more on macro-management of China's economic development (Wang and Gong 2007).

During the reform in 2003 led by Premier Wen Jiabao, the SETC was removed and its functions were transferred to three government institutions: the National Development and Reform Committee (NDRC, formerly the National Development and Planning Committee), the newly established State Assets Supervision and Administration Commission (SASAC) and the Ministry of Commerce (by merging the Ministries of Domestic Trade and of Foreign Trade and Economic Cooperation) (*Xinhua* 2003). The NDRC assumed responsibilities of approval of NOCs' investment both at home and overseas (en.ndrc.gov.cn). At ministerial ranking, SASAC was directly under the States Council to handle all the central enterprises (*yangqi)* that owned by the central government, including 'performs investor's responsibilities, supervises and manages the state-owned assets of the enterprises under the supervision of the Central Government (excluding financial enterprises), and enhances the management of the state-owned assets.' (sasac.gov.cn) According to Mattlin (2009, 8), 'by taking all central enterprises away from the control of various government agencies and putting them under the unitary supervision of an organ that reports directly to the State Council, the central government asserted its authority.' MLR was given the authority to grant and administrate licenses for mineral exploration and production, while the Ministry of Commerce was in charge of energy imports and exports (Kong 2006).

Also in 2003, Beijing established an Energy Bureau within the NDRC to control the energy industry by examining industrial projects and supervising energy-affiliated activities (*China Daily* 2005b). But with only 30 staff members, the Energy Bureau clearly lacked authority, mandate and capacity to pursue the designated duties. Even worse, its bureaucratic ranking was lower than that of the SOCs (at vice-ministerial level but often headed by ministerial level officials), which made it impossible for the Energy Bureau to effectively administrate and coordinate the energy sector. Soon after, the State Council took another move to reinforce the nation's energy governance, after extensive consultations (Zhao 2007).[1]

On 27 May 2005, the National Energy Leading Group was established, headed by Premier Wen Jiabao, involving 13 other government ministers. The Leading Group was assumed duties for the development of blueprint, energy exploitation, energy conservation and international cooperation. Subordinate to the Group, a National Energy Office (NEO) (vice-ministerial ranking) was formulated to oversee macro energy growth trends, to organize research, and to aid the leading group's administration. Comprised of 24 members, the NEO was led by Ma Kai (Director of the NDRC), with Ma Fucai (former General Manager of CNPC who resigned after a gas-field accident that killed 243 people in December 2003) and Xu Dingming (Director of NDRC's Energy Bureau) as vice directors (*China Daily* 2005a).

Nonetheless, the debates over an Energy Ministry had never stopped but became ever heated prior to the 11th National People's Congress (NPC) in March 2008. Referring to the experiences of advanced countries, many Chinese scholars were in favour of building super-ministries, including a Super-Energy Ministry. Luo (2008), from the Institute of American Studies under the Chinese Academy of Social Sciences, proposed 'four principles' to help define the relationship between the government and the energy industry. First, the Energy Ministry should only be responsible for policy-making, and not for policy implementation and inspection. Second, the Energy Ministry should manage the industrial sectors at a macro level, such as setting standard and providing financial support, but should not directly intervene operations at the micro level. Third, the Energy Ministry should provide services to energy corporations by supplying information of new technology and professional training. Finally, the Energy Ministry should have sufficient power to control energy investments and access to markets, and to advise CEO appointments of the NOCs. Many agreed that an Energy Ministry should be resumed under the Energy Leading Group to help ensure a consistent and coherent energy policy, assisted by inspection agencies who were to supervise specific industries (Luo 2008).

Yet some of the key issues, such as how to rectify the relations between the Energy Ministry and NOCs, and what implications of a new Energy Ministry might have on other government Departments (Qian 2007), were missed in the debates. In the end, the Ministry of Energy did not come up; instead, a vice-ministerial level National Energy Administration (NEA) was created under the NDRC, with the Energy Leading Group and the NEO both abolished. Headed by Zhang Guobao, Vice Director of NDRC, the NEA assumed responsibilities for drafting and carrying out energy policies and regulations related to the industry, and for development of renewable and clean energy in China

(Interfax 2008, 8). Still, the NEA had no authority over the key issues relating to energy policy, such as the strategy of China's energy development, reform of the energy system and energy pricing mechanism, etc.

On 27 January 2010, the National Energy Commission (NEC) was established, headed by Premier Wen Jiabao and Vice Premier Li Keqiang, involving 21 additional ministers. The high-profiled NEC was viewed as 'super-commission' to demonstrate the great importance assigned by central leaders to the issue of energy. It had two main duties: to help enhance NEA's authority, and to facilitate coordination between government departments over energy policy-making. The involvement of top officials from the national security ministry and the military also led observers to believe that 'the issue of energy had now involved China's core national interest' (*BBC Energy Monitory* 2010). Yet some insiders sounded more cautious. Li Junfeng from the NDRC Research Institute for Energy, for instance, held that the NEC was still a policy coordinator and an Energy Ministry was needed for China's energy governance (*BBC Energy Monitory* 2010). In March 2013 during the 12th NPC, the idea of setting an Energy Ministry reappeared but failed again unfortunately. The NEA remained and being restructured, led by Premier Li Keqiang, to ensure better coherence of energy policy, and the State Electricity Regulatory Commission was dissolved (Table 1) (*Xinhua* 2013, nea.gov.cn). It seems that as long as power struggles existed between government ministries and with NOCs, it would be difficult for Beijing to rebuild an Energy Ministry in charge of China's energy policy-making.

Table 1.   Composition of the NEC, July 2013 – Present.

Director	
LI Keqiang	Premier of the State Council
Deputy-director	
Zhang Gaoli	Vice-Premier of the State Council
Members	
Xiao Jie	Deputy Secretary-General of the State Council General Office
Liu He	Director of the General Office of the CPC Central Finance Office
Wang Yi	Minister of Foreign Affairs
Xu Shaoshi	Director of the National Development and Reform Commission
Wan Gang	Minister of Science and Technology
Miao Yu	Minister of Industry and Information Technology
Geng Huichang	Minister of National Security
Lou Jiwei	Minister of Finance
Jiang Daming	Minister of Land and Resources
Zhou Shengxian	Minister of Environmental Protection
Yang Chuantang	Minister of Transport
Chen Lei	Minister of Water Resources
Gao Hucheng	Minister of Commerce
Liu Shiyu	Vice-Director of the People's Bank Corporation
Jiang Jiemin	Director of the State-Owned Assets Supervision and Administration Commission (until September 2013)
Wang Jun	Director of the State Administration of Taxation
Yang Dongliang	Director of the State Administration for Work Safety
Shang Fulin	Chairman of the China Banking Regulatory Commission
Wang Guanzhong	Assistant Chief of General Staff of the PLA
Wu Xinxiong	Deputy Director of the National Development and Reform Commission and Director of the NEA

Source: State Council of PRC (2013); Jiang (2014).

Incomplete reform of the national oil companies

As above mentioned, the remaining government function associated with CNPC and Sinopec was completely removed in the 1998 reform, and Beijing employed SASAC to show its ownership of a major stake in the 121 large and powerful *yangqi* (centrally administered SOEs), including NOCs (Downs and Meidan 2012). In terms of government policy planning, the NOCs were expected to bear responsibility for China's oil security, and to put the nation's interests first while faced with potential risks (Shi 2007). CNPC and Sinopec were also restructured, in May 1998, as vertically integrated corporations, from the previous upstream and downstream divisions. The restructuring was believed to promote competitions between the NOCs, and also to provide them the capacity to cover financial losses caused by price regulation with profits from other parts of their operations (Tu 2012), and probably to create 'national champions' to compete internationally as well.

However, with no new players introduced into the market, the NOCs' monopoly in upstream and downstream was only replaced by regional domination: divided by the Yangtze River, CNPC controlled the north against Sinopec's ruling in the south; CNOOC still controlled offshore explorations. In 2004, further efforts were made to break up business territories among the NOCs, when CNPC and Sinopec were allowed to enter offshore E&P business, while CNOOC received the rights for onshore development. Private oil companies were also granted rights for oil imports, and the retail market for refined oil was opened to foreign oil companies as well (Kong 2006). Between April 2000 and February 2001, CNPC's subsidiary PetroChina, Sinopec and CNOOC were further listed at the international stock markets, allowing the NOCs to better integrate with the international system. Yet again, as the majority of their shares were owned by the Chinese government, the NOCs did not become commercial companies through international listing. The NOCs were asked to share a responsibility to ensure China's stable oil supply, and in return, the government provided protection to NOCs from facing competitions from private companies via laws and regulations, and even stated in the terms of WTO accession that the oil industry was relevant to China's national interests (Shi 2007).

Looking from the surface, Beijing had the ultimate authority over the NOCs through the control of majority shares and the dominance of NOCs' leadership. The CEOs were assessed 'not only on how well they run their companies, but also on how well they serve the CCP's [Chinese Communist Party] interests'. If they could demonstrate success in both areas, the NOCs' executives would have a chance to be promoted to higher positions (Downs 2006, 23). Meanwhile, the frequent interchange between CEOs and government posts had enabled a close political network that could informally affect the careers of the CEOs. For instance, there was a so-called 'Petroleum Clique' in Chinese politics, whose power peaked in the 1960s and early 1980s, with Yu Qiuli, Kang Shi'en, Song Zhenming and Tang Ke as key members (Liao 2006, 201–204), but still remained influential in China today. As all NOCs' executives were also government officials, the separation of the government and NOCs did not but their political networks; and those who had closer links with the 'Petroleum Clique' could have even better career path. Taking Wang Tao as an example, who used to be the Petroleum Minister (1985–1988) after Tang Ke, and then served as CNPC's first General Manager (1988–1996). Thereafter, Wang stayed as CNPC's Senior Advisor for two more years before elected into the Standing Committee of the NPC in 1998 (Wang Tao's Resume). Wang's successor Zhou Yongkang (1996–98) was also a ministerial-level CEO and served various government posts after his term at CNPC. Zhou's membership at the CCP Politburo Standing Committee (PSC, the highest decision-making body in China) since 2007 was said due to the support by Zeng

Qinghong, who used to be Yu Qiuli's secretary. The former PetroChina CEO (2006–2013) Jiang Jiemin (Chairman of SASAC March–August 2013), Sinopec Chairman Fu Chengyu (2011 – present, former CEO of CNOOC) and CNOOC Chairman Wang Yilin were also said to have close ties with Zeng and Zhou, which was essential for their career development, in addition to their own merit (Downs and Meidan 2012). Such a political network has facilitated the NOCs to influence government's policy-making and has also led to an unusual P–A relationship.

Of course, the political demise of the 'Petroleum Clique' could have negative effects on the heirs as well, and indicated by Zhou Yongkang's down from power recently. When Jiang Jiemin was dismissed in August 2013 for corruption probe, following similar scandals of a few other CNPC senior officials, many believed that it was a prelude to remove Zhou Yongkang, who was viewed as the backer of a large group of corrupted officials, including Bo Xilai (Rabinovitch 2013a; *SCMP* 2013). Before long, Zhou was reportedly being under corruption investigations, on 7 December 2013, together with his son Zhou Bin and other family members (*RFA* 2013). Although Beijing has not formally publicized the case to date, probably because of Zhou's PSC membership (the first ever PSC member to face corruption charges) (*SCMP* 2014), the investigation of Zhou's wrongdoings has made NOCs the centre of the extensive corruption scrutiny: among the 11 high-ranking *yangqi* officials under investigation five were from NOCs (Hornby 2014; *Caijing* 2014). But it remains to be seen whether the NOCs would lose their political influence completely if their CEOs remain as government officials.

Market monopoly is another instrument of the NOCs. According to statistics, PetroChina and Sinopec accounted for 65% and 22.3% of the nation's crude oil output, and for 50% and 25% of refined oil output, respectively (Shi 2007, 115). This was often used as a leverage by NOCs to bargain with the government. In Downs' words (2006), the NOCs could be so powerful that the State Energy Office was made a 'corporate-driven think tank', at times. The NOCs also enjoyed substantial autonomy in business operation, such as deciding how to deal with their 'profits' and to whom to sell their oil products. The government could not inspect NOCs activities partially due to information asymmetry, but the agents' political influence should not be neglected either.

Reforms of the fuel pricing system

China's fuel pricing reform was another example to show the problematic P–A relationship. Following various reforms in the energy sector, the Chinese government has pursued oil-pricing reforms since the 1980s via four phases. Yet again, the remaining government control over the petrol price and the only partially liberalized domestic oil market has caused repeated shortages of petrol supply over the past decade, and the question that arose was how should China's fuel prices be decided and by whom?

Moving away from the planned economy, Beijing pursued the first price reform between 1981 and 1994, during which the centralized pricing system was replaced by the so-called 'two-track system' (*shuanggui zhi*), under which two types of oil price were set domestically. One was a fixed price (*ping jia*) set by the government for the quotas allocated to the NOCs which had to be followed, and the other was a higher price (*gao jia*) set by the market for the NOCs to sell the petrol beyond their quotas (Chen 2008). Phase two of the price reform started in 1994 when the 'two-track system' was abandoned, which boosted China's domestic oil price to a higher level following the market demand. The third oil price reform in 1998 aligned domestic crude price in China with the international oil market, to meet the WTO obligations (Yang 2003). These reforms did not affect the monopoly by CNPC and Sinopec in crude oil production and imports, and in wholesale of refined oil; their dominance was rather strengthened by two State Council Circulars in 1999 and 2001.[2]According to Article 3 of the 1999 Circular, all the crude oil (domestically produced and imported) must be 'allocated by the state', which would actually be handled by the NOCs. Article 4.1 of the same document stipulated that oil products from ALL refineries should be passed to the enterprises affiliated with CNPC or Sinopec, and only they had exclusive rights for wholesale of oil products. Article 2.1 of the 2001 Circular further said that no new fuel retailing stations outside CNPC and Sinopec control would be allowed to operate; and new applications for wholesale business should be submitted, via the two NOCs, to the SETC for approval.

Fuel prices in China, however, did not follow suit of the crude price but was under the control of NDRC due to 'insufficient market competition and imperfect market mechanisms', though it also hoped that 'fuel prices would eventually be determined by market forces' (*Xinhua* 2009). Against NOCs' market monopoly, the Chinese government had a dilemma in fuel price setting. On the one hand, Beijing faced enormous pressure from NOCs to raise petrol price constantly in order to offset their costs triggered by record high international crude price. As shown in Chart 1, the international oil price hiked from US$28/barrel in 2003 to US$138/barrel in June 2008, and down slightly to US$104.96/barrel in 2012 (*BP* 2013). Between 2003 and 2008, petrol price in China had been raised by 2/3, but it was still 'a reflection of $60 per barrel instead of the $100 per barrel in the international market' (Jiang 2012).

On the other hand, Beijing attempted to suppress inflation risk to retain social stability and thus, chose to provide subsidies and tax rebate to NOCs, to offset their claimed losses and to ensure undisrupted petrol supply (Xian 2008; *AP* 2008). In January 2008, Vice Premier Zeng Peiyan urged NOCs to bear their responsibilities to ensure petroleum and power supply, because these 'industries are the basic sectors and the lifeline of the national economy' (*Xinhua* 2008a). In order to enhance transparency in petrol pricing, on 5 December 2008, the NDRC issued a draft scheme, jointly with the Ministry of Finance, Ministry of Transport and State Administration of Taxation, on fuel taxation and fuel price reform, to be effective starting 2009. The draft held that 'pricing of domestic fuel prices should not only reflect fluctuations of international oil prices and production cost, but should also take into account of domestic oil supply and demand' (*Xinhua* 2008b). Six months later, another NDRC Circular was issued on the *Measures for Oil Price*

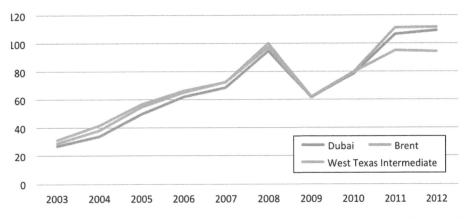

Chart 1. Spot crude prices, 2003–2012 ($/bbl). *Source*: Adapted according to the data from the *BP Statistical Review of World Energy* (2013, 15).

Administration, specifying that fuel price would be changed when the international crude price rises or falls by a daily average of 4% for consecutive 22 working days (NDRC 2009). In March 2013, the NDRC again decided to shorten the fuel price adjustment span to 10 working days and removed the 4% requirement to better reflect the international prices (Caing 2013a; Hornby 2013). Between January 2009 and 24 April 2014, NDRC adjusted fuel prices 43 times: up 24 occasions and down 19 times. By April 2014, China's petrol wholesale price was 8795 yuan/tonne (3080 yuan higher than in 2008), and the wholesale price for diesel was 7675 yuan/tonne (2715 yuan higher) (see Chart 2 below).

During this period of time, the NOCs repeatedly required price lifts claiming that the price adjustments made were insufficient for them to absorb the international crude price hike. But when the retail price for 90 octane gasoline in China ($3.31/gallon) surpassed that of the USA ($2.68/gallon) in late 2009 (Zaobao 2009; Bloomberg 2009), public opinion began to challenge the sensibility of the pricing mechanism over the 'cost of refinery' and the reliability of information provided by the NOCs. Many argued that as the NOCs faced little competition from private refineries, the 'cost of refinery' could be whatever they want it to be, and there were no incentives for them to reduce the cost. Meanwhile, the cost information provided by the NOCs could be either misleading or twisted due to the lack of government monitory (*Xinhua* 2009; Jiang et al. 2009; Tang 2014).

In addition to NOCs' monopoly, two more factors were believed as also responsible for China's high fuel prices – high taxation and environment concerns – but the consumers seem to have born most of the cost associated. Taxation was said counting for only 12–13% of the US petrol price, including the road tax and highway fees; but it counted for 28–30% in China's petrol price even excluding road tax and highway fees (china.com 2012). When the NDRC decided to upgrade fuel standard from grade IV–V to enhance air quality in major Chinese cities in September 2013, 70% of the price hike was shouldered by consumers, while the NOCs managed to receive government subsidies, 'to offset the losses caused by price gaps between the crude and refined oil', and to compensate other relevant losses (Caing 2013b). Since 2004, CNPC and Sinopec have received nearly 126bn yuan of the government subsidies and forced many private refineries/retailers out of the market (*Xinjing Bao* 2014).

The NOCs' monopoly was believed not only causing higher fuel prices in China, but also damaging Chinese overall economy, which led a 4.8% of GDP loss in 2011. Analysts urged Beijing to boost NOCs' efficiency by increasing 'market players', and by selecting CEOs based on market needs (Sheng 2013). The proposals on ownership change were also

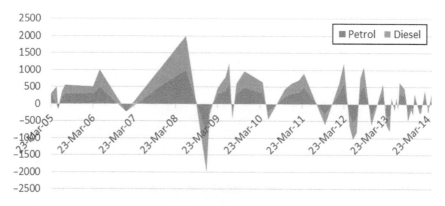

Chart 2.   Changes of refined oil prices in China, 23 March 2005–24 April 2014 (yuan/tonne). *Sources*: Adapted by author from the data at china.com.cn (2014) and NDRC (2014).

raised for SOEs' efficiency enhancement, with suggestions that the fate of SOEs should be decided by the market through fairer competitions (Zhou 2014).

Conclusions

The analysis has indicated that the hypothesis set for the study is valid: due to the incomplete government and NOCs reforms, the Chinese government has not been able to make the NOCs acting like an agent. They do face similar problems suggested by the P–A theory, such as information asymmetry and conflicts of goals, but the government was not always the principal, owing to NOCs' political influence and market monopoly.

This finding can help explain the nature of the government–NOCs' relationship in China, but has also got theoretical implications to the P–A theory. It seems sensible to argue that the P–A theory can help explain a relationship that involves little political factors, but does not make much sense in the case of China. In terms of practical implications, the research has uncovered that the factor of information asymmetry did affect the government–NOCs relationship, but was less significant than NOCs' political influence and monopoly. The conflict of the goals also existed, but the government often had to yield to NOCs' requests for the security of oil supply, while the NOCs could pursue their interests based on their special status.

Zhou Yongkang's fall from power has certainly undermined NOCs' political potential, but it may take another while for Beijing to remove NOCs' political muscle completely (Wang 2013). Beijing has urged the SOEs become 'more efficient and more profit-focused – in short, more like private companies' (Rabinovitch 2013b), but it is uneasy to break NOCs' market monopoly as well. It seems unlikely for the Chinese government to privatize SOEs/NOCs for the moment, two options could be sensible to help reinforce a P–A relationship. One is to further remove NOCs' political functions and to consolidate China's market mechanism. Once a better environment for competition is established, there will be no need for the government to directly intervene the energy market or fuel pricing. The other is to establish a Super-Energy Ministry that can assert fundamental authority over the NOCs, and to manage the energy sector via a more coherent and effective system. Beijing has got the plan in its policy agenda for more than a decade and to see a Super-Energy Ministry in Chinese politics should only be a matter of time. Hopefully, we can also expect a more constructive role played by the NOCs, as an agent of the government, in advancing the Chinese economy, together with their counterparts in private sector and from foreign countries.

Acknowledgements

The author would like to express her great appreciation to Dr Hongyi Lai and Dr Xiaoyi Mu for their helpful insights on her draft paper. She was also highly grateful for the comments from the anonymous reviewers, which have helped improve the quality of the study significantly

Notes

1. Four options were raised for consideration: (1) to establish a Ministry of Energy; (2) to follow the case of the USA and form a National Energy Commission; (3) to set up an Energy Office under the State Council and (4) to raise the Energy Bureau to vice-ministerial level.
2. The State Council of PRC: 'Circular on Cleaning up and Rectification of Small Refineries and Regulation of the Distribution Order of Crude and Refined Oil Product Markets', 6 May 1999 and 'The Circular on Further Rectification and Regulation of the Rectified Oil Product Market', 31 August 2001.

References

Note: The sources without access date specified were accessed on the same day as publication

Aivazian, V. A., Y. Ge, and J. Qiu. 2005. "Can Corporatization Improve the Performance of State-Owned Enterprises Even Without Privatization?" *Journal of Corporate Finance* 11: 791–808.

AP. 2008. "Chinese State Oil Companies Promised Tax Rebate Amid Losses Blamed on Price Controls." April 15.

BBC Energy Monitory. 2010. "China Announces the Formation of the High-Profile National Energy Commission, and Attention is Drawn to the Fact That High-Ranking Officers from the Military are Members of the Commission." January 28.

Bloomberg. 2009. "China Raises Fuel Prices; Sinopec, PetroChina Gain." November10. http://www.bloomberg.com/apps/news?pid=20601089&sid=aeqCu7fbtenQ

BP Statistical Review of World Energy. 2013.

Caing. 2013a. "New Version of Fuel Price Setting Cycle Shortened to Ten Working Days." [In Chinese.] March 26.

Caing. 2013b. "70% of Fuel-Upgrade Cost to be on Consumers While Vehicle Owners to Pay Extra 30 Yuan per Month." [In Chinese.] September 24.

Cajing. 2014. "CNPC got the Most Officials Under Investigation Among Central Enterprises." [In Chinese.] April 16. http://www.politics.caijing.com.cn/2014-04-16/114103093.html

Chen, G. 2008. "Revisiting and Thinking of the Reform and Opening of the Oil Industry Over the Past 30 Years." [In Chinese.] November 12. http://www.ccnews.people.com.cn/GB/87320/8328880.html

China.com.cn. 2012. "The Issue of Taxation Behind China's 'Higher Petrol Prices than the United States.'." July 12. Accessed April 20, 2014. http://www.finance.china.com.cn/industry/special/2013yjxt/20120712/ 920393.shtml

China.com.cn. 2014. "An Overview of Domestic Petrol Price Adjustments in Recent Years." [In Chinese.] February 26. Accessed April 20. http://www.finance.china.com.cn/industry/energy/special/2014yjst1/20140226/ 2216462.shtml

China Daily,. 2005a. "New Energy Office Confirmed." April 30.

China Daily. 2005b. "Premier Wen Heads New Energy Group." May 27.

CNOOC 2008 Annual Report, 2009. 2009. April 10. Accessed November 8. http://www.cnoocltd.com/cnoocltd/tzzgx/dqbg/ nianbao/images/2009410577.pdf

Crooks, E. 2013. "China Tops US As Leading Net Oil Importer." *Financial Times,* October 9.

Downs, E. 2006. "Brookings Foreign Policy Studies Energy Security Series: China." Accessed October 6, 2007. http://www.brookings.edu/~/media/research/files/reports/2006/12/china/12china.pdf

Downs, E., and M. Meidan. 2012. "Business and Politics in China: The Oil Executive Reshuffle of 2011." Accessed July 15. http://www.chinasecurity.us/images/stories/DownsMeidanCS19.pdf

Eller, S. L., P. R. Hartley, and K. B. Medlock III. 2011. "Empirical Evidence on the Operational Efficiency of National Oil Companies." *Empirical Economics* 40 (3): 623–643.

Ewing, R. D. 2005. "Chinese Corporate Governance and Prospects for Reform." *Journal of Contemporary China* 14 (43): 317–338.

Fortune Global 500. 2013. Accessed November 10. http://www.money.cnn.com/magazines/fortune/global500/2013/full_list/

Griffin, James M., and Henry B. Steele. 1980. *Energy Economics and Policy*. 1st ed. New York: Academic Press.

Guo, S. 2007. "The Business Development of China's National Oil Companies: The Government to Business Relationship in China." Accessed July 9, 2009. http://www.bakerinstitute.org/ programs /energy-forum/publications/energy-studies/docs/NOCs/Papers/NOCGuo%20China. pdf

Han, X. 2006. "Personal Views on the Reform of the Chinese Petroleum Economic System." [In Chinese.] *International Petroleum Economics* 4: 19–21.

Hornby, L. 2013. "PetroChina and Sinopec Struggle to Contain Upstream Costs." *FT*, October 29.

Hornby, L. 2014. "CNPC Launches Project to Lift Oil Production in China's Northeast." *FT*, April 22.

Hua, J. 2008. "Illustration of the Plans Over Reform of the Departments Under the State Council." March 11. http://www.politicalchina.org/NewsInfo.asp?NewsID=124157

Huyghebaert, N., and Q. Quan. 2011. "Ownership Dynamics After Partial Privatization: Evidence from China." *Journal of Law and Economics* 54 (2): 389–429.

Interfax, China Energy Report. 2008. "Chinese National Energy Bureau May Signal Preparations for Energy Ministry – analyst." March 6–12, p. 8.

Jensen, M., and W. Meckling. 1976. "Theory of the Firm: Managerial Behaviour, Agency Costs, and Ownership Structure." *Journal of Financial Economics* 3: 305–360.

Jiang, B. 2012. "China National Petroleum Corporation (CNPC): A Balancing Act Between Enterprise and Government." In *Oil and Governance: State-Owned Enterprises and the World Energy Supply*, edited by D. G. Victor, D. R. Hults and M. C. Thurber, 379–417. New York: Cambridge University Press.

Jiang, H., M. Wu, J. Yang, and L. Wan. 2009. "An Analysis of Our Country's Current Reform in Oil Products Pricing." [In Chinese.] *Journal of Southwest Petroleum University* (Social Sciences Edition) 2 (3): 9–13.

Jiang, Jiemin C. V. 2014. "Jiang Jiemin's Bio." [in Chinese.] Accessed July 10, 2014. http://cpc. people.com.cn/gbzl/html/121000593.html

Kassim, H., and A. Menon. 2003. "The Principal–Agent Approach and the Study of the European Union: Promise Unfulfilled?" *Journal of European Public Policy*. 10 (1): 121–139.

Kong, B. 2006. "Institutional Insecurity." *China Security* (Summer): 64–88.

Lianhe Zaobao. 2009. "Chinese Refineries may Request Further Price Rise." [In Chinese.] June 1.

Liao, X. 2006. *Chinese Foreign Policy Think Tanks and China's Policy Towards Japan*. Hong Kong: Chinese University of Hong Kong Press.

Lin, X. 2012. "Privatisation or Monopoly? – The Choices Facing the SOEs' Reform." [In Chinese.] *Cultural Perspectives* 4: 68–76.

Luo, Z. 2008. "Relevant Specialists Envisage the Function and Structure of the Coming Energy Ministry." *Economics Reference Daily*, [In Chinese.] January 29.

Marcel, V., and J. V. Mitchell. 2006. *Oil Titans: National Oil Companies in the Middle East*. Washington, DC: Chatham House/ Brookings Institution Press.

Mattlin, M. 2009. "Chinese Strategic State-Owned Enterprises and Ownership Control." *BICCS Asia Paper* 4 (6): 1–28.

Miller, G. J., and A. B. Whitford. 2002. "Trust and Incentives in Principal–Agent Negotiations: The 'Insurance/Incentive Trade-Off." *Journal of Theoretical Politics* 12 (2): 231–267.

mlr.gov.cn. 2012. Ministry of Land and Resources (of PRC). Accessed March 15. http://www.mlr. gov.cn/mlrenglish

NDRC (National Development and Planning Committee). 2009. "Measures for Oil Price Administration." [In Chinese.] May 7. Accessed November 15. http://www.sdpc. gov.cn/zcfb/ zcfbtz/2009tz/W020090508568402700156.pdf

NDRC (National Development and Planning Committee). 2014. "Circular on Raising Prices of Refined Oil Products." April 24. http://www.economy.caixun.com/clyfz/20140424-CX03ch4n. html

nea.gov.cn. 2013. National Energy Administration. Accessed July 5, 2014. http://www.nea.gov.cn/ gjnyw/index.htm

PD (People's Daily). 2008. "China's Government Reform." [In Chinese.] February 26. http://www. politics.people.com.cn/GB/30178/6922745.html

Qian, M. 2007. [In Chinese.] October 9 "An Energy Ministry Seems Less Likely." *China Business Daily*.

Rabinovitch, S. 2013a. "China Probes Regulator of State Companies." *Financial Times*, September 1.

Rabinovitch, S. 2013b. "China Reforms Chip Away at Privileges of State-Owned Companies." *Financial Times* November 9.

RFA (Radio Free Asia). 2013. "Further Reports Emerge of Chinese Probe into Zhou Yongkang." December 7.

Saam, N. J. 2007. "Asymmetry in Information Versus Asymmetry in Power: Implicit Assumptions of Agency Theory?" *The Journal of Socio-Economics* 36: 825–840.

sasac.gov.cn. 2013. "Main Functions and Responsibilities of SASAC." Accessed February 15. http://www.sasac.gov.cn/n2963340/ n2963393/2965120.html

SCMP (South China Morning Post). 2013. "Xi Jinping Sets Up Special Unit to Probe Zhou Yongkang Corruption." October 21.

SCMP (South China Morning Post). 2014. "Briefings Point to Conclusion of Graft Investigation into Zhou Yongkang." January 29.

Sheng, H. 2013. "State-Owned Enterprises are Subsidised by All the Chinese People." [In Chinese.] http://www.economy.caijing.com.cn/2013-11-08/113540379.html

Shi, D. 2007. "Structural Reforms in China's Oil Industry: Achievements, Problems and Measures for Further Reforms." In *Shaping China's Energy Security: The Inside Perspective*, edited by M. Meidan, 113–124. Paris: Asia Centre.

Sinopec Website Accessed November 12. http://www.sinopecgroup.com/gsjs/Pages/fzlc2012.aspx 2012.

Smith, D. A. C., and M. J. Trebilcock. 2001. "State-Owned Enterprises in Less Developed Countries: Privatization and Alternative Reform Strategies." *European Journal of Law and Economics* 12: 217–252.

Stevens, P. 2003. "National Oil Companies: Good or Bad? – A Literature Survey." Accessed May 5, 2011. http://www.dundee.ac.uk/cepmlp/journal/html/Vol14/Vol14_10.pdf

Tang, Z. 2014. "It is More Difficult to Monitor SOEs than to Monitor the Government." [In Chinese.] April 22. http://www.comments.caijing.com.cn/2014-04-22/114120703.html

The State Council of PRC. 1999. "The Circular on Cleaning Up and Rectification of Small Refineries and Regulation of the Distribution Order of Crude and Refined Oil Product Markets." May 6. Accessed April 15, 2008. http://www.cnnsr.com.cn/jtym/fgk/1999/ 19990506000000011186.shtml

The State Council of PRC. 2001. "The Circular on Further Rectification and Regulation of the Rectified Oil Product Market." [In Chinese.] October 26. Accessed April 15, 2008. http://www.china.com.cn/chinese/PI-c/70619.htm

The State Council of PRC. 2013. "The Circular on Personnel Changes of the NEC." [In Chinese.] July 11. Accessed March 30, 2014. http://www.gov.cn/zwgk/2013-07/11/content_2444996.htm

Tu, K. J. 2012. "Chinese Oil: An Evolving Strategy." *China Dialogue*, April 24. Accessed June 15. http://www.carnegieendowment.org/2012/04/24/chinese-oil-evolving-strategy

Victor, D. G., D. R. Hults, and M. C. Thurber. 2012. *Oil and Governance: State-Owned Enterprises and the World Energy Supply*. New York: Cambridge University Press.

Wang, J. 2013. "Disappointed at the Reform Held at the 3rd Plenary Session of the18th CCP Central Committee for Not Aiming at the SOEs." [In Chinese.] November 14. http://www.estate,caijing.com.cn/2013-11-14/113562855.html

Wang, Y., and J. Gong. 2007. "The Reform of Chinese Administration System: From a Comprehensive Government to a Limited Government?" [In Chinese.] June 7. Accessed February 26, 2008. http://www.politics.people.com.cn/GB/5831337.html

Wang Tao's Resume. Accessed February 15, 2013. http://www.cnfatong.com.cn/main/home/ns_detail.php?id=6988 &nowmenuid=47&catid=0

Xian, Y. 2008. "Special Interest Groups Behind the Policy of 'Subsidizing Sinopec'." [In Chinese.] March 18. http://www.news.creaders.net/comment/newsViewer.php?nid=338176 &id=787308

Xinhua. 2003. "State Economic and Trade Commission was Calm Over 'Fading Out'." [In Chinese.] March 11.

Xinhua. 2008a. "Vice Premier Urges More Energy Output to Ensure Supply." January 20.

Xinhua. 2008b. "China to Kick-Start Fuel Tax Reform on Jan 1." December 5.

Xinhua. 2009. "How to Explain Higher Petrol Price in China than That in the Unites States?" [In Chinese.] July 5.

Xinhua. 2013. "China to Restructure National Energy Administration." March 10. http://www.news.xinhuanet.com/english/china/2013-03/10/c_132221775.htm

Xinjing Bao. 2014. "Why Should CNPC Obtain Billions of Subsidies from the Government?." [In Chinese.] April 15. http://www.bjnews.com.cn/graphic/2014/04/15/313080.html

Xu, X., and Y. Wang. 1999. "Ownership Structure and Corporate Governance in Chinese Stock Companies." *Chinese Economic Review* 10: 75–98.

Yang, J., ed. 2003. *The Modern Oil Market.* [In Chinese.]. Beijing: Petroleum Industry Press.

Yao, J., and Y. Zhang. 2013. "The Problems and Solutions of the Chinese SOEs' Reform." [In Chinese.] *Chinese Business Sector* 1: 252–253.

Zhao, J. 2007. "Debates About the Energy Ministry." [In Chinese.] *Caing,* May 17. Accessed April 5, 2008. http://www.info.jrj.com.cn/news/2007-05-17/000002243465.html

Zhao, J. 2011. "An Analysis on the Reform of Our Country's Petrochemical Industrial Structure." [In Chinese.] *International Petroleum Economics* 12: 71–75.

Zhou, Q. 2014. "The Institutions with Conflicted Interests Cannot Lead the Reform." [In Chinese.] April 4. http://www.politics.caijing.com.cn/2014-04-04/114071890.html

Corporate governance or governance by corporates? Testing governmentality in the context of China's national oil and petrochemical business groups

Tyler M. Rooker[a,b]

[a]University of Nottingham, Nottingham, UK; [b]Peking University, Beijing, China

Like other industrial sectors with significant – 'pillar' – importance in China's overall economy and development, oil and petrochemicals are governed by state-owned business groups. In this context, 'corporate governance' of these groups is of fundamental interest. This study probes corporate governance of 31 national oil and petrochemical business groups by examining their structure, development and business activities in the period from 2007 to 2011. The post-1998 restructuring of China's qiyejituan business groups, their related party transactions and related party corporate finance all yield insight into how property rights are decisive in how corporate governance based on governmentality – or the interrelation of corporate, state and social relations – is structured. This study sheds light on how China's big business policy and governance of the state-business interface progresses in a socialist market economy. It has clear implications international trade and investment as well as multinational corporations doing business with China.

Introduction

There has been an astonishing growth in China's oil and petrochemical industry since the late 1990s, when state-controlled business groups formed through institutional separation from the state. This study probes a group of 31 domestically listed (in Shanghai and Shenzhen) national oil and petrochemical companies (NOPCs) in the period from 2007 to 2011. It entails examining the post-1998 restructuring of China's *qiyejituan* business groups, their related party transactions (RPTs) and related party corporate finance. The results point to how property rights are decisive in how corporate governance based on China's governmentality, the state-business interface, in a socialist market economy works.

Recent work (Ong and Zhang 2008; Sigley 2006) has attempted to understand governmentality of China's socialist market economy as a combination of socialist authoritarianism by a still-dominant party state and neoliberal self governance by calculating subjects. This study takes Mancur Olson's (Olson and Kähkönen 2000; Olson 1982) 'encompassing interest' or 'encompassing organization' as the core concept governing property rights in China, explaining not only forms of corporate governance but the development and business of NOPCs and beyond. Thus crucial idea is derived from important work on China's corporate governance by Lin and Milahupt (2013; see also Clarke 2003), as well as Yeo's (2013) contextualization of corporate governance, though it differs in explaining how corporate groups, rather than SASAC (the state-owned assets supervision and administration commission), are governing China today.

The following study starts from rethinking property rights to understanding the governance of oil and petrochemical corporates over the past five years. The next section of the study reviews relevant literature in the field of corporate governance and business groups, which is followed by the development of four hypotheses that derive from rethinking of property rights in context of governmentality. Following this, method and data analysis are discussed, including statistics and case studies of 31 NOPCs. Finally, the study concludes by discussing the implications of the findings and their significance.

Literature

Corporate governance

Property rights of business groups necessitate a different tact on corporate governance. The classic separation of principal investors (financiers) from agents (business executives and managers) of Berle and Means (1932) is not applicable because a central authority unifies majority ownership across multiple listed companies with their management by delegated authorities. The central authority associated with many of China's business groups, the parent company, SASAC and ultimately the state, is often negatively identified as a barrier preventing listed companies from responding to forces from the financial market (Morck, Wolfenzon, and Yeung 2005) while continuing a form of 'fragmented authoritarianism' (Howson 2014). The lack of a market for corporate control, i.e. merger or takeover activity, means that capital markets do not serve the function of disciplining management (Clarke 2003). Yet the introduction of business group parent firms as intermediaries between the state and listed company provides a layer of separation from government intervention in decision-making, reducing political 'cost' and empowering managers (Fan, Wong, and Zhang 2007), while shielding them from the grabbing hand of the state (Su 2005). Hence, business groups fill an institutional void or create institutional separation in de-centering the locus of corporate governance for formerly state-owned business groups, even if the majority of assets are traceable back to the state.

'Rationalization' of the oil and petrochemical industry

Radical restructuring of state-owned enterprises (SOEs) was pushed nationally for the first time in 1997/1998. Various experiments in decentralization of management (Morris, Hassard, and Sheehan 2002; Cao 2000), trials of business group functions (Sutherland 2001) and closing down of industrial ministries (on the oil and petrochemical industry in particular, Lin 2008) were a prelude to the radical changes of 1997/1998. Oi (2011) points to the 15th Chinese Communist Party Congress in 1997 as the official start to a radical wave, while Oi and Han (2011, 22) declare the 'late 1990s was the watershed period in China's corporate restructuring when the nationwide pattern and speed of reform changed markedly'. Brødsgaard (2012) explicitly names Zhu Rongji and the 1998 administrative reform as crucial for NOPCs. Yet while the organizational form of the business group – known as the *qiyejituan* – first emerged in the late 1980s and early 1990s (Keister 2000; Sutherland 2001; Hahn and Lee 2006), post 1997/1998 brought a wave of reorganization (*chongzu*) and restructuring (*gaizhi*). Whether referred to as their privatization, securitization or corporatization, SOEs nationwide transformed in earnest only after 1997/1998 (Morris, Hassard, and Sheehan 2002; Cao 2000; Smyth 2000; Green and Liu

2005). Not coincidentally, it was only at this point that the main players in the oil and petrochemical industry were restructured and reorganized (alternatively, see Lin 2008). Hence, former SOEs have come to rule not only China but make up an increasingly significant part of the Global Fortune 500.

Role of RPTs in business groups

'Related party transactions' (*guanlianfangjiaoyi*; RPTs) in business groups are exchanges between a group's listed company and another company in the group. NOPCs' regular RPTs, both purchases and sales, provide a proxy for gauging reliance on market-supporting institutions or the entrenchment of intra-group transactions despite the changing external environment (Carney, Shapiro, and Tang 2009). Lu, Yao, and Lan (2004) study RPTs, distinguishing between related party purchases and related party sales, of listed firms in 2001 and find that related party sales are more important to control product distribution. Yeh et al. (2009) and Berkman, Cole, and Fu (2010) use RPTs as a direct proxy for corporate governance (or lack thereof). As Cheung et al. (2009) also show, analysing RPTs in China's business groups allows understanding the degree to which listed companies are supported by these transactions, i.e. transactions are valued above or below market rates, and thus represent either a premium paid by the listed company or a discount enjoyed by it. Jian and Wong (2004) find that RPTs minimize transaction costs and help manage earnings between different group firms. RPTs allow the diversion of corporate wealth into other uses by the business group (Jian and Xu 2012). Despite their importance to NOPC corporate organization and operation, RPTs are often only viewed as either propping up or tunnelling away the listed firm's assets and profits (Jian and Wong 2010; Williams and Taylor 2014), instead of as key features of the operation and governance of NOPC business groups.

Related party finance

Prior to the late 1990s, SOEs viewed 'banks' as simply another name for state resource dispersal institutions: rather than direct budgetary allocations, loans underwritten by banks fulfilled the state's purposes. As with the reform of the state-owned industrial sector above, however, this changed radically in the late 1990s with a bank bailout, the restructuring (and listing) of banks, the hardening of loan requirements and payments and the creation of institutions. While their existing debt was written off and triangular debt retired through debt-equity swaps and legal person shares, newly organized business groups would no longer have access to soft loans with easy repayment terms (Morris, Hassard, and Sheehan 2002). Yet it is still true that corporate finance comes mostly from loans at state-controlled banks, and that these loans are mostly made to state-controlled businesses accessed through political connections (Sutherland 2001; Su 2005; Jian and Xu 2012). Beside these external financing options, business groups have internal financing options such as 'finance companies' (*caiwugongsi*) that take group subsidiaries' deposits, make loans and provide credit for business operations that otherwise could not take place (Keister 2000). Other internal financing mechanisms include direct loans from controlling shareholders or shareholders' subsidiaries, loan guarantees and 'informal' finance, such as net receivables and net other receivables. These represent business goods and services already sold or purchased, respectively, but not yet paid for. While these are standard measures for listed companies' balance sheets to account for assets and liabilities, they take a different valence in the context of related parties. In particular, 'other' accounts receivable (*qitayingshoukuan*) refers to transactions where capital is due to be paid to the listed company outside ordinary business operations (Jiang, Lee, and Yue 2010), which again can be from a related party. Governance of the different financial and capital strategies between the listed company and the business group of which it is a part are quite broad.

Research hypotheses

Utilizing these four aspects of rethinking property rights organically generates four hypotheses that annual reports of listed NOPCs from 2007 to 2011 can probe. To the extent that NOPCs, over the period 2007–2011, are moving towards a neoliberal view of property rights, the state as ultimate controlling shareholder and its shareholding percentage of NOPCs will be decreasing, minority shareholder influence on recurring and one-off RPTs will be increasing, the amount of RPTs will be decreasing and takeovers or bankruptcy will be evident. On the contrary, if blocks of shares remain in the state's hands, RPTs continue and shareholder activism and takeover threats are suppressed, this is evidence that market institutions are not emerging or even declining over the period. Thus, the first *research hypothesis*:

Hypothesis 1:   The extent to which NOPC governmentality of property rights has shifted from 2007 to 2011 is reflected in changes to institutions of corporate governance.

Integrating both radical restructuring and reorganization in 1997/1998 with business groups as the primary organizational form of business yields further questions against which research data can be tested, namely, the extent to which China's listed NOPCs have consolidated their groups into a single, multidivisional firm with majority outside ownership mirroring Western managerial capitalist forms of corporate organization (Chandler 1977). Thus:

Hypothesis 2:   The nature and direction of changes in industrial structure and corporate organization of NOPC business groups since the 1997/1998 restructuring and reorganization indicates that types of governmentality NOPCs are evolving.

This is important to examine to assess the extent to which Western and neoliberal ideas have shaped the development of NOPCs from 2007 to 2011. In this study, RPTs measure the extent of market institution internalization. Over time, increasing volume and ratio of RPTs indicates worsening market institutional environment, while decreasing volume and ratio indicates improving market institutions. Increased RPTs also demonstrate a trend towards business group organization rather than the multidivisional firm of the West. This generates a third *research hypothesis*:

Hypothesis 3:   The volume, ratio and direction of RPTs for NOPCs between 2007 and 2011 determine the extent of market institution development.

Increased NOPC access to capital markets and gradual withdrawal from internal, business group sources of capital indicates external capital markets and corporate financial institutions are growing in importance. The corollary is that debt-based and business group related party finances are increasing and thus institutions supporting capital market development for NOPCs are deteriorating or ineffective. Hence, the final *research hypothesis*:

Hypothesis 4:   Over the period 2007–2011, NOPC financing decreases internally in response to group-external, financial market institutional development if capital markets based on neoliberal property rights are adopted.

Method

The selection of NOPCs for this study comes from the Shenzhen (SZSE) and Shanghai (SSE) A-share bourses. Some of the companies are listed under the SSE 'Energy Industry Index' and the SZSE 'Petrochemical, Plastic and Rubber Index'. Others were found by consulting stock market information websites, including *Sina Finance*, *East Money* and *Emoney*,[1] and securities company websites for specialized oil and petrochemical industry 'boards'. The selection was limited to companies that had listed by 2007, so that a full five years of annual reports are available for comparison. In addition, companies connected to the three major NOPCs or large industry players in the petroleum industry are included if they are majority held or the majority of their business is in the NOPC industry.

Data comes from reviewing the 2007–2011 annual reports of 31 listed companies. First, property rights and governance are explored by reflecting on the one and a half decades of NOPC development since restructuring and reorganization. Then, business and non-business related party costs and sales are noted. Financing among the NOPCS is surveyed by analysing leverage, loans, loan guarantees, accounts receivable and other accounts receivables from the annual reports. To understand corporate finance of the NOPCs, the presence or absence of a finance company within the business group has already been noted. Finally, several case studies of individual NOPCs are reviewed in terms of property rights.

Findings

Ownership

All NOPC business groups possess varying amounts of block share ownership by their controlling shareholder: for the central state-owned enterprises (CSOEs), they control an average of over 48% of the shares, though the majority have well over 50% of shares. For the local state-owned enterprises (LSOEs), controlling shareholders exert a similar amount of dominance, with only one company, owned by a municipal district in the Xinjiang city of Karamay, having less than 50%. Finally, private companies' controlling shareholders average ownership of 22% of all shares, though three have less than 20%. From 2007 to 2011, the population of companies increased operating revenue to 4.81 trillion yuan from 2.19 trillion yuan, an average annual growth rate of 23.85%. The majority of this increase in revenue came from the growth of PetroChina and Sinopec, who together grew to a combined 4.51 trillion yuan from 2.04 trillion yuan, with an average growth rate of 24.21%. Reflecting this dominance by the two industry titans, the CSOEs in the group averaged growth of 23.91%, ahead of the LSOEs at 18.02% and private enterprises with 13.57%. Operating costs for all enterprises increased faster than revenues, growing at an average annual rate of 26.17%, again led by PetroChina and Sinopec who had average growth in operating costs of 26.91%.

CNPC and Sinopec Group

The organization of CNPC, Sinopec Group and CNOOC Group assets into PetroChina, Sinopec and CNOOC and their subsequent listing on domestic and international stock markets is well known (Zhang 2004; Lin 2008; Wu 2002; Nolan 2001). Of more significance for this study, is the subsequent period, 2001–2011, of NOPC development that forms the backdrop for the data under study. Some 18 listed companies were disposed of by CNPC/PetroChina and Sinopec Group/Sinopec in the period from 2002 to 2009, with the CSOE buybacks from the stock market concentrated in 2005–2006. In addition to PetroChina, CNPC, the parent of the business group, still holds controlling ownership of three other listed companies, while Sinopec Group and Sinopec together control five other listed companies (see Appendix 1).

CNPC has 3.03 trillion in assets in 2011, up from 2.63 trillion in 2010 and 2.22 trillion in 2009. Its debt-to-asset ratios in these years are 14.78%, 14.99% and 14.51%, respectively. In terms of return on equity (ROE) and return on assets (ROA), CNPC averages 7.25% and 20.97% over the three-year period. According to Lianhe Credit (2012a, 4), CNPC has 78 enterprises designated as second-grade subsidiaries that it includes in its consolidated income sheet. In 2011, PetroChina's assets amounted to only 63.33% of CNPC's assets, but provided 84.15% of operating income (see Table 1). This is the lowest asset ratio over the five-year period, and has declined slowly but steadily from 66.77%. While the pace of change is slower than in the case of Sinopec Limited and Sinopec Group below, there is still an indication that CNPC's asset growth is outpacing PetroChina, at a rate of 17.9% versus 15.9%, respectively.

Sinopec Limited accounts for 64.75% of Sinopec Group's total assets, but provided a much larger percentage of the Group's operating income, accounting for 98.12% (see Table 2). The percentage of assets held in Sinopec Limited is also declining, from a high in 2007 of 73.31%, and dropping each successive year by 2–3%. This indicates that, while the assets of Sinopec Limited are growing, those of Sinopec Group are growing even faster – 11.0% versus 15.1% annually.

In addition to sales and asset swaps, PetroChina and Sinopec Limited engaged in a number of share buybacks or 'privatizations' of listed companies, mostly in 2005–2006. PetroChina's buyback strategy came into force in late 2005 when it issued takeover bids totalling 6.15 billion yuan to acquire three listed companies: Jilin Petrochemical, Jinzhou Petrochemical and Liaohe Oil Field (Xu 2006). Sinopec began the exercise in early 2006, issuing bids for outstanding shares of Qilu Petrochemical, Yangzi Petrochemical,

Table 1. CNPC versus PetroChina, 2011.

	Assets (bn RMB)	Liabilities (bn RMB)	Debt-asset ratio (%)	Operating income (bn RMB)	Operating cost (bn RMB)	ROE (%)	ROA (%)
CNPC	3027.88	1327.19	43.83	2381.28	1716.45	7.68	21.96
PetroChina	1917.53	834.96	43.54	2003.84	1425.28	13.60	30.17

Source: Lianhe Credit (2012a), PetroChina 2011 Annual Report.

Table 2. Sinopec Group versus Sinopec Limited, 2011.

	Assets (bn RMB)	Liabilities (bn RMB)	Debt-asset ratio (%)	Operating income (bn RMB)	Operating cost (bn RMB)	ROE (%)	ROA (%)
Group	1745.307	1022.965	58.61	2551.951	2087.161	11.51	26.63
Limited	1130	621	43.54	2506	2093.20	15.93	30.17

Source: Lianhe Credit (2012b), Sinopec 2011 Annual Report.

Zhongyuan Oil and Gas and Daming Oil in the amount of 14.3 billion yuan (An 2006). The implementation of this mass 'privatization' was tested out in years prior. Sinopec, for example, had initiated the consolidation of Yanshan Petrochemical,[2] listed in Hong Kong, in late 2004 and again for Zhenhai Refinery, also in Hong Kong, in late 2005, with the deals costing 3.85 billion HKD and 7.67 billion HKD, respectively.

Related party transactions

In 2007, NOPCs had approximately 11% of all operating revenue and 22% of all operating cost arising from RPTs. When Sinopec Limited, with 12% of both revenue and cost coming from related parties, and PetroChina, with 6% and 36%, are excluded, NOPCs percentages rise to 26% and 44%, indicating a much higher amount of RPTs in the oil and petrochemical industry outside the two oligopolistic players. Yet if the figures are calculated excluding not only Sinopec Limited and PetroChina, but all their related affiliates, the numbers are 19% for related party sales and 13% for related party purchases. Thus, Sinopec Limited and PetroChina affiliates rely to a much larger extent on supplies and sales channels from the two oligarchs, while NOPCs unrelated to Sinopec Limited and PetroChina have more reliance on their group affiliates for sales channels than supplies – perhaps understandable, if oil and petrochemical inputs are coming from Sinopec and PetroChina. Sales represent a downstream orientation for NOPCs. The higher ratios of related party purchases versus sales can be understood if the supply of oil is dominated by Sinopec Limited and PetroChina, as their listed affiliates have little choice but to purchase upstream inputs from their parent or its affiliates. Indeed, all of the companies with more than 30% of operating cost coming from related party purchases were either CNPC, Sinopec Group or Sinopec Limited affiliates.

In 2011, the weighted average ratios of related party sales and purchases to total operating revenue and cost for the entire group of NOPCs are 10% and 16%, respectively. When Sinopec Limited, with 12% related sales and 10% related purchases, and PetroChina, with 5% and 22%, are excluded, the weighted averages for the group are 29% and 38%, respectively. Excluding all of Sinopec Group and CNPC affiliates brings these averages down to 19% and 26%, respectively. Again, the high figures when excluding only Sinopec and PetroChina but not necessarily their affiliates can be understood because the remaining population of NOPCs includes important affiliates, such as Shanghai Petrochemical and YueyangXingchang (part of Sinopec Limited and Sinopec Group, respectively), that rely on the group for inputs of crude oil and comprehensive services as well as output channels for sales. What is not readily apparent is why the ratio of related party purchases to operating cost has risen so dramatically: PetroChina has reduced its reliance on CNPC affiliates to 22% from 36% in 2007, which to some extent explains the overall figure for the group, but excluding Sinopec Group and CNPC affiliates gives a rise in the ratio of related party purchases to operating cost – to 26% from 13% in 2007. One conclusion is that for this group of domestically listed NOPCs, their development over the past five years has led to an increasing reliance on other companies within their own business groups, rather than the external market, for a range of inputs, services and sales outlets, a conclusion that would support the increasing lack of market-supporting institutions in China.

Thus, increasing inputs from related party suppliers seems to be an important trend, though one bucked by both Sinopec Limited and PetroChina. While the interpretation is mixed, it is clear that for important central state NOPCs such as Liaotong Chemical, YueyangXingchang, DaqingHuake, Yizheng Chemical Fibre and Shanghai Petrochemical, tapping related party suppliers is increasingly the strategy of choice.

Corporate finance

Finance companies and business group loans

Over the five-year period, overall debt to asset ratios increased to 46.01% from 42.44%. Also apparent in the data is a debt to asset ratio that increased some 200% for Sinopec during this period. The CSOEs with finance companies include CNOOC Finance Company, China Petroleum Finance Company and Sinopec Finance Company, as well as SinoChem Finance Company, Norinco Finance Company, SinoTrans-CSC Finance Company, and ChemChina Finance Company. These finance companies are all controlled by the group parent company, though the listed company may own shares of them.

The final piece of the corporate finance picture explored here is loans to or guarantees for related parties and loans, guarantees and short-term borrowing from related parties. Sinopec Limited provided 9.8 billion yuan in guarantees to its joint venture and cooperative enterprises. In 2007, PetroChina had a total of 46.7 billion yuan in loans, 24.4 billion of which came from the China Petroleum Finance. One of these loans, for 19.9 billion yuan, originated in November 2008 and is for a period until April 2032; the other, for 4.5 billion yuan, is until September, 2020. Both are charged a band of interest rates around 5%. In 2007, CNPC subsidiary Jichai Diesel reported that it obtained short-term loans of an addition 150 million for a total of 500 million yuan from China Petroleum Finance. Jichai Diesel paid 1 million yuan as 'guarantee fee' to its controlling shareholder for the loan in 2007. Another controlling shareholder, Jichai Diesel Factory, provided guarantees for Jichai Diesel's borrowing of close to 190 million yuan in loans.

Sinopec Limited had 11.9 billion yuan in short-term loans from Sinopec Group and its affiliates in 2011. The total amount listed at the end of the report is 53.0 billion yuan. Sinopec Limited provided 782 million in guarantees for its joint and cooperatively operated companies, versus a total of 4.5 billion yuan in guarantees. For loans maturing in less than one year, PetroChina had 37.9 billion yuan worth that were guaranteed by CNPC and its affiliates. It had 113 billion yuan in long-term loans, at least 40 billion of which came from China Petroleum Finance. By the end of 2011, PetroChina had borrowed 134.2 billion yuan from CNPC and its affiliates. Shanghai Petrochemical in 2011 borrowed 4.8 billion yuan from Sinopec Finance Company. It began listing Sinopec Finance as a related party in 2008 and noted loans of 230 million from this company in 2009. A loan of 5.2 billion yuan was made by Sinopec Finance to Shanghai Petrochemical in 2010. It lists a single loan guarantee of 200 million for a related subsidiary.

Outstanding accounts

Examining informal means of finance in 2007, the group of domestically listed NOPCs had an average of 457 million yuan in related party receivables and 1.69 billion yuan in related party payables in 2007. This indicates a net flow of capital into listed vehicles from related parties. The influence of Sinopec Limited and PetroChina on this average are heavy, as Sinopec had 3.99 billion in receivables and 5.47 billion in payables to related parties, while PetroChina had 4.09 billion in receivables and 29.5 billion in payables, topping the ranks of both financial categories. Twenty-five billion in payables to PetroChina indicates that CNPC is directing cash into propping PetroChina away from two smaller companies, though the absolute amount – totalling less than 50 million yuan – is likely of little importance.

Related party other receivables differ from related party receivables in being classified as involving debts arising from transactions outside the scope of a company's main business. Sinopec Limited and PetroChina again lead the list with 6.8 billion yuan and 4.7 billion yuan, amounting to less than 1% of operating income for 2007, but accounting for 57% and 30% of all other receivables. This large ratio of other receivables arising from related parties, averaging 54% but ranging from 7% to 91% for companies with more than 1.5 million yuan outstanding in this category, indicates whatever the nature of transactions with related parties outside of main business, the flow of capital outward is strongly oriented to related parties. This contrasts with the analysis of business-related receivables and payables above. A final observation is that there are extensive other receivables for firms such as Nanjing Tanker, Shanghai Petrochemical, Sinochem International, China Oilfield Services Limited (COSL) and Shandong Haihua, all of which have between 200 million and 450 million yuan in other receivables.

In 2011, the NOPCs averaged 1.07 billion yuan in receivables and 2.7 billion yuan in payables to related parties. Sinopec Limited and PetroChina lead the companies in total amount of related party receivables and payables, with 15.4 billion and 10.9 billion in receivables and 64.0 billion and 9.8 billion in payables, respectively. CNOOC's Offshore Oil Engineering and COSL rank highest among related party receivables with 21% and 18% of revenue. The two companies have a much lower ratio of payables to total operating income, at 3% and 5%, respectively. For Sinopec Limited and PetroChina, none of their related party receivables or payables account for more than 1% of total operating revenue and cost, with the exception of PetroChina's payables, which are 5% of the cost. While only slightly increasing from the previous year when it had 63.8 billion in payables, PetroChina has more than doubled the amount it owes to related parties, as it has added 10 billion or more in each of the years 2008, 2009 and 2010, suggesting that CNPC is deploying this tactic to keep more cash inside PetroChina. Sinopec Limited is also worthy of mention, as it went from 1.5 billion yuan in net payables in 2007 to 5.6 billion in receivables in 2011. Of the five LSOEs, Yanchang Petrochemical Engineering's net receivables have skyrocketed, growing from 4.6 million in 2007 to over 1 billion in 2011. In part this is due to escalating trade with its parent company, Shaanxi Yanchang Petroleum Group, as receivables have increased from 200 million in 2008 to 250 million in 2009 and 580 million in 2010. The large and increasing balance indicates that other group members are using Yanchang as a source of temporary financing and even outright appropriation of funds.

The largest amount of other receivables in 2011 was from Sinopec who had 1.5 billion yuan. This is predictably followed by PetroChina's 552 million. Yet these numbers have fallen significantly from 2007, and related party other receivables make up only 21% and 6% of all other receivables for Sinopec and PetroChina, respectively. Excluding Sinopec and PetroChina yields an average of 4.4 million yuan per company in related party other receivables, down from the 8.3 million yuan average in 2007, pointing to less influences for this informal financing mechanism.

Case studies

Liaotong Chemicals

Liaoning HuajinTongda Chemicals Company Limited is one of nine listed companies in the Norinco Group, which holds 51% of shares through a 60% stake of North Huajin Chemical Industries Group. Its growth rate over the 2007–2011 period is astonishing, with revenue growing from 3.4 billion yuan to 37.6 billion yuan by 2011. In 2011, it had the highest percentage, 91.85%, of purchases from related parties over total costs, buying almost six times the percentage of operating cost from related parties that it did in 2007. In

2008, Liaotong Chemical began to list 'Norinco Finance' as a related party. That is because, in 2008, it was floated four massive, long-term loans of 3.2 billion yuan (its 2008 total revenue was 3.7 billion). It also obtained 5.6 billion from two loans guaranteed by its controlling shareholders, Liaoning Huajin Chemical Group and its owner the group parent Norinco Group. Liaotong listed four subsidiary companies and 24 related parties held by North Huajin or Norinco. Aside from business-related entities such as import and export, fine chemicals and catalyst production firms, the related parties includes a hospital, a hotel, geotechnical and engineering design research companies and a finance company. Liaotong in 2009 began to sign a series of 'Crude Oil Purchasing Agreements' with Norinco-affiliated firms. In 2009 alone, it actually bought 2.89 billion yuan worth of crude oil, surpassing its entire operating revenue in cost. This practice was repeated in 2010 and 2011, raising to close to 100% the ratio of related party purchases to total cost; it purchased 16.10 billion and 27.02 billion yuan of crude in these years. Sales to related parties similarly reflect a jump in company operations – in 2010 and 2011, operating revenue skyrocketed to 23.93 billion yuan and 37.56 billion yuan from 2.75 billion yuan; related party sales accounted for 20% and 31% of this new income. Liaotong Chemical illustrates a massive, business group financed and led expansion of Norinco group's internal capabilities without influence of group-external institutions, markets or strategy. Sales of petrochemical products to group members guarantees the massive build up in production capacity will be covered by non-market demand. Norinco's strategy represents a significant model of development among the NOPCs.

Sinopec versus SASAC

Qiu (2010), a well-known media commentator and industrial analyst, asked, tongue-in-cheek, 'Who is Sinopec trying to bamboozle by selling its equity in real estate property for 1 yuan?' In April, 2010, Sinopec indeed sold its 50% interest in Zhuhai Huarui Property Management and Construction Company held by Sinopec's Yanshan Petrochemical subsidiary. In a statement responding to criticism, Yanshan clarified that the 1 yuan price was justified as the real estate company was burdened 14.6 million in debt and had negative net assets. As Qiu notes, however, Sinopec is sandwiched between SASAC/ government and shareholders/market. One month prior, in response to overheating real estate market, central SASAC issued the infamous 'exit order' (*qingtui ling*), requiring that with the exception of 16 CSOEs that specialize in real estate, all other CSOEs must exit the industry (amounting to over 220 subsidiaries under 78 different CSOEs) within six months. Sinopec Limited's sale could be interpreted as its anger at SASAC's order. By the end of 2010, Sinopec and PetroChina were joined only by five other CSOEs in jettisoning their real estate assets, leaving some 71 other CSOEs with more than 200 subsidiaries still continuing their real estate businesses (Zheng 2010). In 2014 alone, CSOEs liquidated 10 billion in real estate assets, with Sinopec selling off a Sichuan real estate company for 1 yuan (Guo et al. 2014). As Cao (2000) has argued in a different context, this selling off of state assets occurred without any regulatory oversight (from SASAC or any other government bureau) or administrative appraisal, incurring a critical response from individuals regardless of stock market performance and viability of real estate businesses.

Schizophrenia: Jilin Chemical Engineering

Jilin Chemical Engineering was listed in Shanghai in 2003, raising 391 million yuan. It was 49% controlled by Jilin Chemical Group, a wholly owned subsidiary of CNPC. Its main business is contracting oil and petrochemical, municipal utility, housing, smelting, power and electrical engineering and construction, with over 50% of its sales coming from CNPC subsidiaries. Only a few short years later, in late 2008, Jilin Chemical Group signed a share transfer and asset swap agreement with Shanxi Coal Import-Export Group. Shanxi Coal paid 620 million yuan for the remaining 39.75% controlling interest of the listed company. Also, in exchange for seven legally independent coal trading companies, CNPC was able to withdraw all assets, liabilities and staff from the listed vehicle, which now trades as Shanxi Coal International Energy. Owing to different values of assets swapped, Jilin Chemical Group was required to pay 52 million yuan to complete the deal.

Despite starting in 2002 selling off, swapping assets or repurchasing shares of numerous listed subsidiaries, reabsorbing and consolidating oil and petrochemical assets that were previously listed under PetroChina, CNPC choose to list, then de-list Jilin Chemical Engineering during this period. Yet this is not an isolated incident, or simply CNPC. On 23 May 2013, Sinopec Group's Sinopec Engineering began trading on the Hong Kong stock market, with Sinopec Group holding 67% block of ownership. Kunlun Energy, another Hong Kong listed firm that is 62% controlled by CNPC, bought key gas pipeline assets by purchasing a majority share of Beijing Natural Gas Pipeline Company in December 2010 (Wang and Zhang 2011). Bucking both the initial promise made to investors at the time of listing and the trend of consolidation of assets under their main listed vehicles PetroChina and Sinopec Limited, CNPC and Sinopec Group have engaged in schizophrenic oscillations between building multidivisional firms like those common in the West and expanding business groups with murky asset transfers and growing RPTs.

Discussion

What were the goals of CNPC and Sinopec Group delisting companies over the past decade? Both Tang, Li, and Meng (2006) and CITIC securities (Yin 2005) outline problems that are solved by 'privatizing' (delisting) subsidiaries. Among these are lack of capital (listed companies quickly lose the ability to attract fresh capital), shareholder interference (important decisions must pass through shareholder meetings), too much competition in the same national product and supply markets (subsidiaries competing for customers and resources) and excessive RPTs (hurt shareholders). The implication is that by making subsidiaries into branches under a dominant parent, similar to a Chandlerian multidivisional firm, these problems will be solved or at least alleviated: less capital to subsidiaries means more capital for parent; less scrutiny from shareholders means less interference in execution of business decisions from above; less competition makes it easier to make and sell products and less RPTs means that all transactions become invisible inside the 'visible hand' of the multidivisional corporation. This would confirm Brødsgaard's (2012; Steinfeld 2010) insight that corporatization of state sector forces firms to act according to global market conditions, fortifying the commercial supremacy of the West. Yet evidence presented both in ownership chains, listing of new subsidiaries and expansion of RPTs belies such a neat convergence. The NOPCs examined here, including some of the most powerful businesses in the world, also present evidence to the contrary. By listing, many of the NOPC group subsidiaries are, in fact, outsourcing scrutiny of and building capability for business operations, pointing to Olson's (1982; Lin and Milahupt 2013) encompassing organization or interest rather than simply access to further capital funds.

Returning to the issue of RPTs addressed in the third hypothesis, they decrease slightly for NOPCs overall, as well as Sinopec Limited and PetroChina. Yet other NOPCs, both including and excluding Sinopec and CNPC subsidiaries, increased RPTs; in the case of purchases, the ratio to total costs has doubled, even as costs overall grew. The findings indicate that business group organization remains a main, and increasingly important, aspect of the oil and petrochemical industry in China. On the one hand, the shift over the period is towards much more reliance on intra-group suppliers to the NOPCs, differing from other findings (Lu, Yao, and Lan 2004) and perhaps indicative of the nature of the industry, with a limited number of suppliers of a scarce resource. On the other hand, Sinopec Limited and PetroChina have reduced their reliance on RPTs, particularly suppliers, as more of upstream oil and petrochemical supplies are transferred to their remit. Movement towards a Western multidivisional firm is reflected in the increasing ratio of RPTs for Sinopec Group/Sinopec Limited's and CNPC/PetroChina's subsidiaries. Thus, there are mixed results in terms of whether China and its NOPCs are operating in an environment where more market-supporting institutions are present.

Evidence on financial market development outside business groups shows clearer evidence that external financial institutions have shown poor growth or effectiveness from 2007 to 2011. Debt-based financing grew, particularly for large, key CSOEs. Increasing utilization of finance companies is evident in the massive loans floated by CNPC, Sinopec Group, CNOOC, Sinochem and Norinco. NOPCs are moving away from external financial markets and scrutiny, suggesting more ineffectual finance markets in 2011 compared with 2007. Informal finance lends evidence to this conclusion. Outstanding payments both to and from listed NOPCs nearly doubled over the five-year period. PetroChina, in particular, utilizes outstanding payments to its group suppliers to keep capital from flowing out. Yet these can be argued to be business accounting expenses, a regular part of transacting in the oil and petrochemical industry. This interpretation is backed up by the significant decrease in 'other' RPTs, which have fallen significantly, and average only a few million yuan per company. Potentially, these transactions provide a small opportunity for graft or malfeasance at a local level, but are increasingly insignificant for overall corporate financing. This, contrary to the examination of debt and finance companies, implies that NOPCs are increasingly utilizing internal finance for business-related expansion.

Implications for theory and practice

It is in this context of property rights and corporate governance over state assets and businesses that listing on the stock market must be understood. Wang Yong, immediately prior to retiring as the head of SASAC, outlined the future direction of reforms to central and local SOEs as further listing on the stock market and creating boards of directors (Chang 2013). The goals of listing are not to access capital, as is often assumed in the literature (e.g. Pan and Brooker 2014), because this is abundantly available through bank loans and internal finance. An *Economist* (2001) story from Yanshan, a town on the outskirts of Beijing built and run by Sinopec Group, suggests another answer. Preparing for the listing of Sinopec Limited in 2000, Sinopec Group divided the town into productive and non-productive assets (including people), while Morgan Stanley and KPMG consultants ran around holding study sessions with managers and employees on how to be a good capitalist. The irony of such a 'campaign' to change Yanshan townspeople's ideology to index their value and daily work to such a fetishistic-financial sign as a stock market ticker was perhaps lost on the author at the time.[3] To list assets, what was needed was to change managerial and employee frameworks of value to facilitate governance arising from the institution of the stock market. Sinopec Group, then as now, faced choices on how to maximize group and limited company resources to engage its historical welfare burden, lifetime commitment to employees, the running of town utilities, administration of local schools and hospitals and management of (employee) apartment complexes. As part of China's encompassing organization, it also must *govern* assets to maximize China's development as a corporate group. Financiers and investors view separation into productive (relative to financed business operations and activities) and non-productive parts as sufficient to ensure property rights of shareholders and resulting corporate governance. Yet the creation of property rights and goals of listing, in and of itself, for groups, and the resulting scrutiny through corporate governance, play out quite differently when the business group nature of the companies is understood.

Conclusions

The findings of the four research hypotheses explored in this study yield important advances in understanding big business policy in China. Rather than 'transitioning' towards a market economy, big businesses have already transitioned, and the key sites at which corporate governance occurs are at the interfaces between state officials/SASAC and business groups and between business group parents and subsidiaries. Following the 'confounding webs' in some groups sheds light on the endless chains of subsidiaries that cloud the organizational understanding of China's largest and most important business like so much octopus' ink (Cao 2000, 41). The limitations of attempting to understand a singular, legally independent 'firm' in the context of China's socialist market economy is apparent through the chains and interfaces highlighted in this study. Not only international trade, investment and expansion policy but multinational firms looking to work with China should take note and pay careful attention to the nature of big business in China today.

Notes

1. The websites that maintain their individual petroleum or petrochemical 'concept boards' (*gainianbankuai*) are finance.sina.com.cn, quote.eastmoney.com and www.emoney.cn, respectively. Sites were accessed in November and December, 2012.
2. This was the first time any Hong Kong-listed company was 'privatized'.
3. The *Economist* author notes that the stock market price of the newly listed Sinopec Limited was subsequently prominently displayed in the lobby of the Sinopec headquarters building in Beijing. The parallel with the idolatry and adulation given to Mao portraits and tchotchkes only two dozen years previous is uncanny.

References

An, Bei. 2006. "The Complete Initiation of Sinopec's Bids to Purchase Four of Its Subsidiaries." [In Chinese.] *Xinhua Net*, June 3. Accessed December 11. http://www.finance.sina.com.cn/stock/s/20060306/15332394619.shtml

Berkman, Henk, Rebel Cole, and Lawrence Fu. 2010. "Political Connections and Minority Shareholder Protection: Evidence from Securities-Market Regulation in China." *Journal of Financial and Quantitative Analysis* 45 (6): 1391–1417.

Berle, Adolf, and Gardiner Means. 1932. *The Modern Corporation and Private Property*. New York: Macmillan.

Brødsgaard, Kjeld. 2012. "Politics and Business Group Formation in China: The Party in Control?" *China Quarterly* 211: 624–648.

Cao, Lan. 2000. "Chinese Privatization: Between Plan and Market." *Law and Contemporary Problems* 63 (4): 13–62.

Carney, Michael, Daniel Shapiro, and Yao Tang. 2009. "Business Group Performance in China: Ownership and Temporal Considerations." *Management and Organization Review* 5 (2): 167–193.

Chandler, Alfred. 1977. *The Visible Hand*. Cambridge: Belknap/Harvard University Press.

Chang, Bao. 2013. "SOEs Make Strong Progress on Listings amid Reforms." *China Daily*, January 11, p. 16.

Cheung, Yan-Leung, Lihua Jing, Tong Lu, P. Raghavendra Rau, and Aris Stouraitis. 2009. "Tunneling and Propping Up: An Analysis of Related Party Transactions by Chinese Listed Companies." *Pacific-Basic Finance Journal* 17: 372–393.

Clarke, Donald. 2003. "Corporate Governance in China: An Overview." *SSRN*. Accessed January 15. http://www.ssrn.com/abstract=424885

Economist. 2001. "Survey: A Lesson in Capitalism." *Economist*, April 7, pp. S14–S15.

Fan, Joseph, T. J. Wong, and Tianyu Zhang. 2007. "Politically Connected CEOs, Corporate Governance, and Post-IPO Performance of China's Newly Partially Privatized Firms." *Journal of Financial Economics* 84 (2): 330–357.

Green, Stephen, and Guy Shaojia Liu. 2005. *Exit the Dragon: Privatisation and State Control in China*. Oxford: Blackwell.

Guo, Haifei, Kai Yan, Jiaxuan Li, and Lei Yang. 2014. "Petrochemicals and Electronics Lead the Way in 'Sale' of Over Ten Billion in Real Estate Assets by Over 70 CSOEs." [In Chinese.] *Economic Observer*, March 28. Accessed March 29. http://:www.eeo.com.cn/2014/0328/258272.shtml

Hahn, Donghoon, and Keun Lee. 2006. "Chinese Business Groups: Their Origins and Development." In *Business Groups in East Asia*, edited by Sea-Jin Chang, 207–231. Oxford: Oxford University Press.

Howson, Nicholas. 2014. "'Quark Corporate Governance' as Traditional Chinese Medicine – The Securities Regulation Cannabilization of China's Corporate Law and a State Regulator's Battle Against Party State Political Economic Power." *Seattle University Law Review* 37 (2): 667–716.

Jian, Ming, and T. J. Wong. 2004. "Earnings Management and Tunneling Through Related Party Transactions: Evidence from Chinese Corporate Groups." European Finance Association Annual Conference Paper No. 549. February, 2004.

Jian, Ming, and T. J. Wong. 2010. "Propping Through Related Party Transactions." *Review of Accounting Studies* 15 (1): 70–105.

Jian, Ming, and Ming Xu. 2012. "Determinants of the Guarantee Circles: The Case of Chinese Listed Firms." *Pacific-Basin Finance Journal* 20: 78–100.

Jiang, Guohua, Charles Lee, and Heng Yue. 2010. "Tunneling Through Intercorporate Loans: The China Experience." *Journal of Financial Economics* 98: 1–20.

Keister, Lisa. 2000. *Chinese Business Groups*. New York: Oxford University Press.

Lianhe Credit Rating Company. 2012a. "CNPC: Credit Rating Report for Medium-Range Bills Issued in First Quarter, 2013." [In Chinese.] Accessed December 15. http://www.lianheratings.com.cn

Lianhe Credit Rating Company. 2012b. "Sinopec Group: Long-Term Corporate Credit Rating Report." [In Chinese.] Accessed December 15. http://www.lianheratings.com.cn

Lin, Kun-Chin. 2008. "Macroeconomic Disequilibria and Enterprise Reform: Restructuring the Chinese Oil and Petrochemical Industries in the 1990s." *China Journal* 60: 49–79.

Lin, Li-Wen, and Curtis Milahupt. 2013. "We are the (National) Champions: Understanding the Mechanisms of State Capitalism in China." *Stanford Law Review* 697: 734–746.

Lu, Yuan, Jun Yao, and Hailin Lan. 2004. "Diversification, Internal Transactions, and Performance in Chinese Firms." Paper submitted to Fourth Asia Academy of Management Conference, Shanghai, December 16–18.

Morck, Randall, Daniel Wolfenzon, and Bernard Yeung. 2005. "Corporate Governance, Economic Entrenchment, and Growth." *Journal of Economic Literature* 43 (3): 655–720.

Morris, Jonathan, John Hassard, and Jackie Sheehan. 2002. "Privatization, Chinese-Style: Economic Reform and the State-Owned Enterprises." *Public Administration* 80 (2): 359–373.

Nolan, Peter. 2001. *China and the Global Economy*. Basingstoke: Palgrave.

Oi, Jean. 2011. "Politics in China's Corporate Restructuring." In *Going Private in China*, edited by Jean Oi, 1–18. Stanford, CA: Walter H. Shorenstein Asia-Pacific Research Centre Books.

Oi, Jean, and Chaohua Han. 2011. "China's Corporate Restructuring: A Multi-Step Process." In *Going Private in China*, edited by Jean Oi, 19–37. Stanford, CA: Walter H. Shorenstein Asia-Pacific Research Centre Books.

Olson, Mancur. 1982. *The Rise and Decline of Nations*. New Haven, CT: Yale University Press.

Olson, Mancur, and Satu Kähkönen. 2000. "Introduction: The Broader View." In *A Not-So-Dismal Science*, edited by Mancur Olson, and Satu Kähkönen, 1–36. Oxford: Oxford University Press.

Ong, Aihwa, and Li Zhang. 2008. "Introduction: Privatizing China." In *Privatizing China: Socialism from Afar*, edited by Li Zhang and Aihwa Ong, 1–19. Stanford, CA: Stanford University Press.

Pan, Fenghua, and Daniel Brooker. 2014. "Going Global? Examining the Geography of Chinese Firms' Overseas Listings on International Stock Exchanges." *Geoforum* 52: 1–11.

Qiu, Lin. 2010. "Who is Sinopec Trying to Bamboozle by Selling Property for 1 Yuan?" [In Chinese.] *Qianjiang Evening News*, April 8, p. B7.

Sigley, Gary. 2006. "Chinese Governmentalities: Government, Governance and the Socialist Market Economy." *Economy and Society* 35 (4): 487–508.

Smyth, Russell. 2000. "Should China be Promoting Large-Scale Enterprises and Enterprise Groups?" *World Development* 28 (4): 721–737.

Steinfeld, Edward. 2010. *Playing Our Game: Why China's Economic Rise Doesn't Threaten the West*. Oxford: Oxford University Press.

Su, Dongwei. 2005. "Corporate Finance and State Enterprise Reform in China." *China Economic Review* 16: 118–148.

Sutherland, Dylan. 2001. "Policies to Build National Champions: China's 'National Team' of Enterprise Groups." In *China and the Global Business Revolution*, edited by Peter Nolan, 67–140. Basingstoke: Palgrave.

Tang, Guliang, Xinfu Li, and Rongli Meng. 2006. "Perspective on Sinopec 'Delisting' Its Listed Companies." [In Chinese.] *Finance & Accounting* 6: 43–47.

Wang, Duan, and Yuzhe Zhang. 2011. "Kunlun's Stock Options: Exercise for the Fat." *Caixin*, December 2.

Williams, Maggie, and Dennis Taylor. 2014. "Measuring and Explaining the Extent of Corporate Propping Transactions: Evidence from China." *Global Review of Accounting and Finance* 5 (1): 76–92.

Wu, Mengfei. 2002. "A Study of Restructuring in the Chinese Petroleum Sector." Unpublished diss., MIT Sloan School of Management.

Xu, Zhifeng. 2006. "PetroChina Takeover Bid for Its Own Listed Companies is Decided." [In Chinese.] *People's Net*, January 12.

Yeh, Yin-Hua, Pei-Gi Shu, Tsun-Siou Lee, and Yu-Hui Su. 2009. "Non-Tradable Share Reform and Corporate Governance in the Chinese Stock Market." *Corporate Governance: An International Review* 17 (4): 457–475.

Yeo, Yukyung. 2013. "Contextualizing China's Corporate Governance: The Case of China's Central State Enterprise Groups." *Journal of Contemporary China* 22 (81): 460–475.

Yin, Xiaodong. 2005. "2006 A-Shares Investment Strategy for Petroleum & Petrochemical Industry." *CITIC Securities Industry Research: Petroleum & Petrochemicals*, December 2005. Accessed December 15. http://www.cs.ecitic.com/ShowDocumentFile.jsp?id=1603400

Zhang, Jin. 2004. *Catch-Up and Competitiveness in China: The Case of Large Firms in the Oil Industry*. London: RoutledgeCurzon.

Zheng, Zhong. 2010. "71 Companies Central-State Enterprises Still Have Not Exited the Real Estate Industry 16 Companies Have Gotten Credit Support." [In Chinese.] *China Securities Journal*, December 6.

Appendix 1.   Profile and 2007–2011 Annual Reports Consulted of NOPCs in 2011

Stock code	Full English name	Ultimate shareholder	Block ownership (2011), %	Nature of shareholder
600248	Shaanxi Yanchang Petroleum Chemical Engineering	Shaanxi province, Yan'an city and Yulin district SASACs	62	LSOE
000637	Maoming Petro-Chemical Shihua	Taiyue Real Estate	30	Private
000819	YueyangXingchang Petro-Chemical	Sinopec Group	23	CSOE
000698	Shenyang Chemical Industry Co., Ltd	Shenyang Chemical Group (ChemChina Group)	34	CSOE
600028	China Petroleum & Chemical Corporation (Sinopec Corp)	Sinopec Group	76	CSOE
002221	Oriental Energy	Zhou Yifeng, Zhou Hanping	51	Private
601857	PetroChina Company Limited	CNPC	86	CSOE
600339	Xinjiang Dushanzi Tianli High & New Tech	Dushanzi district (Karamay city) SASAC	23	LSOE
000554	Sinopec Shandong Taishan Petroleum	Sinopec Limited	25	CSOE
000096	Shenzhen Guangju Energy	Shennan Oil Group (Nanshan district (Shenzhen) SASAC, COSCO, Shenzhen Investment)	58	LSOE
600688	Sinopec Shanghai Petrochemical	Sinopec Limited	56	CSOE
601808	COSL	CNOOC	54	CSOE
600387	Zhejiang Haiyue Co., Ltd	Haiyue Economic Development Limited	22	Private
002207	Xinjiang Zhundong Petroleum Technology	Qin Yong	8	Private
600087	Nanjing Tanker Corporation	Nanjing Changjiang Oil Transport (CSC-SinoTrans)	55	CSOE
600583	Offshore Oil Engineering	CNOOC	49	CSOE
600500	Sinochem International	SinoChem Ltd	56	CSOE
000617	Jinan Diesel Engine	Jichai Power Equipment Company (CNPC)	60	CSOE
600871	Sinopec Yizheng Chemical Fibre	Sinopec Ltd	42	CSOE
000731	Sichuan Meifeng Chemical Industry	Huachuan Oil and Gas Exploration Company (Sinopec Group)	14	CSOE
000985	Daqing Huake	Daqing Petrochemical Factory, Linyuan Refinery (CNPC)	55	CSOE
000159	Xinjiang International Industry	Xinjiang Foreign Economic & Trade Group	31	Private

(*Continued*)

Appendix 1 – *continued*

Stock code	Full English name	Ultimate shareholder	Block ownership (2011), %	Nature of shareholder
000059	Liaoning Huajin Tongda Chemicals	Huajin Chemical Industries Group (Norinco)	51	CSOE
002192	Luxiang	KeRongqing	21	Private
000510	Sichuan Jinlu Group	Hongda Group	5	Private
000822	Shandong Haihua	Haihua Group (CNOOC)	40	CSOE
002040	Nanjing Port	Nanjing SASAC	63	LSOE
000852	Kingdream Public Limited Company	CNPC	68	CSOE
000155	Sichuan Chemical Company Limited	Sichuan SASAC	63	LSOE
000407	Shandong Shengli	43 individuals	9	Private
600378	Sichuan Tianyi Science & Technology	Haohua Group (ChemChina Group)	23	CSOE

Note: Annual reports downloaded from the SSE website, www.sse.com.cn, and SZSE website, www.szse.cn, and the "Annual Reports" section of vip.stock.finance.sina.com.cn, all accessed from July, 2012 through December, 2013.

Rationale of internationalization of China's national oil companies: seeking natural resources, strategic assets or sectoral specialization?

Hongyi Lai[a], Sarah O'Hara[b] and Karolina Wysoczanska[a]

[a]School of Contemporary Chinese Studies, University of Nottingham, Nottingham, UK; [b]School of Geography, University of Nottingham, Nottingham, UK

The bulk of the existing literature emphasized that China's companies sought strategic assets (technology, brands and access to markets) through internationalization in order to overcome latecomers' comparative disadvantage, while some studies suggested that these firms went after natural resources to address China's rising oil imports. The third argument (which we coin the 'sectoral strength' hypothesis) suggested that the upstream firms in extractive business would seek natural resources, whereas downstream ones would seek strategic assets. In this study, we examine the rationale of main overseas investment deals ('going out') of China's two largest national oil companies during 2002–2010 which were also China's top two non-financial firms with the largest outward investment stocks during 2004–2010. We conclude that these deals can be best explained by the 'sectoral specialisation' hypothesis supplemented with a consideration for strategic assets.

Introduction: China's soaring profile in outward foreign direct investment

One of the most significant developments in global investment in the last several years has been the rapid ascent of Chinese firms. Since its opening in the late 1970s China has made progressive, but impressive efforts to attract foreign direct investments (FDI) inflows. Moreover, since 1999, China has pursued a parallel strategy, coined the 'go out' (or go global, *zouchuqu*) corporate strategy, whereby it has encouraged increased internationalization of Chinese firms.

The pace of international investment of Chinese firms has accelerated in the last decade. As illustrated in Figure 1, outward foreign direct investment (OFDI) flows from China grew from US\$ 2.7 billion in 2002 to almost US\$ 70 billion in 2010, making it the largest source of capital among developing countries and fifth in the world (MOFCOM 2010). This marked increase in OFDI occurred against an overall global decline in FDI flows since the latter peaked in 2007. From 2008 when the financial crisis struck till 2010, developed economies even pulled back on their OFDI investments (UNCTAD 2011, 24; 2013, xvi, 4). In sharp contrast, China, thanks to its huge foreign reserve and its robust economic growth at home, has seized the opportunity to expand significantly its OFDI. By 2012, China's OFDI had reached US\$ 84 billion and as a result ranked third in the world in this arena, accounting for an impressive 6% of the world total US\$ 1.39 trillion OFDI (UNCTAD 2013, xv, xvi). Significantly, 60% of the respondents from the investment promotion agencies surveyed for the *World Investment Report 2013* regarded

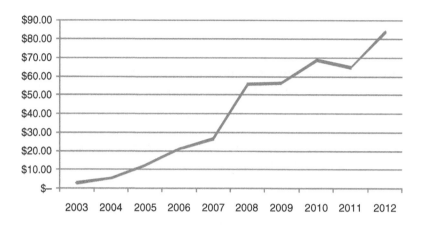

Figure 1.   China's outward direct investment flows, 2002–2012 (US$ billions). Source: MOFCOM, *2010 Statistical Bulletin of China's Outward Foreign Direct Investment*, http://images.mofcom.gov. cn/hzs/accessory/201109/1316069658609.pdf, accessed 4 May 2014. Data of 2011–2012 came from UNCTAD, *World Investment Report*, 2012, 2013.

China as the most promising source of FDI in the world for the period of 2013–2015, enabling China, instead of the US to claim this top spot (UNCTAD 2013, 21). China's stellar performance far outperformed the overall post-crisis decline or stagnation of OFDI of Russia, India and especially Brazil, the other members of the BRIC (UNCTAD 2013, 214–216). Meanwhile, the number of Chinese multinational enterprises (MNEs) on the Fortune Global 500 list expanded from zero in 1990 to 61 firms in 2010 (Peng 2012).

However, compared to outward investments from other major economies, China's share in the OFDI stock (i.e. cumulative total) is still comparably small (see Figure 2). According to the *World Investment Report (WIR)* 2013, the world's FDI stock reached US $23.6 trillion by the end of 2012 (UNCTAD 2013). China's OFDI stock in 2012 amounted to US$476.1 billion and constituted only 2% of the world's total (Figure 2).

Nevertheless, China's national oil companies (NOCs) are significant players in the world investment movement and world business. Leasing and business services, and

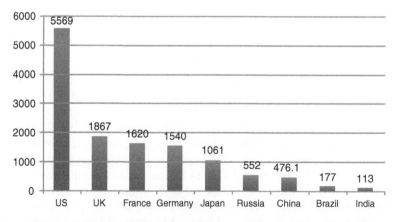

Figure 2.   OFDI stock of major economies (US$ billion), 2012. Source: Data for OFDI stock up to 2010 come from MOFCOM, *2010 Statistical Bulletin of China's Outward Foreign Direct Investment*, http://images.mofcom.gov.cn/hzs/accessory/201109/1316069658609.pdf, accessed 4 May 2014. Data of 2011–2012 came from UNCTAD, *World Investment Report, 2013*.

banking were the two largest sources of Chinese OFDI stock in 2010, accounting for US $97.2 billion and US$55.3 billion, respectively (MOFCOM 2010). Mining including oil and gas and other commodities exploration and mining activities accounted for US$44.7 billion of investment stock (MOFCOM 2010).

China's national oil companies (NOCs) 'have emerged as significant players in global mergers and acquisitions in upstream oil and natural gas' (namely, exploration and extraction of oil and gas). For example, Chinese companies invested US$18.2 billion on merger and acquisition (M&A) deals in 2009, accounting for 13% of the total US$144 billion of global oil and gas acquisitions, and for 61% of total US$30 billion of acquisitions by national oil companies (CNPC Research Institute of Economics and Technology 2010; quoted from Jiang and Sinton 2011).

The prominent role of China's NOCs in global investment in mining is due to several reasons. First of all, China's largest NOCs are among the world's top firms. In 2012, Sinopec and CNPC were ranked fifth and sixth, respectively, among the Fortune 500 Firms – the highest ranks among Chinese firms. Both Sinopec and CNPC (or PetroChina, the publicly-listed company and the most important branch of the latter) were the largest firms in China. Second, China has become the largest net oil importer since September 2013 (EIA 2014), largely thanks to the growing demand from the transport sector. Compared to coal of which China has rich deposits, oil consumption generates less pollution and causes less damage to the environment. However, China has a far smaller reserve as far as oil is concerned. In order to meet the rapidly growing oil consumption, China's oil and gas companies have been actively searching for resources abroad. China's demand for gas has increased drastically in the recent years and this trend seems to be continuing in the coming decade (O'hara and Lai 2011).

Research questions

This contribution aims to address the question *'What is the rationale for China's national oil companies (NOCs) to invest abroad?'* against two contexts. The first is the speed at which Chinese firms have entered the world stage with respect to OFDI and the second is to add to the existing debates within the literature on the rationale for internationalization of firms from emerging economies and developing countries.

To explore this question, we have conducted an analysis of the cases of foreign investment projects by Sinopec and CNPC over the last decade and tested the three following hypotheses derived from the literature on internationalization of firms – namely that: (1) China's companies seek strategic assets (technology, know-how, brands, and privileged access to markets) in order to overcome late comers' comparative disadvantage, (2) China's NOCs are primarily interested in natural resources to accommodate China's rising reliance on oil imports and (3) the upstream firms in the extractive business look for natural resources, whereas downstream firms are mainly interested in strategic assets and efficiency (which we coin the 'sectoral specialisation' hypothesis). We conclude that the 'sectoral specialisation' hypothesis supplemented by a heavy consideration for strategic assets best explain these international deals.

Literature on internationalization of business and the Chinese case

The existing literature offers useful insights as to the rationale of internationalization of business. Most of the mainstream international business theories are based on the experience of MNEs originating from developed economies. They propose that internal strength is an important prerequisite for a firm's internationalization. Dunning's eclectic model (1981) suggested that a firm would engage in international production when it possessed certain ownership-specific advantages that were not possessed by other firms. Only when a firm possessed such an advantage in ownership could it increase profits by exploiting its assets in overseas markets. The choice of host country location was believed to be determined by one or more of four types of motivations (Dunning 1998; Dunning and Lundan 2008, 67) – market-seeking, efficiency-seeking, resource-seeking and strategic asset-seeking. The aim of market seeking was to protect the existing markets or to exploit new markets (Dunning and Lundan 2008, p.70). Efficiency-seeking referred to the scenarios where firms seek to exploit differences in the costs of production between countries (UNCTAD 2007). Firms were regarded as seeking natural resources when they secured a continual supply of raw materials for companies' own industrial operations (Deng 2004). Strategic assets-seeking firms endeavoured to augment their comparative advantages or to overcome their comparative disadvantages by investing abroad in strategic assets such as research and development capacity, technology, brands and reputation or distribution and production networks (Deng 2012; Teece, Pisano, and Shuen 1997). These strategic assets were 'a set of complementary and specialized *Resources* and *Capabilities* which are scarce, durable, not easily traded, and difficult to imitate, may enable the firm to earn economic rents' (Amit and Schoemaker 1993, 37).

Much of the literature which considers China's international business focuses on whether conventional theories can explain the motivations behind China's OFDI (e.g. Child and Rodrigues 2005; Liu, Buck, and Shu 2005; Luo and Tung 2007; Buckley et al. 2007). Two major issues have been highlighted by recent studies. First, firms from emerging economies like China have weak ownership advantages (Deng 2009; Buckley et al. 2007; Alcácer and Chung 2007; Child and Rodrigues 2005). Second, these firms often leap-frog certain stages of internationalization process (Mathews 2006). From this perspective, Chinese companies go abroad not to exploit existing firm-specific advantages, but rather to explore and acquire strategic assets from developed market economies to overcome their latecomer disadvantages (Child and Rodrigues 2005; Luo and Tung 2007; Yiu, Lau, and Bruton 2007; March 1991). Indeed, some researchers (Nolan 2001) showed that the gap between top Chinese firms and their foreign counterparts was bigger than many had thought. For example, in 2012, PetroChina overtook Exxon as the world's biggest oil producer. However, in terms of total assets, profits and technological capacity, PetroChina is still behind the US giant (BBC News, 2012). Thus Chinese firms often resorted to a more aggressive approach to compensate for their competitive weakness and to gain sustainable competitive advantage (Cui and Jiang 2010; Rui and Yip 2008).

Several scholars (Ning 2009; Morck, Yeung, and Zhao 2008; Deng 2007; Buckley et al. 2007; Cai 1999) provide evidence for the argument that Chinese firms, especially multinational corporations (MNCs) and large state-owned firms (SOEs) are driven by their need to catch up through acquiring strategic assets such as technological know-how and managerial expertise. Some widely acknowledged institutional advantages for Chinese MNCs and large SOEs in the existing research include government support through diplomatic assistances, supplies of financial resources, access to state-supported scientific and technical research, benefits of state ownership (while not losing autonomy), and administrative regulations favouring outward investments.

Although there has been some doubt that the investment behaviour of Chinese firms has been significantly influenced by government policies, some researchers claim that Chinese OFDI was becoming more commercial and that internal corporate motives are now playing a more important role (Chen 2009; Houser 2008; Hong and Sun 2006).

Because the exploration of new markets is the most common type of strategy for companies from developing economies (UNCTAD 2007), several studies point to the rise of market-seeking Chinese firms (Buckley et al 2007, Taylor 2002). These studies have concluded that on the one hand, market-seeking motives were the logical consequence of China's export oriented policy, especially in the 1980s and 1990s (Zhan 1995), while on the other hand, growing competitive pressure from western MNEs in the Chinese domestic market and sliding profit margins gave incentive for Chinese companies to expand abroad, especially towards large markets (Deng 2004; Cai 1999).

With respect to natural resources, a number of existing studies have emphasized that China invests in resource-rich countries to secure a stable supply of raw materials to support China's high economic growth (Leung, Li, and Low 2011; Ellings and Friedberg 2006; Taylor 2002). Indeed, China's increased demand for oil and gas reflects not only the country's impressive economic performance, but also its lack of domestic reserves with China holding only 1% of oil and 1.5% of gas total world reserves (BP 2011). Some studies indicated that the resource-seeking OFDI of Chinese NOCs is directly associated with the government's policy of national energy security (Salidjanova 2011; Frynas and Paolo 2007). However, there are no conclusive findings on the significance of natural resources as a primary factor for Chinese NOCs to invest abroad. While Globerman and Shapiro (2009) conclude that securing resources is a relatively unimportant motive for Chinese OFDI, several researchers (e.g. Buckley et al. 2007; Kolstad and Wiig 2012) suggest that China's OFDI has concentrated on natural resources in countries with a weak institutional environment. In addition, Amighinia, Rabellottic, and Sanfilippob (2013) have suggested that state owned enterprises SOEs are not only more risk taking and attracted to natural resources, but are also driven by the strategic needs of their home country when investing abroad, while private enterprises are more risk averse and more motivated by tapping into the markets in their overseas investment. There is a growing body of literature, for example, a study by Lu et al. (2014) that emphasizes the role of institutions in the developed host countries that attracts China's OFDI. However, this argument seems to be less relevant for our study, as the previous study by Amighinia, Rabellottic, and Sanfilippob (2013) and our dataset suggest, China's large state energy firms have made a huge amount of investment in developing countries which lack good institutions.

Arguably, comparatively less has been written on efficiency-seeking motives in Chinese companies. According to the UNCTAD report (2007), efficiency-seeking outward investments were relatively unimportant for Chinese firms because of low costs in their domestic market. Several scholars proposed that factors such as increasing labour costs, infrastructure bottlenecks and power shortage might have resulted in the growing role of efficiency-seeking motives in China's OFDI in recent years (Ning and Sutherland 2012).

A number of studies have also emphasized the rapid expansion of outward investment from China into the world's tax havens (Ning and Sutherland 2012). The preferred tax havens for Chinese investors are Hong Kong, the Cayman Islands and the British Virgin Islands. By 2010, these destinations accounted for almost 76% of total Chinese OFDI stock (MOFCOM 2010). Although much of this investment was considered exclusively 'round-tripping' – assets recycled through tax havens for the purpose of obtaining preferential treatment as foreign capital (UNCTAD 2007; Luo and Tung 2007); a number of studies have also noted the importance of raising capital on foreign capital markets in such havens (Xiao 2004). In our dataset, we cannot find much information on investment of NOCs or acquisitions in these tax havens. We thus decide not to pursue this line of inquiry.

Hypotheses: strategic assets, natural resources and sectoral strength

Given the contending views on business internationalization, we believe that a careful analysis of overseas investment projects by China's NOCs can help shed light on the relevance of these theories for China. To explore this issue, we analysed the main reasons for OFDI projects over the period 2000–2010 which coincides with a period of increased activity by the NOCs.

As the literature suggests, there are four main reasons for internationalization of a business – seeking strategic assets, markets, efficiency and natural resources (Dunning 1998; Dunning and Lundan 2008, p. 67). By strategic assets, we mean *technology, research and development capacity, good management practice, brand names and reputation, access to international markets or distribution and production networks*. Strategic assets seeking in this study thus incorporates the assets- and market-seeking explanations. In particular, we focused on the explanations of strategic assets seeking versus natural resources seeking. We focus our analyses on these two explanations, though we still take note of other motivations such as efficiency. We do so for the following reasons.

As stated, the bulk of the literature on the internationalization of Chinese business converges towards the argument that the Chinese seek strategic assets and market access especially from developed market economies. It suggests that Chinese firms do so because they have a particularly strong desire to overcome their disadvantages of being latecomers, close a large gap with their foreign counterparts (Nolan 2001) and catch up with internationally leading firms (Child and Rodrigues 2005; Luo and Tung 2007; Yiu et al. 2007; March 1991).

In contrast, most of the studies generally hold that given China's low production costs the role of efficiency-seeking plays a minor role in the internationalization of Chinese business (UNCTAD 2007; Buckley et al. 2007). Despite changes in recent years, low production costs remained a key competitive edge in the 2000s, the period this study focuses on. Hence we develop the following strategic assets-seeking hypothesis – (1) *In concluding international deals, China's national oil companies primarily seek strategic assets.*

(2) The apparent alternative hypothesis is the natural resources seeking explanation. This hypothesis arises from major developments in recent years where over half of China's oil consumption has to be imported and where this share has also been increasing. Thus, it is imperative for China's oil firms to secure supplies of natural resources. This hypothesis is also drawn from numerous existing studies on China's overseas investment in resource-rich countries (Leung, Li, and Low 2011; Ellings and Friedberg 2006; Taylor 2002). This hypothesis is as follows – *In concluding international deals, China's national oil companies primarily seek natural resources (in this case, oil and gas resources).*

(3) According to the UNCTD report, there may be a potentially third alternative hypothesis in addition to strategic assets seeking and natural resources seeking hypotheses (UNCTD 2007, 99–126). This hypothesis suggests that China's NOCs may seek strategic assets or natural resources depending on where are they located in the chain of energy production and whether they are upstream or downstream. This hypothesis is as follows – *in their international deals, an upstream NOC will seek natural resources, whereas a downstream one would seek strategic assets.* Obviously, for a firm whose business is mainly upstream (extraction and exploration of oil and gas), it makes economic sense for it to acquire mostly oil and gas resources in international deals. On the other hand, for a firm that is specialized in downstream business (i.e. refined oil products), it will naturally seek strategic assets such as technology including better refinery technology, brand names or market accesses because these assets will help it to produce and sell downstream products.

We coin the last hypothesis as the 'sectoral specialisation' hypothesis. By definition, a primarily upstream firm has strengths and an edge in competition in upstream business whereas a primarily downstream firm is relatively strong and possesses considerable skills in downstream business. Thus far, these three hypotheses have not been tested using the overseas projects of China's NOCs. Nor has the third hypothesis been carefully and empirically tested in the case of internationalization of China's firms.

Data and methods

We assessed the relevance of the three hypotheses against the overseas investment projects that CNPC and the Sinopec embarked upon between 2002 and 2010. These two firms are selected as they are China's largest players in overseas energy deals. In fact, the Sinopec and CNPC were China's top two non-financial firms in 2010 in terms of OFDI stocks and foreign revenue (MOFCOM 2010). In addition, each of them dominates the upstream (CNPC) and downstream (Sinopec) oil and gas business in China. Therefore, their international deals can shed a good light on the validity of these three hypotheses.[1]

The list of the international deals of the two NOCs initially came from an Information Paper on Overseas Investment by the International Energy Agency (IEA) in 2011 (Jiang and Sinton 2011). Tables 1 and 2 are a list of Chinese foreign oil and gas acquisition since 2002. The list included 11 deals by CNPC (Table 1) and 14 deals by Sinopec (Table 2). According to Jiang and Sinton 2011, the sources were as follows – (1) FACTS Global Energy (2010), FACTS Global Energy (2010), personal communication with analyst, April; (2) Interfax; (3) company websites; (4) CNPC Research Institute of Economics and Technology (2010), Report on Domestic and Overseas Oil and Gas Industry Development in 2009, Beijing: CNPC Research Institute of Economics and Technology; (5) IEA research and (6) Chinese media reports (Jiang and Sinton 2011).

However, details of these international investments were very brief and did not provide an in-depth analysis of the rationale of the two companies in concluding these deals. Thus in order to ascertain the primary reason for the deal, we collected information for each deal through Factiva, a database that compiles hundreds of news reports and sources. The relevant information we gathered on each deal includes the deal date, parties of the deal, the amount of investment by CNPC or Sinopec, the primary reason for CNPC or Sinopec to conclude the deal and a description of the project. In a few cases, the collected data either point to the final outcome of the deals such as their termination or suggest new deals that were not included in the Jiang and Sinton's (2011) paper. The data provide useful information and allowed us to determine what motivated the NOCs to seal a given deal. A summary of the main issues is for each of the deals concluded over the period is provided in Tables 1 and 2. We refer to our dataset as the Dataset on Overseas Investment of China's NOCs. Our findings are reported below.

Data analyses and findings – internationalization of China's CNPC and Sinopec

China's NOCs started their international operations as early as the early 1990s, long before the Chinese government's call for them to 'go out'. CNPC invested in Sudan, Peru and Kazakhstan and opened offices for trading and finance in London and New York (Jiang and Sinton 2011, 10). Since the 2000s, China's NOCs have intensified their international activities in the wake of China's entry into the World Trade Organisation (WTO) and in response to the government's call for 'going out'. As stated, our data base starts from 2002. For CNPC, its overseas investment occurred in two main peaks, 2005 and 2009 (Figure 3).

Table 1.   International investment deals by CNPC, 2002–2010.

Deal number	Deal date, parties, summary of the project amount and main reasons	Description of the rationale of project
1	In April 2002, PetroChina bought stakes in Devon Energy Corporation in Indonesia for $0.216 billion. Primary reason: Assets-seeking (technology and market).	President Huang Yan of PetroChina Co. Ltd, the publicly-listed arm of CNPC, said that the small deal allowed the company to begin building its foreign operations and that PetroChina was pursuing acquisitions in technologies and geographic areas where it could compete aggressively.
2	In April 2003, PetroChina Intl. bought 50% share in Amerada Hess Indonesia Holdings in Indonesia for $0.082 billion. Primary reason: Asset-seeking (market); secondary reason: resources-seeking.	PetroChina sought to increase its foreign business holdings. With the acquisition, PetroChina gained a 45% stake in the Jabung Block Production Sharing Contract (JBPSC) that would supply Singapore with natural gas for 20 years beginning in 2003.
3	In September 2005, CNPC purchased all common shares in PetroKazakhstan in Kazakhstan. $4.18 billion. Primary reason: Resources-seeking; secondary reason: assets-seeking.	This project primarily allowed CNPC to access PetroKazakhstan's proven and suspected oil and natural gas reserves. It also fitted in well with CNPC's other investments in the Central Asian country.
4	In December 2005, CNPC and India's Oil and Natural Gas Co. (ONGC), each paying for $0.575 billion, won the joint bid for Petro-Canada's 38% share in the Al Furat oil and natural fields, located in Syria. Primary reason: Assets-seeking (technology, brands and access to markets).	Chinese national oil companies had increased their pursuit of strategic assets. The partners in the deal might be collaborating to reduce acquisition costs and share risks.
5	In 2006, CNPC acquired all of EnCana's Equity in Block H in Chad at a price of $0.202 billion. Primary reason: Resources-seeking; secondary reason: Assets-seeking (market).	CNPC proceeded to discover significant and new oil reserves that would expand its reserves. The EnCana deal might also allow China to create a significant presence in Chad's oil region.
6	In April 2009 with equal shares, CNPC (CNPC Exploration and Development Company Ltd) and KazMunayGas, Kazakhstan's state oil company, bought Kazakhstan-based MangistauMunaiGaz. Half of the price of $3.3 billion came from CNPC. Primary reason: Resources-seeking.	The project's oil could be transported to China, providing CNPC with a stable oil supply. The company's primary goal was providing a sustained oil supply for the new pipeline.
7	In June 2009, PetroChinabought a 45.5% share of Singapore Petroleum Co. for US$1 billion. Primary reason: Assets-seeking (market); secondary reason: efficiency-seeking.	The deal could allow PetroChina to increase its presence in Singapore. PetroChina would significantly increase its impact on contract prices in a major Asian trading centre.
8	In August 2009, PetroChina bought a 60% stake in the Mackay River and Dover oil sands projects of Calgary-based Athabasca Oil Sands Corp. in Canada for $1.73 billion. Athabasca will operate the project. Primary reason: Assets-seeking (managerial knowhow).	Bill Gallacher, Athabasca's chairman, said PetroChina was attracted by the company's superior management.

(Continued)

Table 1 – *continued*

Deal number	Deal date, parties, summary of the project amount and main reasons	Description of the rationale of project
9	In March 2010, PetroChina and Shell Oil Co. in Australia jointly paid $3.13 billion, each buying a 50% stake in Arrow Energy. Primary reason: Resources-seeking; secondary reasons: assets-seeking (technology and market) and efficiency-seeking.	With the deal, PetroChina and Shell would own 37% of Australia's coal seam gas reserves. They would supply liquefied natural gas to Asian countries, primarily China, expanding PetroChina's sources of natural resources. It would merge Shell Oil's knowledge of liquefied natural gas and regional natural gas market access with PetroChina's knowledge of operations.
10	In May 2010, CNPC and Shell Oil Co. reached a deal with Qatar Petroleum to search for natural gas in Qatar. Primary reason: Resources-seeking; secondary reason: Assets-seeking (technology)	CNPC owned a 25% share of the joint venture in Qatar's Block D region and gain another source of natural gas for China's energy needs. The project would provide PetroChina with technological experience.
11	In May 2010, CNPC bought a 35% share of Shell Oil's Syria Shell Petroleum Development subsidiary for $1.5 billion. Primary reason: Assets-seeking (market, technology, material know-how). Secondary reason: Resources-seeking.	The deal could allow CNPC to increase its upstream business presence in Syria, provide additional energy resources for the company's portfolio and give China another source of energy supplies. It also could allow CNPC to become globally integrated and learn from Shell Oil's operational knowledge.

Note: One deal not included in this table is a project joined by CNPC and Sinopec in Ecuador. See deal No. 17 in Table 2, where CPNC invested $0.781 billion for strategic assets.
Source: Dataset on Overseas Investment of China's NOCs.

International investment by Sinopec followed a somewhat different trajectory with investments growing strongly from 2007 onwards (Figure 4).

When comparing the relative magnitudes of investment of both giants, Sinopec clearly outweighed CNPC. During 2002–2010 Sinopec's total OFDI amounted to US$25.5 billion, compared to US$13.6 billion for CNPC. The annual average of OFDI for Sinopec reached US$2.8 billion, but only US$1.5 billion for CNPC (Figure 4).

Next we analyse each of the cases of OFDI by CNPC and Sinopec and distil the relevant information in our database concerning the primary reasons for the NOCs to conclude a particular deal.

On the basis of the analysis, we classify each of these deals by CNPC and Sinopec by the primary reason (and in some cases, the secondary reason) into strategic assets-seeking, natural resources-seeking or efficiency-seeking. The results are presented in Tables 1 and 2. The summary information on these deals (such as the year, the amount of each deal and their location) by CNPC is presented in Table 3 and Figure 5. The same thing is done for Sinopec and the results are seen in Table 4 and Figure 6.

The pattern for overseas investment of CNPC is somewhat complex, but can be clearly understood at a closer look. There were seven assets-seeking investment projects, compared to five resources-seeking projects. However, the amount of investment has far greater importance than the number of projects. In this regard, resource-seeking investments clearly exceeded assets-seeking investment, being $7.7 billion for the former compared to $5.9 billion for the latter (Table 3). Out of the total investment of $13.6 billion by CNPC, 56.6% was natural resources-seeking (Figure 5).

Table 2.   International investment deals by Sinopec, 2002–2010.

Project number	Deal date, parties, amount and main reasons	Description of the project and its rationale
12	In October 2002, Sinopec Group won a contract of $0.394 billion for increasing the crude oil production of the Zaraitine field in Algeria. Primary reason: Resources-seeking; secondary reason: Assets-seeking.	The project would increase Sinopec Group's crude oil production volume and would also provide Sinopec with technical experience with injecting gas and water underground for increasing the oil yield rate.
13	In December 2003, Sinopec (Shengli Oilfield) bought an interest in three oil blocks located in Kazakhstan's Caspian Sea region for $2.3 million. Primary reason: Resources-seeking.	Along with Big Sky Energy Kazakhstan Ltd, Sinopec would pursue oil exploration and development in the region. Shangli is the most experienced and largest of Sinopec's upstream subsidiaries.
14	In August 2004, Sinopec secured an upstream project in Kazakhstan by buying U.S.-based First International Oil Corp for $0.153 billion. Primary reasons: Assets-seeking.	The purchase allowed Sinopec to control numerous onshore oil exploration blocks in Kazakhstan along with Atyrau province's onshore Sazankurak oil field. As both oil fields had reached their production plateaus, the deal was an effort to obtain strategic assets.
15	In December 2004, Sinopec and Sonangol created a joint venture for developing the offshore oilfield Block 18in Angola, which was operated by British Petroleum. Primary reason: Assets-seeking (market and technology); secondary Reason: resources-seeking.	Most importantly, Sinopec reached a deal with Angola State Petroleum Company to jointly invest $3 billion in building the largest oil refinery in southern Africa (SA). Sinopec could also acquire the stakes and technology in Block 18 from British Petroleum.Sinopec Group would increase its foreign oil production by 5 million tonnes annually by 2007.
16	In May 2005, SinoCanada and Synenco Energy, Canada purchased 40% and 60% shares, respectively, in northeastern Alberta's Northern Lights oil sands project. SinoCanada paid $0.105 billion. Primary reason: Assets-seeking (technology); Secondary Reasons: resources-seeking; efficiency-seeking.	Most importantly, the joint venture would use the skills and technology of both Canada and China to produce an environmentally sound, innovative and energy efficient project. The purchase also allowed Sinopec to expand its energy supplies and efficiency.
17	In February 2006, EnCana sold its Ecuadorian oil and pipeline interests to Andes Petroleum (controlled by CNPC and Sinopec) for a $1.42 billion. Primary reason: Assets-seeking (market); secondary reason: resources-seeking.	The purchase allowed Andes Petroleum and its co-owners Sinopec to boost production and market share as well as to export to Pacific Rim markets.
18	In June 2006, Sinopec won the bidding to buy a 96.9% share of the Udmurtneft oil field from TNK-BP. The company then reassigned 51% of the Udmurtneft shares to Rosneft. The deal was $3.5 billion. Primary reason: Assets-seeking (market); secondary reason: resources-seeking.	The joint venture allowed Sinopec to access international markets including Russian oil and natural gas production and feed its domestic oil supply.
19	In August 2006, Sinopec International and India's Oil and Natural Gas Corp. Ltd. bought Texas-based Omimex Resources Inc.'s Colombian oil assets for $0.8 billion (jointly). Primary reason: Assets-seeking (market).	The joint venture spread the risk of doing business in countries with modest potential growth and unstable business environments. It also enabled Sinopec to expand in the region.

(Continued)

Table 2 – *continued*

Project number	Deal date, parties, amount and main reasons	Description of the project and its rationale
20	In March 2008, Sinopec Group bought a 60% equity interest in Australia's AED Oil Ltd for $0.561 billion. Primary reason: Assets-seeking (market).	The joint venture expanded both companies' interests in the world energy market. Both planned to cooperate in pursuing other similar projects in the region.
21	In September 2008, Sinopec paid Calgary-based Tanganyika Oil Co $1.9 billion for the latter's natural gas and oil assets in Syria. Primary reason: Assets-seeking (technology and market); Secondary Reason: efficiency-seeking.	Energy market analysts noted Tanganyika's enhanced oil recovery technology. This technology would increase production at Sinopec's mature legacy fields. The deal would increase Sinopec refineries' supply of heavier crude oil from overseas to expand its supply sources and bring down costs.
22	In June 2009, Sinopec purchased Addax Petroleum Corp., a Swiss oil explorer, for $7.24 billion. Primary reason: Assets-seeking (market and diversified assets); secondary reason: resources-seeking and efficiency seeking.	Addax has interesting and enticing assets in Africa. The purchase allowed Sinopec to create a stronger presence in West Africa. It would also increase the company's foreign production.
23	In April 2010, Sinopec (SIPC) bought a 9.03% share of Syncrude, a Canadian oil sands company, from U.S.-based ConocoPhillips for $4.675 billion. Primary reason: Assets-seeking (market and technology).	The purchase allowed Sinopec to continue to move into the Canadian oil sands region. Sinopec wanted to make a profit from the purchase rather than shipping the crude oil to China. The company could benefit from the technical knowledge of other partners.
24	In October 2010, Sinopec bought a 40% share of the Spanish oil company Repsol's Brazilian subsidiary for $7.1 billion. Primary reason: Assets-seeking (market and managerial knowhow); secondary reason: resources-seeking.	The purchase allowed Sinopec to improve China's energy security, strengthen its energy sector position in Latin America, develop stronger operations and improve its portfolio of offshore oil and natural gas assets. The company also gained operating experience in Brazil.
25	In December 2010, Sinopec bought 18% of the Gendalo-Gehemdeep water natural gas project in Indonesia owned by Chevron for $680 million. Primary reason: Assets-seeking (technology, market and managerial knowhow).	The purchase permitted Sinopec to improve the company's technical deepwater drilling skills along with its management and production of complex projects. An estimated 25% of the project's natural gas would be sold in Indonesia's domestic market.

Source: Dataset on Overseas Investment of China's NOCs.

The situation for Sinopec is different, and in fact, the opposite. During 2002–2010, there were 13 investment projects primarily aimed at valuable assets, while two projects were seeking natural resources. In terms of the amount of investment, the pattern was even clearer with $25.1 billion of investment primarily devoted to pursuit of valuable assets, dwarfing the meagre $0.4 billion investment primarily aiming at natural resources.

Discussion

The next issue we will investigate is the validity of the three hypotheses. One quick approach is to examine the primary reason for investment by combining that of CNPC with that of Sinopec. Out of $39 billion total investment by CNPC and Sinopec, 79.3% was aimed primarily at assets seeking compared to 20.7% natural resources seeking (Table 5).

CNPC's Investment, 2002–10 (US$ billion)

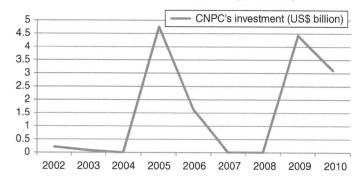

Figure 3.   Total outward investment flows from CNPC between 2002 and 2010 (in US$ billion). Note: One investment (investment in Qatar in 2010) is excluded due to lack of data leaving 11 projects in the figure. Source: Dataset on Overseas Investment of China's NOCs.

Thus, taken together, it appears that the asset-seeking hypothesis has the most mileage in explaining the investment patterns of China's biggest NOCs with both going after valuable and strategic assets in their OFDI such as technologies, brands and, importantly, access to foreign markets.

For example, in May 2009, PetroChina, the main branch of CNPC, agreed to pay US$1 billion for a 45.5% stake in the Singapore Petroleum Company (SPC) increasing its stake to 70.1% in July the same year. This was the first major move by CNPC into an international downstream business and allowed it to gain a strategic foothold in Asia's largest oil trading centre. The SPC investment not only allowed CNPC to build on its existing position in Singapore and gain access to refining capacity and other infrastructure, but also provided CNPC an opportunity to exploit new options in supplying its distribution network in southern China, where it had no major refining capacity at that time. Significantly, it also allowed CNPC to use SPC as a vehicle for other international deals, thereby diluting the political risks. In another massive deal which took place about the same time, Sinopec International Petroleum Exploration and Production (SIPC), a branch of Sinopec, bought Swiss oil explorer Addax Petroleum Corp for $7.24 billion, making it China's biggest overseas acquisition up to that time.

Sinopec's Investment, 2002-10 (US$ billion)

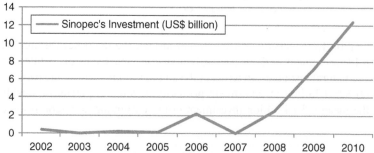

Figure 4.   Total outward investment flows from Sinopec between 2002 and 2010 (in US$ billion). Note: Two investment projects are excluded – one was cancelled; for the other one, we could not find the amount of investment (2004 Angola). In the case of the deal with Russia in 2006, we calculated the amount paid by Sinopec after the company reassigned 51% to Rosneft. Source: Dataset on Overseas Investment of China's NOCs.

Table 3. Primary reason for international investment deals of CNPC, 2002–2010.

Year	Amount ($billion)	Location
Deals with assets-seeking as the primary reason		
2002	0.216	Indonesia
2003	0.082	Indonesia
2005	0.575	Syria
2006	0.781	Ecuador
2009	over 1.0	Singapore
2009	1.73	Canada
2010	1.5	Syria
Subtotal	5.884	
Deals with resources-seeking as the primary reason		
2005	4.18	Kazakhstan
2006	0.202	Chad
2009	1.7	Kazakhstan
2010	1.6	Australia
2010		Qatar
Subtotal	7.682	

Note: See note in Table 2 for information on the deal in Ecuador.

Addax had a number of attractive assets in the Gulf of Guinea, with promising acreage offshore Nigeria, Gabon and Cameroon. Through this deal, Sinopec hoped to build a stronger presence and operations in West Africa and Iraq, accelerating its international growth strategy. It also tried to increase the company's overseas production and increase the proportion of crude it refined from its own assets. The deal also enabled Sinopec to diversify its foreign assets holdings away from 'financial' assets such as foreign government securities into more 'real' assets such as energy and natural resource companies. Thus, the primary reason for the deal was seeking strategic assets, followed by seeking natural resources.

However, this quick assessment of the first two hypotheses is rough. Our analysis can be refined through a close examination of the third hypothesis (the 'sectoral specialisation'

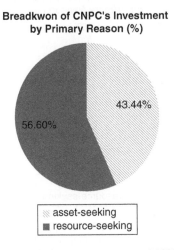

Breakdwon of CNPC's Investment by Primary Reason (%)

43.44%

56.60%

- asset-seeking
- resource-seeking

Figure 5. Breakdown of CNPC's international investment of 2002–2010 by the primary reason. Note: In case of resource-seeking, one project (Qatar in 2010) is excluded due to a lack of investment data. So, 11 deals are included in the data. Source: Dataset on Overseas Investment of China's NOCs.

Table 4.   Primary reason for international investment deals of Sinopec, 2002–2010.

Year	Amount ($ billion)	Location
Deals with assets-seeking as the primary reason		
2004		Angola
2004	0.153	Kazakhstan
2005	0.105	Canada
2006	0.4	Columbia
2006	1.658	Russia
2006	0.639	Ecuador
2008	0.561	Australia
2008	1.9	Syria
2009	7.2	West Africa and Iraq
2010	4.675	Canada
2010	7.1	Brazil
2010	0.680	Indonesia
Subtotal	25.071	
Deals with resources-seeking as the primary reason		
2002	0.394	Algeria
2003	0.0023	Kazakhstan
Subtotal	0.3964	

hypothesis). To do this, we need to know whether CNPC and Sinopec operate mainly in upstream or downstream sectors.

It is generally believed that CNPC traditionally specializes in the extraction of oil and gas, while Sinopec focuses more on downstream business such as the distribution and sale of oil and gas products. Energy production and processing data from the two NOCs suggest that this remains true (Table 6). In 2010, CNPC produced far more crude oil than Sinopec at home (105.41 million metric tonnes or mmt for CNPC versus 42.56 mmt for Sinopec). However, Sinopec outstripped CNPC in terms of processing crude oil (213 mmt versus 160 mmt) and in producing refined domestic oil product (140 mmt versus 102

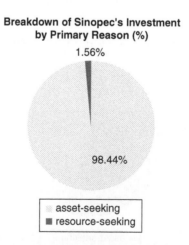

Figure 6.   Breakdown of overseas investment by Sinopec during 2002–2010 by primary reason. Note: Thirteen projects were included in the data. Out of the 14 projects, one project is excluded due to a lack of investment data. It was investment in Angola in 2004 with the aim for asset-seeking. Source: Dataset on Overseas Investment of China's NOCs.

Table 5. International investment of CNPC and Sinopec by primary reason, 2002–2010.

NOC	Amount ($billion)
Assets seeking	
CNPC	5.884
Sinopec	25.071
Subtotal	30.955
Resources seeking	
CNPC	7.682
Sinopec	0.396
Subtotal	8.078
Total (assets and resources seeking)	39.033
Breakdown of total investment (%)	
Assets seeking	79.3
Resources seeking	20.7

mmt). Apparently and in addition, about 45 mmt of Sinopec's refined oil product was produced outside China (Table 6 and its sources).

According to the third (or the 'sectoral specialisation') hypothesis, we should expect Sinopec to invest more overseas in strategic assets which relate primarily to its downstream business and expect CNPC to invest more in natural resources which are associated more closely with its upstream business. From what we have seen (Tables 3–6 and Figures 5–6), this is indeed the case. CNPC, which is primarily an upstream energy firm, focused mainly on natural resources seeking projects in investing abroad. In contrast, Sinopec, a predominantly downstream energy firm, invested overwhelmingly in strategic assets in undertaking international projects. Therefore, the 'sectoral specialisation' hypothesis is supported by the evidence.

Nevertheless, there is a subtly heavy consideration for strategic assets for both firms in investing abroad. Take CNPC for an example, as Figure 7 illustrates and as explained above, in general, CNPC is driven by a consideration for natural resources in its international deals. However, the significance of natural resources to its OFDI portfolio had been in decline since peaking in 2005 and rebounded modestly during 2006–2010. In contrast, the significance of strategic assets to its OFDI had been increasing since 2003 and surpassed that of natural resources during 2006–2009. It thus appears that even though CNPC is primarily interested in natural resources when investing abroad, the significance of strategic assets had loomed large in the backdrop and had increased since 2002 (except for a downturn in 2010). Therefore, the patterns of overseas investment by Sinopec and CNPC can be best explained by the 'sectoral specialisation' hypothesis which is supplemented by an argument for strategic assets.

Table 6. Oil and gas production and processing of CNPC and Sinopec, 2010.

	CNPC	Sinopec
Oil production at home (mmt)	105.41	42.56
Gas production at home (bcm)	72.53	12.50
Crude oil processed (mmt)	160.08	212.97
Domestic refined products sales (mmt)	102.47	140.00

Sources: Annual Report of Sinopec Group 2010 and CNPC – Annual Report 2011, http://www.cnpc.com.cn/en/press/publications/annualrepore/2011/Operation_Highlights.htm?COLLCC=2452502946&.

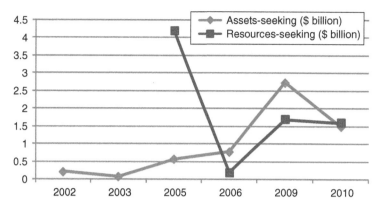

Figure 7.   Resources-seeking deals versus assets-seeking deals by CNPC over the years. Source: Dataset on Overseas Investment of China's NOCs.

Implications for theory and practice

This study has a number of implications for the conventional perception of the motivations of China's NOCs and for theories on internationalization business. The conventional view would regard natural resources-seeking as a key factor that motivates China's NOCs to invest abroad. The findings of this study suggest that this is not the case and that strategic assets-seeking has played a more important role.

Much of the literature on internationalization business would suggest that China's NOCs endeavour to overcome the latecomers' disadvantages by obtaining better technologies, more established brands and accesses to international markets. Indeed, assets-seeking has apparently been a significant factor that drives international investment of major firms from the emerging markets like China. However, in doing so, firms will also play to their own advantages and invest in areas where they have already had significant strengths in a specific sector and apparently aim to reduce risks in investing away from their home countries. Firms apparently still play to their strength in given sectors (as seen from their dominant business in upstream versus downstream sectors) and may aim to reduce risks in new international projects as well. While giving a very serious consideration of strategic assets, upstream firms will pay more attention to natural resources whereas downstream firms may focus predominantly on strategic assets. In the case of China's two major NOCs, one that is specialized in downstream business has chosen to invest more in downstream projects that are clearly associated with strategic assets, and the other, that has a traditional strength in upstream business, has preferred to invest primarily in upstream business, which is closely related to natural resources. Based on these findings, we see merits in exercising caution when attempting any generalized arguments about a single motivation in internationalization of firms from developing countries. There is also merit in considering calculated multiple motivations reflecting firms' strength in a given major sector and the needs to overcome their latecomer disadvantages through acquiring strategic assets. The findings of this study can help to shed light on the dynamics and the logic of growing and massive investment of these Chinese corporate giants around the world, and probably investment of firms from other emerging markets as well.

Conclusions

In recent decades, China has emerged as an increasingly important player in global investment outflows. Its NOCs in particular are among the most active investors in the global extractive business. Meanwhile, as stated in the aforementioned review of literature, there have been discussions and debates among scholars on internationalization of business in general and that in China in particular.

In this study, we set out to test three hypotheses regarding the OFDI of China's NOCs – the natural resources seeking hypothesis, the strategic resources seeking hypothesis, and the 'sectorial specialisation' hypothesis. We examine the overseas investment deals by the two largest Chinese NOCs, namely, CNPC and Sinopec during 2002–2010 and try to find the primary reason for each of these deals. Overall, we find that in investing outside China, CNPC was more interested in natural resources whereas Sinopec was overwhelmingly focusing on securing strategic assets. If we take into account the total investment from both NOCs, the majority of the investment poured into assets-seeking projects.

On the face value or in terms of the breakdown of total investment by the two NOCs, the assets-seeking hypothesis seems to be supported. This is so as nearly 80% of the investment was primarily for obtaining strategic assets, such as technology, brand and access to foreign markets. However, at a closer look at the investment rationale of individual NOC and their position in upstream and downstream business, it is clear that the 'sectoral strength' hypothesis stands out the best in our test using the collected data analysis. It emerges from our analysis that CNPC, a main upstream company, was more interested in getting natural resources in its overseas investment. On the other hand, Sinopec, an oil and gas company specialized more in downstream business than upstream, single-mindedly sought strategic assets in its investment projects abroad. Each NOC apparently wanted to augment their economic advantage and existing sectoral strengths. They might also want to invest in areas where they knew the best to avoid unnecessary risks. Therefore, the 'sectoral specialisation' hypothesis best explains the OFDI of CNPC and Sinopec and the assets-seeking hypothesis receives some support simply because the Sinopec's assets-seeking investment overwhelmed CNPC's resources-seeking-dominant investment outflows.

Our study has important implications for the global energy business world with the findings indicating that China's NOCs have actively embarked upon investments abroad by prudently tapping on their existing strength in the specific downstream or upstream sectors while increasingly focusing on strategic assets such as technology and market accesses. Backed by huge foreign reserves and the largest energy market in the world, this shrewd investment strategy may well enable China's NOCs, latecomers from an emerging market, to play a quick catch-up game against the existing prominent Western energy conglomerates in the global energy business. In the coming decades China's NOCs may become strong rivals in certain sectors and regions, thereby intensifying corporate competition in the world energy business.

Acknowledgements

Hongyi Lai acknowledges the support from the British Academy/Leverhulme Small Research Grant for data collection and analyses in this study.

Note

1. China National Offshore Oil Corporation (CNOOC) is not included. This firm has far smaller overseas investment compared to CNPC and Sinopec that are already included in the study. CNOOC is an upstream firm similar to CNPC. Given the main importance the study attaches to the amount of investment, the exclusion of CNCCO will not change the conclusion.

References

Alcácer, J., and W. Chung. 2007. "Location Strategies and Knowledge Spillovers." *Management Science* 53: 760–776.

Amighinia, A., R. Rabellottic, and M. Sanfilippob. 2013. "Do Chinese State-Owned and Private Enterprises Differ in Their Internationalization Strategies?" *China Economic Review* 27: 312–325.

Amit, R., and P. J. H. Schoemaker. 1993. "Strategic Assets and Organizational Rent." *Strategic Management Journal* 14 (1): 33–46.

BP. 2011. *BP Statistical Review of World Energy June 2011*. London: BP.

Buckley, P. J., J. Clegg, A. R. Cross, X. Liu, H. Voss, and P. Zheng. 2007. "The Determinants of Chinese Outward Foreign Direct Investment." *Journal of International Business Studies* 38 (4): 499–518.

Cai, K. 1999. "Outward Foreign Direct Investment." *China Quarterly* 160: 856–880.

Chen, S. 2009. "Marketization and China's Energy Security." *Policy and Society* 27: 249–260.

Child, J., and S. B. Rodrigues. 2005. "The Internationalization of Chinese Firms." *Management and Organization Review* 1 (3): 318–410.

Cui, L., and F. Jiang. 2010. "Behind Ownership Decision of Chinese Outward FDI." *Asia Pacific Journal of Management* 27: 751–774.

Deng, P. 2004. "Outward Investment by Chinese MNCs." *Business Horizons* 47 (3): 8–16.

Deng, P. 2007. "Investing for Strategic Resources and Its Rationale." *Business Horizons* 50: 71–81.

Deng, P. 2009. "Why Do Chinese Firms Tend to Acquire Strategic Assets in International Expansion?" *Journal of World Business* 44 (1): 74–84.

Deng, P. 2012. "The Internationalization of Chinese Firms." *International Journal of Management Review* 14 (4): 408–427.

Dunning, J. H. 1981. *International Production and the Multinational Enterprises*. London: Allen &Unwin.

Dunning, J. H. 1998. "Location and Multinational Enterprise." *Journal of International Business Studies* 29 (1): 45–66.

Dunning, J. H., and S. M. Lundan. 2008. *Multinational Enterprises and the Global Economy*. Cheltenham: Edward Elgar.

EIA (US Energy Information Administration). 2014. "China Is Now the World's Largest Net Importer of Petroleum and Other Liquid Fuels." Accessed 21 April 2014. http://www.eia.gov/todayinenergy/detail.cfm?id=15531

Ellings, R. J., and A. L. Friedberg. 2006. "Going Out: China's Pursuit of Natural Resources and Implications for the PRC's Grand Strategy." *NBR Analysis* 17 (3): 65–98.

Frynas, J. G., and M. Paolo. 2007. "A New Scramble for African Oil?" *African Affairs* 106 (423): 229–251.

Globerman, S., and D. Shapiro. 2009. "Economic and Strategic Considerations Surrounding Chinese FDI in the United States." *Asia Pacific Journal of Management* 1: 163–183.

Hong, E., and L. Sun. 2006. "Dynamics of Internationalization and Outward Investment: Chinese Corporations' Strategies." *The China Quarterly* 187: 610–634.

Houser, T. 2008. "The Roots of Chinese Oil Investment Abroad." *Asia Policy* 5: 141–166.

Jiang, J., and J. Sinton. 2011. *Overseas Investments by Chinese National Oil Companies: Assessing the Drivers and Impacts*. Paris: IEA Information Paper.

Kolstad, I., and A. Wiig. 2012. "What Determines Chinese Outward FDI?" *Journal of World Business* 47: 26–34.

Leung, G. C., R. Li, and M. Low. 2011. "Transitions in China's Oil Economy, 1990–2010." *Eurasian Geography and Economics* 52 (4): 483–500.

Liu, X., T. Buck, and Ch. Shu. 2005. "Chinese Economic Development, the Next Stage: Outward FDI?" *International Business Review* 14: 97–115.

Lu, J., X. Liu, M. Wright, and I. Filatotchev. 2014. "International Experience and FDI Location Choices of Chinese Firms." *Journal of International Business Studies*. doi:10.1057/jibs.2013.68.

Luo, Y., and R. L. Tung. 2007. "International Expansion of Emerging Market Enterprises." *Journal of International Business Studies* 38 (4): 481–498.

March, J. G. 1991. "Exploration and Exploitation in Organizational Learning." *Organization Science* 2: 71–87.

Mathews, J. 2006. "Dragon Multinationals." *Asia Pacific Journal of Management* 23 (1): 5–27.

MOFCOM (The Chinese Ministry of Commerce). 2010. *2010 Statistical Bulletin of China's Outward Direct Investment*. Beijing: MOFCOM.

Morck, R., B. Yeung, and M. Zhao. 2008. "Perspectives on China's Outward Foreign Direct Investment." *Journal of International Business Studies* 39 (3): 337–350.

Ning, L. 2009. "China's Lead-Taking in the World ICT Industry." *Pacific Affairs* 82 (1): 67–91.

Ning, L., and D. Sutherland. 2012. "Internationalization of China's Private Sector MNEs." *Thunderbird International Business Review* 54 (2): 169–182.

Nolan, P. 2001. *China and the Global Economy*. London: Palgrave Macmillan.

O'Hara, S., and H. Lai. 2011. "China's 'Dash for Gas': Challenges and Potential Impacts on Global Markets." *Eurasian Geography and Economics* 52 (4): 501–522.

Peng, M. W. 2012. "The Global Strategy of Emerging Multinationals from China." *Global Strategy Journal* 2: 97–107.

BBC News, March 29, 2012. http://www.bbc.co.uk/news/business-17556938

Rui, H., and G. S. Yip. 2008. "Foreign Acquisition by Chinese Firms: A Strategic Intent Perspective." *Journal of World Business* 43: 213–226.

Salidjanova, N., "Going Out: An Overview of China's Outward Direct Investments." USCC Staff Research Report, U.S.–China economic and Security Review Commission, March 30, 2011.

Taylor, R. 2002. "Globalization Strategies of Chinese Companies." *Asian Business and Management* 1 (2): 209–225.

Teece, D., G. Pisano, and A. Shuen. 1997. "Dynamic Capabilities and Strategic Management." *Strategic Management Journal* 18: 509–533.

UNCTAD (United Nations Conference on Trade and Development). 2007. *World Investment Report: Transnational Corporations, Extractive Industries and Development*. New York: United Nations.

UNCTAD (United Nations Conference on Trade and Development). 2011. *World Investment Report*. New York: United Nations.

UNCTAD (United Nations Conference on Trade and Development). 2012. *World Investment Report*. New York: United Nations.

UNCTAD (United Nations Conference on Trade and Development). 2013. *World Investment Report*. New York: United Nations.

Xiao, G. 2004. "People's Republic of China's Round-Tripping FDI: Scale, Causes and Implications." Asia Development Bank Institute Discussion Paper No. 7.

Yiu, D. W., C. M. Lau, and G. D. Bruton. 2007. "International Venturing by Emerging Economy Firms." *Journal of International Business Studies* 38: 519–540.

Zhan, J. X. 1995. "Transnationalization and Outward Investment: The Case of Chinese Firms." *Transnational Corporations* 4 (3): 67–100.

From mercantile strategy to domestic demand stimulation: changes in China's solar PV subsidies

Gang Chen

East Asian Institute, National University of Singapore, Singapore

Through scrutinizing China's industrial subsidies towards its solar photovoltaic (PV) sector from a theoretical perspective constructed by Michael Porter on the government's role in forging national comparative advantages, this study tries to capture recent dynamics in China's state capitalism, which has been evolving from a mercantile stage in which most subsidies were designed to influence factor conditions and supporting industries, to a new stage of domestic demand with more subsidies aimed at reshaping domestic demand conditions to absorb redundant manufacture capacity. China has emerged as the world's largest solar panel producer, but compared to its fast-expanding wind power market that has congenital advantages in attracting policy support, China's domestic solar PV market has been underdeveloped and failed to absorb a large part of its inflated production capacity. Empirical evidences have shown that in sync with the state's recent policy shift to domestic demand from export-orientated mercantile strategy, the government's role in supporting the solar PV industry has been transforming from subsidizing the production side to subsiding the demand side. As solar PV power generation is approaching the breaking point of grid parity with existing subsidies and feed-in tariffs, China could witness its PV installed capacity grow exponentially in the near future.

1. Introduction

The Chinese model of state capitalism has been prominently discussed in the study of the country's meteoric economic growth in the past two decades, of which a fascinating part is the massive subsidies of various forms conferred by the state to a wide range of domestic industries that have aggressively expanded their shares in the global market (McGregor 2012; Lin and Jiang 2011; Fligstein and Zhang 2011; Nolan 2007). There have been studies revealing that the Chinese government, in the form of producer subsidies, research grants, tax rebate, low-interest loans and cheap land, has substantially subsidized a motley of capital-intensive industries, from steel, auto to paper-making and shipbuilding, in which the labour-intensive country had not had much competitive advantages in the first place if not for such governmental intervention (Haley and Haley 2013; The Economist 2012; Bremmer 2010; Huang and Wang 2010; McGregor 2010; Nolan 2007). Most of the aforementioned research argued that a glut of government subsidies, in comparison with other factors, has played a decisive role in helping these China-based industries to gain comparative advantages vis-à-vis their foreign competitors. This is incompatible with the viewpoint of Porter (1998, 72–127) on the competitive advantages of nations, which purported that the role of government, instead of being included in the 'diamond' of four determinants of national advantages, should be categorized as an indirect variable (another indirect variable is the factor of chance) that influences each of the four determinants, i.e. factor conditions; demand conditions; related and supporting industries and firm strategy, structure and rivalry, either positively or negatively (Figure 1). In other words, provided government policies and practices are associated with the success the home-based firms have enjoyed, the role of the state can only indirectly help or hurt the nation's industry through reshaping the circumstances of the four determinants rather than imposing direct influence upon national comparative advantages.

2. Hypothesis

If China's industrial subsidies are being scrutinized through such a theoretical lens framed by Porter, observers will find that the policy tool kit of China's state capitalism, driven by mercantile national strategies that aim at export expansion and trade surpluses, has thus far been intently reshaping all the four determinants, with increasing emphasis on the demand conditions. As the exponential expansion of China's industrial production has led to frequent trade disputes with major economies and grievous overcapacity at home, the Chinese government has been talking about economic restructure with emphasis on activating domestic demand since the outbreak of global financial crisis in 2008.

Following this logic, the study is putting forward a hypothesis that China's state capitalism, facing a downturn external demand and severe internal overcapacity, has been forced to evolve from a mercantile stage, in which most subsidies were designed to influence factor conditions and supporting industries, to a new stage of domestic consumption with a policy on reshaping demand conditions prioritized to absorb redundant capacity and achieve such non-economic goals as environmental protection and social stability.

3. Methodology

With a case study on the dynamics of how governmental subsidies have been helping out the expansion of China's solar panel industry, the study is designed to prove that a shift in subsidy directions and functions shows that China has been paying more attention towards structural change that focuses on domestic demand and low-carbon pathway instead of pure

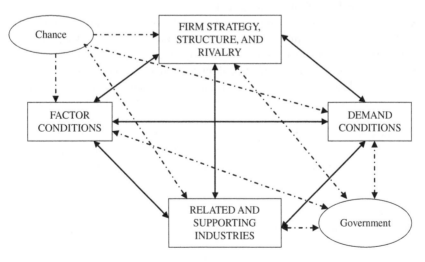

Figure 1. The complete system of the determinants of national advantage and the roles of government and chance (Porter 1998, 127).

mercantile benefits associated with export expansion and accumulation of foreign exchange reserve. A methodology of comparing China's bifurcated policy approaches in supporting wind and solar sectors, in combination with evidences collected during a fieldwork (Beijing, March 2012) in the Energy Research Institute of the National Development and Reform Commission (NDRC), which formulates China's energy strategy, may help convince people of the valid transformation that will not only boost domestic consumption of merit goods (solar panels) that previously were mostly demanded by foreign consumers, but also furnish continuous support to sustain domestic photovoltaic (PV) producers.

4. Literature

China, a latecomer to modernization, has been swiftly emerging as the world's clean energy powerhouse, with strong national policies aimed at incentivizing the use of new renewables such as solar and wind (Salim and Rafiq 2012, 1051; Chen 2012, 46). A report from PEW Charitable Trusts (2010, 15) found that as early as 2009, China's clean energy investments soared more than 50% to US$34.6 billion, taking the lead among G-20 nations for the first time and pushing the United States into the second place. The Economist (2012, 13) in a special issue connected China's great leap forward in solar and wind with its formidable state capitalism model that can enjoy some success in tackling second-generation infrastructure problems and mandating higher environmental standards. Farsighted researchers (Li 2010; Yang and Pan 2010b) had foretold the potential overcapacity problems as a result of over-subsidy and overinvestment when over 80,000 tons of multi-crystalline silicon production facilities were under construction in China in the second half 2009 (Chen 2012, 55). Li heeded China's over-reliance upon external demand when boosting its solar panel manufacture in the infant stage, categorizing the asymmetrical problem as Both-Ends-Out (*liangtou zaiwai*), which implied that China imported 95% of its PV raw materials and exported 95% of its finished products due to an underdeveloped domestic market (Li 2010, 38). Such a topic caught attention from a research team led by Zhang and Andrews-Speed, who attributed China's solar overcapacity and over-dependence on foreign market to the lack of appropriate interactions between renewable energy policy and renewable energy industrial (manufacturing) policy (Zhang et al. 2013).

Despite existing studies on China's solar panel production (see, for example, the study of Douglas Gress on how Chinese producers enrolled in global networks in this issue) and related government policies to promote the industry, there is no updated research to capture the recent change, albeit subtle and gradual, in government approaches of subsidizing and supporting the industry in favour of the domestic demand side. Under the dynamic context of China's state capitalism that is evolving from a mercantile phase to a new stage with policy priority on domestic demand, Zhang and Andrews-Speed's concern has been partially answered by the latest fine-tuning in the direction of government subsidies, although such policy shift is yet to be significant enough to breed a domestic market of sufficient scale to absorb manufacture oversupply that has encountered an overseas boycott.

5. Findings

5.1 Overheated solar PV manufacture decoupled from underdeveloped solar power generation

Over the past decade, the gravity of solar PV production has shifted from the United States, to Japan, to Europe and to Asia, especially China, which has quadrupled its polysilicon solar panel manufacture capacity between 2009 and 2011. A total of 63% and 64% of cells and modules produced in 2012 were made in mainland China, which is a marginal increase over 2011 (62% and 59%) (Mehta 2013). As mentioned by Gress, price sensitivity in the global solar PV market has persisted, with price competitiveness of Chinese products leaving Chinese firms well positioned globally. China's existing production capacity of solar panels is about 150% of the global real demand, and in just four years between 2009 and 2012, the international price of solar panels had been cut by more than 75% largely due to an aggressive capacity build-up in China. The share of made-in-Europe modules continued to fall, from 14% in 2011 to 11% in 2012, and Japan's share dropped from 6% to 5% (REN21 2013, 47). The top 15 solar PV module manufacturers accounted for half of the 36 GW (gigawatt) produced globally; nine of these companies hailed from China (Figure 2).

One of the major chronic challenges facing China's solar PV industry is the asymmetrical supply-demand problem, in which China has to export more than 90% of its finished products to other parts of the world due to an underdeveloped domestic market (Li 2010, 38). Although China has already become the largest solar PV producer in the world, its domestic demand for such products far lags behind environment-conscious Germany and Italy. In 2012, China doubled its capacity to about 7 GW, only 7% of the global total installed capacity that stood at 100 GW, less than one-fourth of Germany's market share and below one-half of Italy's share (Figure 3). Europe still dominated the market, adding 16.9 GW and accounting for about 57% of newly installed capacity, to end 2012 with 70 GW in operation (REN21 2013, 44). In the long run, the overdependence on overseas markets increases the vulnerability of China's PV industry as declining foreign demand and increasing trade disputes may become a major constraint to its development.

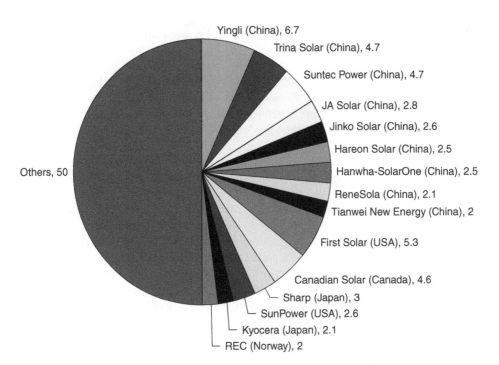

Figure 2. Market shares (%) of top 15 solar PV module manufacturers, 2012. *Source:* REN21, 2013, *Renewables 2013 – Global Status Report*, p. 41.

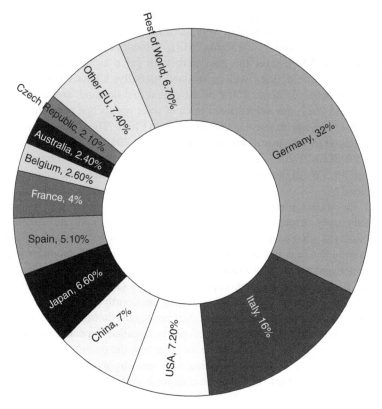

Figure 3. Solar PV global capacity, shares of top 10 countries, 2012 (Global Total: 100 GW). *Source:* REN21, 2013, *Renewables 2013 – Global Status Report*, p. 41.

5.2 How solar subsidies affected determinants of national advantages

China is a game-changer in solar PV manufacture, as its revenue share in the world market surged from an insignificant portion before 2005 to more than 50% in 2011 and 2012. Because the production of solar cell and modules is a capital and tech-intensive industry that China had no comparative advantage a decade ago, its swift success in snatching up the high ground from the control of formidable peers in the United States and Europe has shocked many industrial observers with expectations that the western world should alleviate trade imbalance through the development of such high-tech sectors. EU ProSun (2013), the main solar panel manufacturers' lobby group, attributed the lower Chinese prices, which contradicted the reality that European production costs are lower than in China, to 'illegal state subsidies' and 'widespread dumping as proven by the EU and US investigations'. Yet amidst increasing global concerns about climate change and energy security, it has become a common practice for many governments in the world, including those in the West, to grant subsidies and other policy support to develop the costly clean energy industry that provides environmentally-friendly merit goods, and in theory, economic rationales have generally ignored the view that industrial subsidies may contribute significantly to aspects of a country's comparative advantage and not just disadvantage (Trebilcock et al. 1982). To understand the powerful role the Chinese government subsidies have played in affecting business strategies and national competitive advantage, one has to revisit Porter's (1998, 72–128) classic description on government's indirect influence on national competitive advantage through the 'diamond' of four determinants (See Figure 1).

In Porter's framework, government policy, which is often associated with East Asian countries' economic success, can only indirectly help or hurt the nation's industry through reshaping the circumstances of the four determinants rather than imposing direct influence upon national comparative advantages (Porter 1998, 126–127). Factors of production that include labour, land, natural resources, capital and infrastructure are often affected by the government through subsidies and policies towards the capital markets, while local demand conditions can be reshaped through the reestablishment of local product standards, government procurement and subsidies to consumers. Government can influence the circumstances of related and supporting industries as well as firm strategy and rivalry, another two determinants of national advantages, through subsidies, regulation of supporting services, capital market regulations, tax policy and antitrust laws.

If Chinese government's role in helping its solar photovoltaic manufacture is being looked at through this theoretical lens, its evident that the government's industrial support has covered all the aforementioned four determinants, focussing on the factor conditions and supporting industries. Anti-subsidy investigations by both the US Department of Commerce (2012) and European Economic and Trade Office (EU ProSun 2013) found that the Chinese solar PV producers had got government subsidies – in the form of discounts on raw materials, electricity and funding as well as export subsidy (export buyer's credits) – of about 15% of their sales in the US case and 11.5% in the EU case (Table 1).

The US and EU findings revealed that Chinese government's massive subsidies had artificially altered the country's factor endowment, or the mix of human resources, physical resources, knowledge resources, capital resources and infrastructure, that used to be unfavourable to its solar panel manufacture. Compared with industrialized nations, China is well-known for its advantages in the supply of cheap labour, but in the solar PV manufacture, a capital and tech-intensive sector, labour accounts for a small part, less than 10%, of total cost. Like many other industries, China's solar production is fragmented, with the majority of local firms enjoying no economies of scale. Compared with industrial pioneers like Germany and the United States, China does not have competitive solar-related knowledge resources that reside in universities, government research institutes, private research facilities, business and scientific literature and market research databases. In terms of capital resources, despite its high national rate of savings, China does not have an efficient and mature capital market that can provide low-cost funds to finance industry. Because it's impossible for a nation to upgrade these factors in a short time, the proper explanation that China can overtake industrial forerunners swiftly can be found through the study of factor distortion under the framework of state capitalism.

China's Renewable Energy Law (2005) and the Medium- and Long-Term Development Plan for Renewable Energy (2007) constructed a legalized framework that justified and encouraged support from governments at various levels for the development of local solar manufacture. Since the outbreak of global financial crisis, more and more local governments have deemed renewable energy industry as a new engine of economic growth. The subsidies – largely from local authorities but also from the national government – took the form of cheap land, tax rebates, research fund, support for loan repayments and straight-up cash Table 1.

Wuxi Suntech Power Co. Ltd, which once was China's largest solar PV manufacturer, got bank loans worth only US$ 56 million at the end of 2005, but the amount shot up to US $3.7 billion at the end of 2012, largely due to municipal government's mandate on local state-owned banks for providing low-interest loans to Suntech (China Business Times, 28

Table 1. China's subsidy rates in the US and EU case.

Producer/exporter	Subsidy rate
EU Investigation	
All Chinese Solar Manufacturers	11.50%
Wuxi Suntech Power Co. Ltd.	
Luoyang Suntech Power Co. Ltd.	
Suntech Power Co., Ltd.	
Yangzhou Rietech Renewal Energy Co., Ltd.	
Zhejiang Huantai Silicon Science & Technology Co., Ltd.	
Kuttler Automation Systems (Suzhou) Co. Ltd.	
Shenzhen Suntech Power Co. Ltd.	
Wuxi Sunshine Power Co. Ltd.	
Wuxi University Science Park International Incubator Co., Ltd.	
Yangzhou Suntech Power Co. Ltd.	
US Investigation	
Zhejiang Rietech New Energy Science & Technology Co. Ltd.	14.78%
Changzhou Trina Solar Energy Co. Ltd and Trina Solar (Changzhou) Science & Technology Co. Ltd.	15.97%
All Others	15.24%

Source: US Department of Commerce 2012 and EU ProSun 2013.

March, 2013). From 2006 to 2011, Wuxi Suntech got tax rebate and other forms of refund amounting to 8.65 billion yuan (about US$ 1.42 billion) from the government for the sake of promoting export (China Business Times, 28 March, 2013). Even when Wuxi Suntech, afflicted with insufficient cash flow and weak sales, was closed due to bankruptcy in 2012, the Wuxi government still required the Bank of China to grant emergency loans worth 200 million yuan (China Business News, 28 September, 2012). The government at various levels also gave technological, infrastructure and personnel support to local solar panel producers to enhance their competitiveness in the tech- and capital-intensive industry. Yingli Solar, the world's biggest manufacturer of solar PV that is based in northern China's Hebei Province, has succeeded in setting up two nation-level laboratories for photovoltaic technology, with substantial tech, financial and personnel support respectively from the Chinese Ministry of Science and Technology and the National Energy Commission under China's NDRC. During the author's fieldwork in NDRC's Energy Research Institute (Beijing, 2 March 2012), local policy researchers revealed that such key state labs on renewable energy represented China's highest research level and helped local enterprises attract top-notch scientists and technicians, with enormous hardware (facility, infrastructure and fund) and software (policy, research staff) support from the central and local government. Yingli Solar claimed on its website on 8 August 2013 that one of its two labs specialized in photovoltaic materials and technology was established in January 2010, with a joint investment of 540 million yuan from the government and Yingli altogether and floor area of 60,800 m².

Considering the high cost of operating the solar PV system, however, the government's help aimed at affecting home demand composition was not comparable to its role in reshaping factors of production. Because national subsidy offered to solar power generation programmes was not enough to ensure a reasonable return on investment, most solar panels produced in China could not be absorbed in the domestic market and had to be shipped overseas due to such shortfalls between production and demand subsidy. Prior to 2011, when the solar power market was small, China had no unified feed-in tariff rate at the national level applied to all the solar PV power projects connected to the grid. During that period, the approved feed-in tariff rate ranged between 4 and 9 yuan per kWh based on the different characteristics of individual projects, 10–20 times that of coal power. The exorbitant cost of producing on-grid solar power, together with enormous cost disparities among projects in various localities, was partially due to the fact that the government had refused to adopt the fixed feed-in tariff, which policy makers had thought would lead to over-capacity and costly power generation in some regions.

6. Discussion

6.1 Incentives under state capitalism: a comparison between wind and solar sector

Considering the relatively high costs and risks often involved in renewable energy production, China's great leap forward in sharpening its competitive edge in both solar and wind sectors has been closely related to the government's robust support for and heavy subsidies to the newly emerging industry. However, in terms of promoting the deployment and consumption of such renewable equipments for power generation, the Chinese government took differentiated policies in these two industries, which resulted in a bifurcated wind and solar power generation market. With the energy policy being positioned for a long time at the centre of its development strategy, China since 2008 has formulated some of the world's most ambitious policies and targets to promote renewable power production and consumption, with wind power being positioned at the centre and solar power generation being promoted less vigorously. As a result of different dynamics between wind/solar energy policy and wind/solar equipment manufacture policy, China has emerged as world's largest producer of wind power, but is still lagging behind among major solar power producers. The outcome of efforts to increase the electricity supply from various renewables is easily visible, but the underlying dynamics in policy-making, which are supposedly a major driving force of this trend, are much harder to observe and explain (Schaffer and Bernauer 2014, 15). Researchers have heeded China's policy approach that prioritizes the development of renewable energy manufacturing industry ahead of the production and consumption of renewable energy itself (Zhang et al. 2013), but few studies have been done to compare the policy nuance related to the government's attitudes towards wind and solar power generation and its consequential impact upon the manufacture industry through affecting domestic demand conditions.

China's promotion of renewables and related equipment manufacture is a natural extension of the country's preferred 'no-regret' strategy that emphasizes mitigation actions providing fringe benefits like profitability and employment to the country, regardless of whether or not the threat of climate change is real. When such renewable energy policies were designed, policy makers may have given more weight to economic factors such as energy supply and jobs rather than environmental care. Under the framework of China's Renewable Energy Law and national green targets, detailed institutional incentives and disincentives have been designed by various layers of the government to promote wind, solar and other renewable energy development in China.

In its efforts institutionalized by the groundbreaking PRC Renewable Energy Law (2005) to develop clean energy capacity, the Chinese government introduced such schemes as 'cost-sharing', 'feed-in tariffs', 'mandatory grid-connection' and 'renewable portfolio standard' (RPS) systems that had been successful in advancing the cause of renewables in some European nations and US states. From the Chinese version of RPS, which has drawn up ambitious plans to increase the proportion of renewable energy (including large hydropower) in the primary energy consumption from 7.5% in 2005 to 15% in 2020, it is evident that the government has prioritized the development of wind power over the solar power generation in the mid-term. Excluding hydropower, the aforementioned RPS target was further broken down by the NDRC as 30 GW from wind, 30 GW from biomass and 1.8 GW from solar photovoltaic (Zhang 2005, 1), in which solar PV would be projected to produce only 6% of the total wind power generation. The Chinese government subsequently revised the RPS goal that aimed at 20% of its energy from renewable sources by 2020, with a widened gap between elevated wind capacity of 100 GW and solar capacity still at 1.8 GW.

Considering the comparable disadvantage of generating electricity from renewable sources, China's Renewable Energy Law addressed the core issues of pricing and fee-sharing for on-grid renewable energy through a government-set or government-guided pricing system. Nevertheless, when the policy-makers had found that compared to solar energy production, wind power was more mature at the moment to be widely commercialized with modest government subsidies needed, they decided to promote the wind power in full swing as the main renewable source while deemed subsidization of solar generation as too costly and inefficient. In 2006, the cost of electricity generated from solar power was some 3 yuan (40 US cents) per kWh, while that from a typical coal-fired power plant was only around 0.22 yuan per kWh and that from a wind power plant was averaged at about 0.6 yuan per kWh (Li 2007).

China's abundant inland and offshore wind energy resources provide enormous potential for large-capacity wind farms. As a latecomer in the utilization of wind power, China's wind power installed capacity increased at a much slower rate than the world's average level before 2004, but even during that early stage, strong policy support played a vital role in promoting wind power generation and turbine manufacture. Prior to 1994, there were only a few demonstration wind farms fully financed by the government, and from 1994 to 2003, in-grid wind power was first developed as a new energy source for electrical power generation in China. To import technology from foreign companies and to establish a high-quality Chinese wind turbine generator sector, the former State Development and Planning Commission, predecessor of NDRC, initiated the 'Ride the Wind Program' (chengfeng jihua) in 1996, leading to the establishment of two joint ventures, NORDEX (Germany) and MADE (Spain), which effectively introduced 600 kilowatts wind turbine generator manufacturing technology into China. The landmark policy came in 2003 when the NDRC launched the 'Wind Power Concession Program' (fengdian texuquan xiangmu) to build large-capacity wind farms and achieve economies of scale through reducing the in-grid wind power tariff. Under the programme, the power grid company signed a long-term power-purchase agreement with the wind power project investor and agreed to purchase the prescribed amount of electricity generated by the project, whose capacity must reach 100 MW. Investors and developers of wind farms were selected through a competitive bidding process that determined the in-grid tariff. All end-users of the grid's electricity shared the tariff increase due to wind power purchase. As incentives, the government waived the import customs tariff and value-added tax on the equipment and accessories. The 'Wind Power Concession Program' that minimized the risks to investors through government-guaranteed power-purchase agreements has pushed China's wind power industry into a fast-growing stage between 2005 and 2009 when the country's installed wind power capacity more than doubled annually in the four years. By the end of 2005, China had built 59 wind farms with 1854 wind turbine generators and a 1.27-GW in-grid wind power installed capacity, ranking it at number 10 globally. In 2009, China's installed wind power capacity reached 25.81 GW, about 20 times that in 2005 and ranking number two after the United States. From 1997 to 2004, however, China's installed wind power capacity maintained only a relatively low level of growth rate, fluctuating between 16.3% and 28.4% (Yang and Pan 2010a, 6).

China's prioritization of wind power over other renewables is largely due to the country's geographic and meteorological advantages in tapping wind energy resources. China Meteorological Administration's survey showed that China's potential wind energy resources on land, measured at 50 m above ground level, are about 2380 GW (China Meteorological Administration 2010). The wind-rich areas in China can be grouped into three 'wind belts', namely the long coastal belt covering Shandong, Jiangsu, Shanghai, Zhejiang, Fujian, Guangdong, Guangxi, and Hainan Province, the northern belt including northwestern Gansu, Xinjiang and Ningxia Province, northern Inner Mongolia and Hebei Province, and northeastern Liaoning, Jilin and Heilongjiang Province and the inland belt that covers regions with special geological and topographic characters (National Development and Reform Commission 2008, 21–22). Inner Mongolia alone accounts for about one-third of China's total installed wind power capacity. In addition, it is estimated that, in the 5–20-m deep sea belt along the eastern coastal areas, 700 GW of wind energy potential can be exploited based on the assessment of wind resources at 10 m height, which may provide vital and sustainable energy for the affluent provinces in East China that lack indigenous fossil fuel supplies.

Since 2008 the Chinese government has adopted a set of preferential pricing schemes to encourage wind power generation. The tariff for wind power was fixed by the NDRC in 2009 and classified into four levels to give differentiated support to projects located in different regions that vary in local wind resources (Table 2).

The Chinese wind power market more than doubled its capacity from 12 GW in 2008 to 25.8 GW in 2009 and added 18.9 GW in 2010 to reach 44.7 GW at the end of 2010. China surpassed India in 2008, and Spain and Germany in 2009, to become the world's second largest wind power producer by the end of 2009. China added a staggering 18.9 GW of new capacity in 2010, thus overtaking the United States to become the world's leading wind power country (Global Wind Energy Council 2011, 10–12). In 2012, largely due to Chinese government's stricter approval procedures, the country installed only 13 GW, slightly lower than the 13.1 GW installed by the United States. In spite of that, in terms of cumulative installed capacity, China was still the largest wind power producer in the world by 2012 (Table 3). During the author's fieldwork in NDRC's Energy Research Institute (Beijing, 2 March 2012), local analysts supported the prediction that by 2020, wind power would probably surpass nuclear power as China's third largest source of electricity, after thermal and hydropower.

In contrast to the government's full-scale support for wind power generation, China had no unified feed-in tariff rate at the national level applied to all grid-connected solar PV power projects until very recently. Prior to 2009, when the market was small, the approved feed-in tariff rate ranged between 4–9 yuan per kWh based on the different characteristics

Table 2.   China's regional wind power tariff.

Region	Wind resource	Wind power tariff (Yuan/kWh)
Resource region I	Rich	0.51
Resource region II	Modest	0.54
Resource region III	Modest	0.58
Resource region IV	Low	0.61

Source: National Development and Reform Commission (2009).

Table 3. Major wind power producers by 2012.

Country	Cumulative capacity (GW)	In world's total (%)
China	75.56	26.8
USA	60.01	21.2
Germany	31.33	11.1
Spain	22.80	8.1
India	18.42	6.5

Source: Global Wind Energy Council (2013, 3).

of individual projects (REN21 2009, 22), 10–20 times that of coal power. The exorbitant cost of producing on-grid solar power, together with enormous cost disparities among projects in various localities, have meant that the government has refused to adopt the fixed feed-in tariff, which policy makers think will lead to over-capacity and costly low-level production in some regions. Despite such hurdles as high costs, technical difficulties and low efficiency, China's solar power industry is still wrestling with the Chinese government in view of the huge potential of the solar industry, has been preparing for the extensive subsidies and other incentives for the deployment of large-scale solar PV projects throughout the country. As of 29 April 2010, the Wall Street Journal on its website quoted Ren Dongming, deputy director of the Center for Renewable Energy Development of the Energy Research Institute under the NDRC, as saying that China would be ready to introduce the fixed feed-in tariff only when the conditions have become more settled, with problems of relevant technical limitation and low efficiency resolved and the wide commercial use of solar PV power achieved, as with wind power. Such a fixed feed-in tariff has been anticipated to have a positive effect in attracting both foreign and domestic capital into the domestic solar power industry, and thus to increase solar power generation capacity substantially.

In certain localities, feed-in tariff and other subsidization programmes benefitting regional solar power projects had been experienced before the central government finally made up its mind to grant nation-level supports. A bidding process for a 10-MW programme in the Dunhuang region of western China's Gansu Province resulted in an on-grid price of 1.09 yuan per kWh in 2009. Such a price level at the moment was applicable to local projects in surrounding regions with similar solar resources and equipment. One year later, in April 2010, the NDRC announced that four solar power stations in western Ningxia Autonomous Region would adopt a new price level of 1.15 yuan per kWh, higher than that applied to the Dunhuang programme, the first large-scale solar power generation programme commercialized in China. Despite all these sporadic examples of regional feed-in tariffs, the central government as well as most local governments had been reluctant to subsidize solar power generation in the same manner as they subsidized wind power production until recently, when the government, in the face of weak external demand and serious industrial overcapacity at home, had to speed up its policy shift onto the stimulation of domestic demand in the aftermath of the global financial crisis.

6.2 From producer subsidies to demand-end subsidies: motives behind policy changes

China's growing interest in low-carbon energy production has been intimately linked with efforts to modernize the economy and the energy strategy employed to fuel that modernization (Hatch 2003, 45), as well as increasing public awareness about climate change consequences. In most emerging economies in Asia that has witnessed rapidly increasing energy demand, renewable energy supply presents a lower emission pathway that could be a viable option for steering off the higher emissions path (Dulal et al. 2013, 301). Although China has an electrification rate of close to 99% (Urmee et al. 2009), four – fifths of the total supply is coming from carbon fuels, mostly coal. Exacerbated urban air pollution associated with increasing airborne particulate matter (PM10 and PM2.5) from burning fossil fuels has forced the government to increase the proportion of renewable power in the national energy mix (Buckeridge et al. 2002) for the sake of public healthcare and ecological protection. As pointed out by Doug Gress and other contributors in this volume, the Chinese government, confronting increasing pressure to protect environment, control pollution and secure energy supply, has been placing great importance on solar power generation domestically.

Having realized that the asymmetrical problem of an over-expanded solar manufacture sector and an immature domestic market may exacerbate overcapacity and trade disputes, Chinese policy-makers started to bolster domestic demand through kicking off the unprecedented national 'Golden Sun' programme in July 2009 with financial incentives and strong R&D support for the installation of at least 500 MW of utility-scale solar PV projects during the period 2009–2011. The Chinese Ministry of Finance announced that it would subsidize 50% of the costs of building demonstration solar power projects and transmitting and distributing the solar power from those projects. In remote areas that lacked the infrastructure to connect to the grid, the incentive would go up to 70% for solar PV projects. Under the Golden Sun programme jointly launched by the Ministry of Finance, Ministry of Science and Technology and National Energy Administration, grid companies were required to buy all surplus electricity output from solar power projects that generate primarily for the developers' own needs, at similar rates to benchmark on-grid tariffs set for coal-fired power generators. The Golden Sun programme, a concrete form of policy support for PV projects at the national level, set a cap of 20 MW for each province, requiring those projects qualified for the subsidies to have a generating capacity of more than the 300–kW peak, while construction had to be completed in one year and operations had to last for at least 20 years. Considering the high cost of operating the systems, however, even the national subsidy offered by the programme was not enough to ensure a reasonable return on investment, so regional and local governments still needed to provide an additional subsidy for solar PV developers to cover the shortfalls. During that period, not many provincial and municipal governments had announced their detailed plans to supplement the national subsidy in this area. To further boost the development of solar energy, the government had been advised to introduce a nationwide feed-in tariff subsidy for large-scale PV projects after the implementation of the Golden Sun programme, but with the problems of low efficiency and excessive governmental expenses in mind, policy makers were still hesitant to institutionalize a national feed-in tariff to all solar power projects across the country.

In 2011, the Chinese government changed its mind on the issue through introducing a new set of solar incentives, extending them throughout the entire country for the first time. The authority decided to offer a nationwide feed-in tariff, which offers above-market-price contracts for the generation of solar electricity in China. Against the backdrop of exacerbated solar PV overcapacity and the launch of antidumping and countervailing duty investigations by the United States and EU over China-produced PV products, the Chinese central government planned to give nationwide subsidy of 0.45 yuan for each kWh of electricity generated by solar PV equipments while many provincial governments decided to offer additional subsidy of 0.25–0.3 yuan on top of that, with the unified term of

20 years. As reported by the 21st Century Economic Report on 20 June 2013, in a solar PV industrial park in Jiaxing City, Zhejiang Province, such subsidy could go as high as 2.8 yuan per kWh, which may imply that investors could easily get back their investment within three years. During the author's fieldwork in NDRC's Energy Research Institute (Beijing, 2 March 2012), local policy researchers expected such additional subsidies to increase the number of solar installations in the country by as much as 50% in 2011 and 70% in 2012. The Chinese government's release of its nationwide feed-in tariff sent a positive signal to the country's solar industry that ultimately, the country's PV installation will soar to absorb a large part of the domestic solar PV production capacity that has encountered foreign sanctions.

In the discussion of interactions between renewable energy policy and renewable energy industrial policy, researchers have found with empirical evidences that there is a natural affinity between these two policies, with the improved competitiveness and capabilities of the manufacturers of renewable energy equipment, components and parts often resulting in price reduction of these facilities that leads in turn to lower costs for the installation and generation of renewable power (Zhang et al. 2013, 2). The cost of a solar cell, as noted in a Bloomberg article on 9 September 2013, was about 41 US cents a watt for the moment, down from US$1.46 in 2010 and about US$3 in 2004, which implied that it would be much more cost-effective for the Chinese government to subsidize domestic solar power generation than it would have done a few years ago. China Renewable Energy Industries Association (2011) projected that solar PV power generation could reach the grid parity as early as 2014, a point at which solar PV can generate electricity at a levelized cost that is less than or equal to the price of purchasing power from the electricity grid, and thus becomes a contender for widespread development vis-à-vis conventional thermal power without government subsidies.

According to this pathway to grid parity depicted by China Renewable Energy Industries Association (2011), if the on-grid solar tariff decreased from 2009 level of 1.5 yuan per kWh at an annual rate of 8%, while the thermal on-grid tariff rose 6% per annum since 2009, the grid parity would be realized in 2014 when the price of solar electricity from the grid would be lower than coal-fired electricity. In reality, the cost of solar electricity has been dropping at a much faster rate due to the price slump of solar panels. Daily Economic News (meiri jingji xinwen) reported on 30 August 2013 that the cost of generating electricity from solar sources in China had been cut to the level of about 0.8 yuan per kWh, and if government subsidies of all kinds were counted, the cost could further go down to less than 0.4 yuan per kWh, which would already be competitive vis-à-vis thermal and wind power. The National Development and Reform Commission (2013) institutionalized the nationwide subsidy to all solar PV power plants through announcing a subsidy level of 0.42 yuan per kWh in a circular released in August 2013, a 20% increase from the planned level of 0.35 yuan per kWh which had been proposed in its draft version half a year ago. With such a higher-than-expected government subsidy granted to local solar power plants, China, now the world's fourth largest solar PV power producer, could witness its PV installed capacity grow exponentially in the next few years, just as its wind power market had performed from 2005 to 2010, a period when the country turned itself into the world's largest wind power producer from the tenth position in the global ranking.

7. Implications for theory and practice

Such a dramatic change in solar policy priority associated with the whereabouts of government subsidies and supportive measures is going to have profound domestic and international implications, with China's overdependence upon external PV demand to be subdued, trade tensions to be alleviated and domestic solar power market to grow explosively. Since an economic slowdown in China has been exacerbating the issue of excess industrial capacity, more domestic suppliers in the solar sectors are expected to be pushed to the edge of collapse without robust governmental subsidization on the domestic solar PV power generation. As indicated in the case of interactions between China's wind energy industrial policy and wind power generation policy (Zhang et al. 2013), there should also be a natural affinity between the country's solar PV manufacture policy and solar power generation policy, in which the improved competitiveness and capabilities of the manufacturers of solar PV equipment, components and parts result in lower costs for the installation and generation of solar power, and meanwhile, the development, generation and consumption of solar power are conducive to enhancing the solar panel manufacturing competitiveness by providing a sustainable and stale domestic market demand. As solar PV power generation in China is approaching the breaking point of grid parity with existing subsidies, feed-in tariffs and other supportive measures, China, now the world's fourth largest solar PV power producer, could witness its PV installed capacity grow exponentially in the next few years, just as its wind power market had performed from 2005 to 2010, a period when the country turned itself into the world's largest wind power producer from the tenth position in the global ranking. Solar's installed capacity remained 0.86 GW until 2010, a paltry proportion of 0.09% in China's total installed capacity, but according to China's finalized 12th Five-Year Plan (2011–2015), the solar installed capacity is expected to grow 89.5% annually, close to the wind power's 89.8% growth per annum between 2005 and 2010 (China's State Council 2013). As global solar panel manufacture has encountered severe overcapacity for the moment, which implies a less elasticity in supply than that in demand under condition of government subsidies, the change of government approaches from producer subsidies to demand-end subsidies will continue to benefit industrial producers more than domestic consumers because the relative elastic demand is bound to increase consumption significantly and thus bolsters equilibrium prices.

8. Conclusions

Thanks to massive government subsidies that having been flowing to renewable energy sectors in recent years helping change factor conditions, both China's solar PV and wind turbine manufacturers have gained competitive advantages over their foreign rivals and thus grown dramatically to leading positions in the world. Nevertheless, compared to its fast-expanding wind power market that has congenital advantages in attracting policy support under China's model of state capitalism, China's domestic solar PV market has been too small to absorb a large part of its inflated production capacity, a fundamental factor that triggered external trade disputes and domestic overcapacity. Empirical evidences in this study have shown that in sync with the state's reorientation on domestic demand and economic restructure from previous mercantile strategy with overdependence on export in the global economic downturn, the government's role in supporting the solar PV industry has also been transforming from subsidizing the production side (solar PV manufacture) to subsiding the demand side (solar PV power generation). Chinese policy-makers, once only interested in capturing foreign market for the sake of developing domestic PV manufacturing, have realized that the indigenous development, generation and consumption of solar power helps enhance the manufacturing competitiveness and capability of solar panels by providing a sustainable and stable domestic renewable energy market that is immune from international trade disputes. This policy shift is meant to provide signals to both local manufacturers and to foreign firms that they have the long-term planning horizon necessary to allow them to reasonably invest in R&D and local manufacturing infrastructure (Lewis and Wiser 2007). Such a policy shift under China's state capitalism could be well explained in the theoretical framework constructed by Porter (1998, 127) on the comparative advantages of nations, in which the role of the state can only indirectly help or hurt the nation's industry through reshaping the circumstances of the four determinants of national advantages, i.e. factor conditions, demand conditions, related and supporting industries and firm strategy. The study of China's solar PV policy is a case in point that showcases a gradual but fundamental change in China's state capitalism model from a mercantile stage, in which most subsidies were designed to influence factor conditions and supporting industries, to a new stage of domestic demand with more subsidies aimed at reshaping demand conditions to absorb redundant capacity. Nevertheless, when the new policy from the central government is being implemented across the nation, local governments, most of which are now vexed with mounting debt problems associated with massive infrastructure and property construction, may find it fiscally difficult to provide specific supporting policies and sufficient subsidies for local PV power stations. It has often been a formidable task to translate top-down directives into localized policy changes under a fragmented model of state capitalism.

References

Bremmer, I. 2010. *The End of the Free Market: Who Wins the War Between States and Corporations?* New York: Portfolio.

Buckeridge, D. L., R. Glazier, B. J. Harvey, M. Escobar, C. Amrhein, and J. Fran. 2002. "Effect of Motor Vehicle Emissions on Respiratory Health in an Urban Area." *Environmental Health Perspectives* 110 (3): 293–300.

Chen, G. 2012. *China's Climate Policy*. London: Routledge.

China Meteorological Administration. 2010. "New Progress Made in Surveying China's Wind Power Resources." [woguo fengneng ziyuan xiangcha he pingjia qude xinjinzhan.] www.cma. gov.cn/mtjj/201001/t20100104_55673.html

China Renewable Energy Industries Association. 2011. "China Roadmap of Photovoltaics Development: A Pathway to Grid Parity." [zhongguo guangfu fadian pingjia shangwang luxiantu]. http://www.creia.net/publish/report/121.html

China's State Council. 2013. "China's 12th Five-Year Plan on Energy Development." [zhongguo nengyuan fazhan shierwu guihua]. Accessed December 2013. http://www.gov.cn/zwgk/2013-01/23/content_2318554.htm

Dulal, H. B., K. U. Shah, C. Sapkota, G. Uma, and B. R. Kandel. 2013. "Renewable Energy Diffusion in Asia: Can it Happen Without Government Support?" *Energy Policy* 59: 301–311.

EU ProSun. 2013. Press Release, Brussels, 28 August "European Commission Confirms Massive Illegal Subsidies to Chinese Solar Manufacturers."

Fligstein, N., and J. Zhang. 2011. "A New Agenda for Research on the Trajectory of Chinese Capitalism." *Management and Organization Review* 7 (1): 39–62.

Global Wind Energy Council. 2011. "Global Wind Report: Annual Market Update 2010." Accessed January 2012. www.gwec.net/fileadmin/images/Publications/GWEC_annual_market_update_2010_-_2nd_edition_April_2011.pdf

Global Wind Energy Council. 2013. "Global Wind Report: Annual Market Update 2012." Accessed March 2013. http://www.gwec.net/wp-content/uploads/2012/06/Annual_report_2012_LowRes.pdf

Haley, U. C. V., and G. T. Haley. 2013. *Subsidies to Chinese Industry: State Capitalism, Business Strategy, and Trade Policy*. New York: Oxford University Press.

Hatch, M. 2003. "Chinese Politics, Energy Policy, and the International Climate Change Negotiations." In *Global Warming and East Asia: The Domestic and International Politics of Climate Change*, edited by P. G. Harris, 43–65. London: Routledge.

Huang, Y., and B. Wang. 2010. "Cost Distortions and Structural Imbalances in China." *China & World Economy* 18 (4): 1–17.

Lewis, J. I., and R. H. Wiser. 2007. "Fostering a Renewable Energy Technology Industry: An International Comparison of Wind Industry Policy Support Mechanisms." *Energy Policy* 35: 1844–1857.

Li, Ling. 2007. "China Urges Electricity Suppliers to Buy 'Green' Power." Accessed January 2012. http://www.renewableenergyworld.com/rea/news/article/2007/09/china-urges-electricity-suppliers-to-buy-green-power-49879

Li, Lei. 2010. "Brief Analysis of Current China's PV industry: Part II.." [woguo guangfuchanye fazhanxianzhuang jianxi zhier.] *Solar & Renewable Energy Sources [yangguang nengyuan]* 2: 36–39.

Lin, B., and Z. Jiang. 2011. "Estimates of Energy Subsidies in China and Impact of Energy Subsidy Reform." *Energy Economics* 33: 273–283.

McGregor, R. 2010. *The Party: The Secret World of China's Communist Rulers*. New York: HarperCollins.

McGregor, J. 2012. *No Ancient Wisdom, No Followers: The Challenges of Chinese Authoritarian Capitalism*. Westport: Prospecta Press.

Mehta, S. 2013. "GTM Research: Yingli Gains Crown as Top Producer in a 36 GW Global PV Market." *Greentechmedia News*, May 1. http://www.greentechmedia.com/articles/read/Yingli-Gains-Crown-As-Top-Producer-in-a-36-GW-Global-PV-Market

National Development and Reform Commission. 2008. "China Renewable Energy Development Overview 2008." Accessed January 2012. www.cresp.org.cn/uploadfiles/7/977/2008en.pdf

National Development and Reform Commission. 2009. "National On-grid Wind Power Tariff List." [quanguo fenglifadian biaogan shangwang dianjiabiao.] www.sdpc.gov.cn/zcfb/zcfbtz/2009tz/W020090727530432780298.pdf

National Development and Reform Commission. 2013. "NDRC's Circular on the Promotion of Solar PV Sector through Price Leverage." [guojia fazhangaigewei guanyu fahui jiage ganggan zuoyong cujin guangfu chanye jiankang fazhan de tongzhi.] 26 August. http://www.sdpc.gov.cn/zfdj/jggg/dian/t20130830_556127.htm

Nolan, P. 2007. *Capitalism and Freedom: The Contradictory Character of Capitalist Globalization*. London: Anthem Press.

The PEW Charitable Trusts. 2010. "Who's Winning the Clean Energy Race?: Growth, Competition and Opportunity in the World's Largest Economies." www.pewtrusts.org/uploadedFiles/wwwpewtrustsorg/Reports/Global_warming/G-20%20Report.pdf?n=5939

Porter, M. E. 1998. *The Comparative Advantage of Nations: With A New Introduction*. New York: The Free Press.

PRC Renewable Energy Law. 2005. www.renewableenergyworld.com/assets/download/China_RE_Law_05.doc

REN21 (Renewable Energy Policy Network for the 21st Century). 2009. "Recommendations for Improving the Effectiveness of Renewable Energy Policies in China." Accessed January 2012. www.ren21.net/pdf/Recommendations_for_RE_Policies_in_China.pdf

REN21 (Renewable Energy Policy Network for the 21st Century). 2013. "Renewables 2013 – Global Status Report." Accessed July 2013. http://www.ren21.net/Portals/0/documents/Resources/GSR/2013/GSR2013_lowres.pdf

Salim, R. A., and S. Rafiq. 2012. "Why Do Some Emerging Economies Proactively Accelerate the Adoption of Renewable Energy?" *Energy Economics* 34 (4): 1051–1057.

Schaffer, LenaMaria, and T. Bernauer. 2014. "Explaining Government Choices for Promoting Renewable Energy." *Energy Policy* 68: 15–27.

The Economist. 2012. *Special Report of State Capitalism: The Visible Hand*, No. 8768, January 21st.

Trebilcock, M. J., D. G. Hartle, J. R. S. Prichard, and D. N. Dewees. 1982. "The Choice of Governing Instrument." , Economic Council of Canada's Regulatory Reference.

Urmee, T., D. Harries, and A. Schlapfer. 2009. "Issues Related to Rural Electrification Using Renewable Energy in Developing Countries of Asia and Pacific." *Renewable Energy* 34 (2): 354–357.

US Department of Commerce. 2012. "Fact Sheet, "Commerce Finds Dumping and Subsidization of Crystalline Silicon Photovoltaic Cells, Whether or Not Assembled into Modules from the People's Republic of China".

Yang, M., and R. Pan. 2010a. *China's Wind Power Industry: From Infant to Growth Stage.* Singapore: EAI (East Asian Institute) Background Brief, No. 525.

Yang, M., and R. Pan. 2010b. *Harvesting sunlight: Solar photovoltaic industry in China.* Singapore: EAI (East Asian Institute) Background Brief, No. 562.

Zhang, G. 2005. "How can energy shortage be blamed on China?" [nengyuan jinzhang zenneng guaizui zhongguo.] People's Daily Overseas Edition, September 21, p. 1.

Zhang, S., P. Andrews-Speed, X. Zhao, and Y. He. 2013. "Interactions Between Renewable Energy Policy and Renewable Energy Industrial Policy: A Critical Analysis of China's Policy Approach to Renewable Energies." *Energy Policy* 62: 342–353.

Enrolling in global networks and contingencies for China's solar PV industry

Douglas R. Gress

Department of Geography Education, Seoul National University, South Korea

This study tests the contention in the Asian business systems literature that interacting with global managers and increasing experience via international education are ways by which Asian firms enroll in global networks, thus potentially leading to changes in their broader network contingencies. Chinese solar PV firms are examined given the competitiveness of Chinese products in the global marketplace and the importance being placed on solar energy domestically as China confronts increasing pressure to protect its environment and control pollution while meeting mounting energy needs. Results indicate an emphasis on extra-firm institutional network relationships both within and outside of China for all firms, characteristic of a bourgeoning energy sector. A unique result is that buyer–supplier networks are spatially influenced by extra-local managerial education. Enrolling in wider networks also matters as firms with internationally educated managers have more non-mainland Chinese managers, which mitigates traditional management practices at home.

Introduction

Globally, the solar photovoltaic (PV from here on) industry is one of the fastest growing of the major 'green energy sectors' and a vital part of green growth strategies (Sachs 2009). Accordingly, there has been a growth in the number of contributions from PV industry-related publications (e.g. Caprotti 2009; Marigo 2007; Potash 2009), and a burgeoning emphasis on the PV industry in management (e.g. Jacobsson and Johnson 2000), economic (e.g. van den Heuvel and van den Bergh 2009), and strategy and policy-related publications (e.g. Marigo, Foxon, and Pearson 2008; OECD 2009; Tyfield and Wilsdon 2009; Aylett 2013). The literature, however, with the recent exception of Klitkou and Coenen (2013), has not been as quick to prioritize multi-actor, multi-spatial research into this segment of clean energy, surprising considering that firm activity and the institutions that shape their competitive environments are defined by embedded, place-specific relational logic (Dicken 2011; Whitley 1994).

These multi-spatial and scalar economic realities are particularly relevant to any analysis of contemporary Chinese firms. Yeung (2006), for example, suggests that as Asian firm actors engage in geographically broader networks, they may undergo transformations that may seem counterintuitive to their historical, cultural and institutional embeddedness. More specifically, interacting with global managers and increasing experience via international education are seen as two specific modes by which Asian firms 'enroll' in global networks (Yeung 2000, 413) in an era when Chinese managerial attitudes and behaviours may be changing (Kao 1993; Ralston et al. 1999). This is largely in line with business systems theorization, for as Whitley (1994, 4) points out, '... since social systems are "open" systems, and so social structures and relations can change endogenously as well as exogenously, market processes and outcomes can alter as a result of learning and changes in preference.'

While broadly theorized, potential change generated by enrolling in global networks on contemporary Chinese firm behaviour, inclusive of impacts to broader network contingencies, has not been tested from a multi-spatial, multi-actor perspective. This study therefore examines mainland Chinese solar PV firm networks. There are two key reasons that these firms and their associated networks are ideal subjects of enquiry. First, China, with 6 of the top 20 largest PV solar firms in the world, and one in the top three, has quickly emerged as a growingly influential global player in this increasingly important segment of clean energy. This emergence can be characterized both in terms of its domestic requirements and capabilities (Denning 2011) and in terms of its firms' position and connectivity vis-à-vis traditional solar leaders (Caprotti 2009). Since 2007, China, for example, has emerged as a prolific creator of solar PV patents domestically while expanding its competitive advantage globally via economies of scale in production (Wu 2014). Second, as will be discussed later, these firms have had no choice but to interact with firms and governments *outside* of China while at the same time undertaking core business activities *in* mainland China in an era of progressively market-oriented policy shifts (Yeung 2004) and local level emphasis on, and funding of, green energy (see Chen 2014).

The firm-network methodology has emerged as one vehicle by which such spatially sensitive analyses of multi-actor networks may be conducted. Rather than approaching firm activity via a narrowly defined, internally oriented construct, or through truncated nodal relationships with individual external firm actors, this perspective suggests a simultaneous examination of intra-firm (within the same firm), inter-firm (between firms in different networks) and extra-firm (e.g. government, trade, business and related R&D) network considerations within and across space (Coe, Dicken, and Hess 2008; Hess and Yeung 2006). In turn, this necessitates an understanding of culturally and socially defined practice in order to identify the influence places have in ongoing economic activity (Poon and Thompson 2003). For example, extra-firm studies by Huggins (1998), Perry and Hui (1998) and Zhou and Xin (2003) provide insight into the extent to which (Asian) governments, seen as competitive and active network participants, contribute to the ability of firms to create inter-firm synergies. In other research (Tan and Yeung 2000; Yeung 1997, 1999, 2000), embedded intra-firm Chinese family relational networks are shown to represent culturally distinct forms of enterprise acting not only locally, but also globally as firms form inter- and extra-firm relationships deployed when choosing locations, acquiring capital, hiring new employees or interacting with governments.

As the title of this contribution suggests, however, network architectures may be contingent on factors associated with Chinese solar PV firms as they enroll (or do not enroll) in wider global networks. In this study, then, 'network contingencies' examined include (1) the perceived importance and use of extra-firm actors at varying locations and scales, (2) the location of buyers and suppliers and the selection criteria employed (inter-firm) and (3) intra-firm factors such as management characteristics and perceptions related to firm management, image and size. The results presented were generated from a survey of 36 solar PV-related mainland Chinese firms.

This contribution proceeds with a review of relevant literature and theory, to include an introduction to, and discussion of, the Chinese solar PV industry. Following this section, the hypotheses are introduced, and then the methodology and discussion sections are presented. Implications for theory development as well as practice are then introduced in conjunction with concluding remarks.

Literature review and theory

The Chinese solar PV market: background and progress

China's economy is one of the fastest growing economies in the world, and this growth is being accompanied by an increasing need for *clean* energy (OECD 2009). China currently meets over 70% of its energy needs via coal, and by 2007 had surpassed the USA in terms of total carbon dioxide emissions (EIA 2014). Under pressure to reduce pollution and protect its local environment, China had therefore worked to become first in the world in terms of solar cell production capacity with 30% of the global market share by 2006 (Koot 2006). By 2008, the solar industry in China had again experienced 50% growth and was staged '...to become a model for the global solar energy market...' (Cockerill 2008). By 2012, China had become the second largest growth market for solar PV (behind Germany) and is projected to exceed the USA in installations by 2016 (Kovalyova 2012). All told, the Chinese government plans on expanding solar PV generated power to over 1.8 GW by 2020, largely via large-scale solar power plants (Campbell 2010).

The price competitiveness of Chinese PV products has also left Chinese firms well positioned globally. In some instances, such as the case of US firm Evergreen Solar, competition from Chinese firms is explicitly stated as a reason for market withdraw. Price sensitivity in the global market has persisted. Most recently, the USA imposed a 31% antidumping tariff on Chinese solar panels (Ma 2012), and the European Commission ruling on Chinese solar panel pricing, while favouring China, cast a dubious light on the manner and extent to which the Chinese government subsidizes its firms (Bussey 2013).

Extra-firm actors and research considerations

For some time now, there has been an increasing emphasis on, and state support of, renewable energy technologies in China. Locally, the solar PV component of China's Renewable Energy Development Project, in conjunction with the Chinese government, the World Bank and the Global Environment Facility, has focused on firm-level direct grants to further China's national solar industry (National Renewable Energy Laboratory 2004). Other national and local solar energy projects championed by the Chinese government have included 'Project Sunshine', the 'Bright Project' and the 'Sending Electricity to the Villages' project, all which have sought to satisfy the energy needs of fringe townships (Ying 2007). The Chinese central government also initiated the Village Electrification Program, targeting another 20,000 villages in China's off-grid western region between 2005 and 2010 (Koot 2006). Projects such as these make solar power a promising long-term, cost-efficient choice for countries such as China that have populations spread out over numerous remote 'off the grid' areas (van den Heuvel and van den Bergh 2009). At the same time, China is also seeking to upgrade smart-grid construction to more effectively utilize power generated from clean energy, an estimated US $60 billion investment over the next 10 years (Oster 2010).

Working to satisfy demand both locally and abroad, local producers remained vulnerable to shocks in the international supply chain. In order to remedy this, China's central government earmarked 400 million Yuan to support its renewable energy sector in 2009 (Xinhua News Agency, March 27, 2009). This was a move to further assist Chinese solar firms to increasingly engage in upstream, technologically oriented production rather than simpler solar cell and module assembly.

While government actors can be viewed as integral to firm performance in this sector, other extra-firm actors are nonetheless potentially critical to their success (see also Chen, 2014, for a discussion of extra-firm actors). R&D institutions, universities, trade and professional organizations, and trade fairs, for example, are also constituent actors in firm networks and particularly important for high-tech firms (Coe, Dicken, and Hess 2008; Liu and Dicken 2006). In the case of mainland Chinese solar PV firms, such relationships with not only research institutes, but also universities exist as firms seek to enhance their competence, overseas exposure and competitiveness (Marigo 2007; Wu 2014).

Inter-firm actors and research considerations

By 2006, roughly 80% of China's solar cells and modules were being exported to Germany and the USA (Marigo 2007), and by late 2009, 46% of the solar panels for use in California's Solar Initiative were supplied by Chinese firms (*The Economist*, April 17–23, 2010, 65). Clearly, inter-firm relationships with buyers should be a topic of interest, and not only where they are located, but also how they are chosen. While more generalized studies of Chinese business practice find a direct predisposition for personal relationships (Jansson, Johanson, and Romström 2007; Redding 1993, 1995), results from studies on Chinese *technology* firms suggest that personal networks are *not* as influential as competence and reputation during the selection of business partners (Hsu and Saxenian 2000; Yeung 1998; Yeung and Tung 1996). The present study examines these network contingencies vis-à-vis the impact of international education and the presence of non-Chinese employees in management.

Relationships with suppliers have played an important role in the genesis and growth of mainland firms as well. By 2006–2007, there was a growing need in the Chinese solar industry to source polysilicon, the raw building block for all PV-related products, from imports (Marigo 2007) with prices peaking in 2008 at roughly four times the 2001 price (Research Report on Chinese Polysilicon Industry 2009–2010). Silicon inputs were, and to some extent still are, imported, thus necessitating extra-local relationships. Indeed, China's rebuttal to the WTO suits brought by the USA in 2012 included the argument that China imports almost as many solar PV inputs from the USA as it exports finished products to it (see also Chen, 2014, for a discussion on raw material and finished product production capacities and import/export imbalances).

The realities meeting mainland Chinese solar PV firms outlined thus far suggest that the success of firms along varying points on the value chain, from silicon manufacturing to installation, may be influenced by government actors at multiple scales, for example by impacting access to financing, preferred locations and infrastructure, and, at the same time, by inter and extra-firm relationships as firms seek to capitalize on opportunities abroad.

Intra-firm research considerations

The firm network methodology promotes an analytical emphasis on how firms' relationships produce structural outcomes (Dicken et al. 2001). A 'structural outcome' is a change in organizational level processes or in network connectivity; at the intra-firm level, this could mean a change in the managerial power structure. For some time now, scholars have suggested that, in turn, intra-firm factors influence firm motivations to create, maintain and further networks within and across spaces (see Coe, Dicken, and Hess 2008). In short, examining varying intra-firm organizational constructs is paramount to understanding how firms, in this case Chinese solar PV firms, are engaging wider inter and extra-firm networks.

These are valuable insights because contemporary firms in the Chinese PV industry hardly conform structurally to the smaller, more traditional view of Chinese family-owned firms that once dominated (and constrained) research into Chinese firms. As the state has sought to increase production in increasingly technologically oriented and competitive markets, size has become important (Keister 1998) and is seen to contribute to access to raw materials, market share and trade opportunities (Chen 2004). Not surprisingly, then, China is currently home to some of the largest solar PV companies in the world, some of which are listed on international bourses.

Yeung (2004) further suggests that the concept of Chinese business itself is evolving, and that research should seek to examine this evolution. As such, the present study does not a priori presuppose macro constructs (e.g. family management, an emphasis on personal relationships and paternalistic management style) on mainland Chinese firm behaviour. Rather, the purpose is to unearth the presence or absence of these more traditional intra-firm attributes, and to ascertain whether or not enrolling in global networks has an influence on intra-firm organizational behaviour and affiliated modes of selecting and maintaining inter-firm relationships.

Geographically, we must still recall that firms are still largely 'placed', meaning that locations exert an influence on firm practices and operations (Dicken 2011). Related to this, research conducted by Tan and Yeung (2000) on ethnic Chinese Singaporean investment *in China* conclude that personal connections, government institutions and ethnically based embedded networks influence firm activity on the mainland, mirroring a more 'classic perception' of Chinese networks than may have been anticipated given the originating country of investment. Later research by Jansson, Johanson, and Romström (2007) finds that Chinese firms tend to place comparatively *less* emphasis on firm performance in their business networks, in part due to the importance placed on relationship-oriented business constructs. Likewise, Ralston et al. (2008) conclude that individual Chinese managers still exhibit much higher collectivist measures based on the influence of national culture.

Hypotheses and research questions

The present study may offer new insights with regard to China's solar energy business. While inter and extra-firm networks, both local and extra-local, may be integral to firm success, these relationships remain underexplored in this industry. Likewise, the impact of enrolling in wider global networks may have contingent impacts on not only intra-firm arrangements, but also on inter-firm relationships. The review of the literature highlighted the importance of several extra-firm actors to firm success in this sector, suggesting that at this stage of development all firms remain dependent on extra-firm relationships for their business opportunities. The following hypothesis may therefore be generated concerning extra-firm relationships:

Hypothesis 1: Enrolling in global networks, whether by international education or by hiring non-mainland Chinese managers, will have no impact on Chinese solar firm extra-firm actor engagement.

Given the information presented in the review of the literature, it is also important to examine the socio-spatial logic of inter-firm supplier and buyer relationships in this high-tech sector. Two hypotheses related to inter-firm relationships may be ventured:

Hypothesis 2:   Product, price and competency will be deciding factors in the selection of suppliers and buyers regardless of whether or not firms are enrolled in global networks via education or the employment of non-mainland Chinese managers. However,

Hypothesis 3:   Enrolling in global networks may influence the degree of emphasis placed on personal relationships, culture and location during the selection of suppliers and buyers.

The literature reviewed also revealed several intra-firm dynamics and possible associated inter-firm relationship impacts to firms in this burgeoning industry. Because the purpose is to unearth the presence or absence of traditional intra-firm attributes in Chinese solar PV firms and then to gauge whether or not enrollment in wider global networks has an impact, analyses can be informed by a more generalized research question:

Research Question:

Does enrollment in global networks via international education or the employment of non-mainland Chinese managers impact traditional Chinese intra-firm characteristics?

Data and methodology

Firm-level data were primarily collected by the author while visiting firms at the International Photovoltaic Solar Conference and Exhibition (IPVSEE) held in Beijing, China, from 17 to 20 November 2009, and at the International Green Energy Expo held in Daegu, Korea, from 6 to 8 April 2011. Conducting research at international trade expositions in this way has become an accepted research method across numerous disciplines as it enables researchers to determine and engage dominant firms in a specific industry (see Bathelt and Schuldt 2008). Prior to the exhibition visits, 12 surveys were collected via the Internet to gauge the effectiveness of the survey instrument. Contact information was obtained from EFN-Energy Focus, an online database of firms in the global solar PV industry. The remaining 24 completed surveys (14 at exhibition 1 and 10 at exhibition 2), of a total of 36, were collected by the author at the two exhibitions. T tests revealed no significant differences in data collected in 2009 and 2011 with regard to age ($p = 0.604$) and size ($p = 0.609$). Also, following Armstrong and Overton's (1977) procedure for response bias testing on early and late samples, additional tests indicated no difference based on the presence of non-mainland Chinese employees ($\chi^2 = 1.35$, $p = 0.245$), or country of education for top management ($\chi^2 = 0.899$, $p = 0.343$).

The survey instrument consisted of four sections covering company information, non-mainland Chinese employees, business relationships and business in China, along with a free response section that solicited input regarding the 'Chinese way of doing business'. All-in-all, there were 74 individual questions plus the open-ended question. The survey was translated into Chinese by a bilingual Chinese graduate student. After responses were gathered, responses to all multiple part questions were subjected to tests of reliability, with Chronbach's α values all above 0.70.

On average, the companies have been in business in China for 6.5 years. Company ages span newer companies (20) in operation for 5 years or less, and older firms (16) in operation for $10-20 +$ years. By natural break, there are 6 companies with $30-100$ employees, 11 companies with $101-400$ employees, 7 companies with $401-999$ employees and 12 companies with over 1000 employees. While small, the database captures a number of China's major solar PV firms. Thirty-six per cent of the firms have senior management educated outside of China, primarily in the USA and, to a lesser extent, Germany, and 42% of the respondent firms have non-mainland Chinese managers. Further, 20 of the firms are privately owned, 8 are joint ventures (JVs from here on) with privately owned Chinese companies, 5 are state owned enterprises (SOEs) and 3 are JVs with SOEs. The majority of the respondent firms (26) are direct manufacturers. Respondent firms are engaged in panel/module assembly (7), cell (11) or wafer (8) manufacturing and processing, and polysilicon ingot/block production (10).

Analysis and discussion
Extra-firm networks

To ascertain the importance of specific extra-firm relationships, respondents were first asked to relate the importance of 10 institutional actors to their business success on seven-point Likert scales (see Table 1). Extra-firm government relationships are clearly considered paramount to firms' success, with the national (5.80) and local governments (5.69) in China figuring predominantly. More specifically, as results presented in Table 2 reflect, firms consider relationships with people in the Chinese government of more than average importance when it comes to securing infrastructure improvements, trying to find a suitable business partner, obtaining export/import assistance, choosing a favourable location and when obtaining financing (see also Chen, 2014, for a discussion of national and local level types of assistance and subsidies). Relationships with national (5.36) and local level governments (5.00) *abroad* are also considered significant.

In conjunction with this, business and trade organizations, both in China (4.81) and abroad (4.94), as well as well as international trade shows and exhibitions abroad (5.44) are also considered of greater than average importance, mirroring Marigo's (2007) observation that Chinese PV firms have been increasingly visible at trade shows globally. As mentioned previously, a large percentage of China's PV products are exported, so this emphasis comes as no surprise. Indeed, taking part in global trade shows is an indicator of a firm's degree of investment in international activities and an integral part of internationalization strategies (Seringhaus and Rosson 1994). The results presented here affirm that mainland Chinese solar PV firms are indeed cognizant of the benefits to be derived from these extra-firm relationships. Some time ago, Redding (1995) characterized

Table 1. Perceived importance of extra-firm actors to business success.

How important are relationships with the following to the success of your business?	Mean	SD
National government in China	5.81	1.19
Local government in China	5.69	1.26
International trade shows/exhibitions abroad	5.44	1.50
National government abroad	5.36	1.69
International trade shows/exhibitions in China	5.06	1.51
Local government abroad	5.00	1.53
Business/trade organizations abroad	4.94	1.45
Business/trade organizations in China	4.81	1.70
University relationships in China	4.34	1.63
University relationships abroad	3.92	1.66

Note: Results based on Likert scale (1 = not important at all; 7 = extremely important).
Source: Author's survey results (n = 36).

Table 2. Perceived importance of government relationships.

Personal relationships with people in the Chinese government are important....	Mean	SD
When trying to find a suitable business partner	3.00	1.49
When choosing a favourable location	2.69	1.62
To obtain export/import assistance	2.64	1.55
To secure infrastructure improvements	2.36	1.39
To obtain financing/loans	2.36	1.71

Note: Results based on Likert scale (1 = very strongly agree; 7 = very strongly disagree).
Source: Author's survey results (*n* = 36).

Chinese firms as being weak at generating market recognition outside of their home territory. The results discussed here, however, suggest that Chinese solar PV firms are more intent on creating market recognition internationally. One manager stated succinctly, 'Chinese managers think the size of their company and their brands are very important.'

Only relationships with universities abroad (3.92) scored under the mid-range point of 4.00, but with a large standard deviation some firms do indeed consider such relationships to be of above average importance. Conversely, university relationships with universities in China are considered of above average importance (4.34). This reinforces Marigo's (2007, 11) findings that Chinese PV firms in her (qualitative) study '...tend to have links with universities and research institutes'. However, Chen (2014), suggests that local Chinese university relationships are not technologically capable of across the board assistance to firms, so this finding may indicate that some Chinese firms are extending their reach to more technologically advanced R&D universities abroad.

Hypothesis 1 specifically inquires after the impact of enrolling in wider global networks on these extra-firm relationships. Non-parametric Mann–Whitney U and Kruskal–Wallis tests indicate no differentiation based on where top management was educated, type of ownership, role or the presence of non-mainland Chinese employees, thus supporting Hypothesis 1. Analyses presented thus far suggest that extra-firm linkages engaged by mainland Chinese solar firms are generally geared toward initiating or maintaining innovation (e.g. through university relationships) and industrial growth (e.g. through factors captured in Table 2), while at the same time capitalizing and expanding upon their competitive strengths internationally via extra-firm links to trade and business organizations, extra-local governments and international trade shows.

Inter-firm networks: selection of suppliers and buyers

The local and extra-local geographic continuum discussed in the previous section is further evidenced by the supplier and buyer networks maintained by the firms. As Table 3 reflects, product quality and technical know how, professional reputation and price figure most predominantly into the selection of both suppliers and buyers. Hypothesis 2 is therefore supported.

Location and understanding of Chinese language and culture figure into supplier selection, but are of less than average importance for the selection of buyers. Personal relationships are of average importance in buyer selection, but less so for the selection of suppliers. Also, firms with managers educated in China show increased emphasis on the understanding of Chinese language and culture, and on personal relationships when choosing suppliers, and on location and personal relationships when choosing buyers. While Mann–Whitney U tests reveal no strong statistical differences per say (at the 0.90

Table 3. Criteria for selection of suppliers and buyers.

	Supplier selection						Buyer selection					
	All firms		Educated in China		Foreign educated		All firms		Educated in China		Foreign educated	
	Mean	SD	Mean	SD	Mean	SD	Mean	SD	Mean	SD	Mean	SD
Quality and technical know how	6.69	1.06	6.55	1.36	6.93	0.267	6.22	1.42	5.91	1.72	6.71	0.469
Professional reputation	6.23	1.16	6.27	1.32	6.29	0.913	6.31	1.19	6.23	1.41	6.43	0.756
Price	6.12	0.91	6.27	0.985	6.00	0.784	6.14	1.20	6.18	1.44	6.07	0.730
Personal relationships	3.75	1.62	4.00	1.72	3.36	1.39	4.00	1.71	4.00	1.85	3.79	1.53
Location	4.03	1.58	3.95	1.79	4.14	1.23	3.92	1.76	4.23	1.80	3.43	1.65
Chinese language and culture	4.02	1.90	4.27	2.05	3.64	1.65	3.61	1.81	3.82	1.92	3.29	1.64

Note: Results based on Likert scale (1 = not important at all; 7 = extremely important).
Source: Author's survey (n = 36).

level of confidence there are differences), open-ended responses from managers at the IPVSEE would seem to confirm this and include, 'Relationships with bosses (in the) solar industry are very important when doing business in China' and 'Managers consider profits and informal personal relationships the most important.' Taken together, results provide tenuous support of Hypothesis 3, suggesting that additional analyses would be of use.

Kendall's τ b correlations lend insight into supplier and buyer selection dynamics given the above findings. Table 4(a) reflects, for example, that in supplier selection, there is an inverse relationship between personal relationships and emphasis on product quality along with a positive correlation between understanding of Chinese culture and importance placed on reputation. Understanding of Chinese culture and language, as well as emphasis on personal relationships, is also positively correlated with location during supplier selection. In terms of buyer selection (Table 4(b)), reputation and quality are positively correlated, and, as with supplier selection, understanding of Chinese culture and an emphasis on personal relationships are positively correlated with location. These results lend credence to prior studies by Fan (2002) and Yeung and Tung (1996), in which relational benefits to business operations play less a part in business in China. Results presented here affirm, for example, that quality, reputation and price are the foremost considerations for the selection of both buyers and suppliers. Still, these factors are mitigated to some extent by knowledge of the language and culture, and by an emphasis on personal relationships. These variables, in turn, are a product of enrolling in global networks via extra-local education.

Briefly referring back to Table 3, location is considered to be of average importance when sourcing inputs, and there is evidence to suggest that where top management is educated may influence network architectures. To explore this further, firms were asked to indicate the percentages of purchases from and sales to ethnic Chinese and foreign supplier and buyer firms located within and/or outside of China. Results are presented in Table 5. Supplier networks include strong linkages with non-Chinese suppliers outside of China, which is consistent with expectations given both the long running upstream shortage of raw materials and the emphasis on downstream assembly oriented manufacturing that have characterized China's PV industry (see also Chen 2014 for a discussion of this topic). Interestingly, though, usage of Ethnic-Chinese suppliers *outside* of China, and to an even larger degree, of Chinese suppliers *inside* of China, is apparent. The latter may reflect the

Table 4. Supplier and buyer selection – variable correlations (Kendall's τ b).

	Quality	Reputation	Price	Culture	Location	Relationships
(a) Supplier selection						
Quality	1.00	0.274	0.012	− 0.055	− 0.256	− 0.388**
Reputation		1.00	0.168	0.358*	0.129	− 0.024
Price			1.00	− 0.015	0.082	− 0.083
Culture				1.00	0.577**	0.477**
Location					1.00	0.679**
Relationships						1.00
(b) Buyer selection						
Quality	1.00	0.428**	0.260	0.005	− 0.091	0.000
Reputation		1.00	0.166	0.224	0.099	0.097
Price			1.00	− 0.160	− 0.067	0.155
Culture				1.00	0.729**	0.540**
Location					1.00	0.585**
Relationships						1.00

Table 5. Supplier and buyer networks by country of origin and location.

Supplier/buyer country of origin and location	Percentage of materials or inputs purchased/products or services sold and associated percentage of firm responses by category					
	0%	1–20%	21–40%	41–60%	61–80%	81–100%
Non-Chinese suppliers/*buyers* outside of China						
Purchases	0.18	0.22	0.36	0.17	0.14	0.00
Sales	0.05	0.25	0.08	0.10	0.25	0.25
Ethnic-Chinese suppliers/*buyers* outside of China						
Purchases	0.28	0.44	0.1	0.08	0.03	0.00
Sales	0.73	0.28	0.08	0.06	0.06	0.03
Chinese suppliers/*buyers* outside of China						
Purchases	0.53	0.33	0.03	0.03	0.06	0.03
Sales	0.39	0.39	0.11	0.08	0.03	0.00
Chinese suppliers/*buyers* inside China						
Purchases	0.03	0.03	0.11	0.47	0.25	0.11
Sales	0.10	0.22	0.28	0.11	0.20	0.08
Ethnic-Chinese suppliers/*buyers* inside China						
Purchases	0.47	0.33	0.03	0.11	0.06	0.00
Sales	0.47	0.36	0.08	0.06	0.03	0.00
Non-Chinese suppliers/*buyers* inside China						
Purchases	0.47	0.36	0.06	0.06	0.03	0.03
Sales	0.53	0.36	0.03	0.06	0.03	0.00
Non-mainland Chinese suppliers/*buyers* inside mainland China						
Purchases	0.42	0.36	0.09	0.11	0.03	0.00
Sales	0.44	0.39	0.00	0.14	0.00	0.00
Non-mainland Chinese suppliers/*buyers* in Taiwan, Hong Kong, or Macao						
Purchases	0.39	0.40	0.08	0.14	0.00	0.00
Sales	0.50	0.40	0.06	0.06	0.00	0.00

Source: Author's survey ($n = 36$).

growing maturity of China's PV industrial capabilities. The Chinese government has recently invested significant sums to offset domestic sourcing shortfalls, so these investments may be coming to fruition. Individual Mann–Whitney U tests indicate no statistical differences in sourcing for companies where managers were educated in China or for companies where managers were educated abroad.

Results presented in Table 5 also reveal that sales are dominated by sales to non-Chinese firms outside of China and to Chinese buyer firms located inside China. Mann–Whitney U tests, however, confirm that there *are* differences in these categories based on whether or not top managers were educated in China or abroad ($U = 0.004$ and $U = 0.001$, respectively). For firms with top management educated abroad, there is heavier usage of non-Chinese buyers outside of China, whereas there is more pronounced usage of Chinese buyers *in* China by firms where managers were educated in China.

In short, enrolling in wider global networks by engaging extra-territorial education has lead to diverging and outward looking buyer networks.

Intra-firm considerations and change

Yeung (2004) suggests that Chinese firms engaging in wider and wider networks may change the way they do business *internationally* while undergoing fewer changes 'at home'. A research question was posed in order to explore broad intra-firm characteristics vis-à-vis enrolling in wider global networks.

Data for intra-firm attributes were gathered via a series of nine questions. On seven-point Likert scales (1 = very strongly disagree to 7 = very strong agree), respondents were asked how each of the statements, adapted from Redding (1995), described their company (Table 6). At first glance, it is apparent that firms in China's solar PV industry are readily describable from an older, static perception of Chinese firms in general. For example, Redding (1995, 64) relates that small scale, family owned businesses focusing on one product market are common aspects of Chinese firms. Here, in contrast, we see an emphasis on size and growth (mean = 5.75), a *minority* of family owned and managed firms (mean = 2.17), and diversified product sector participation ('We focus on a limited number of related products', mean = 3.72).

Table 6. Chinese PV intra-firm attributes.

	All firms		Firms with non-mainland Chinese employees		Firms with no non-mainland Chinese employees	
	Mean	SD	Mean	SD	Mean	SD
The president of our company was very knowledgeable about the products we make or the service we provide even before we opened our company	5.81	1.65	5.73	1.53	5.86	1.77
Growth in size is an important goal of our company	5.75	1.38	5.47	1.13	5.95	1.53
We actively learn about and use new ways of doing business	5.69	1.31	5.80	1.01	5.62	1.50
We do business with non-Chinese companies differently that we do business with Chinese companies	4.89	1.41	4.80	1.66	4.95	1.24
All decisions at our company are made by the owner or one top executive	3.94	1.95	3.27	1.94	4.23	1.91
We expect non-Chinese-owned foreign companies to adapt to the Chinese way of doing business	3.92	1.54	3.67	1.80	4.10	1.33
We focus on a limited number of related products	3.72	1.88	3.53	1.96	3.86	1.85
When possible, we try to do business with companies owned by Chinese people, either in China or abroad	2.58	1.50	2.47	1.36	2.67	1.62
We are family owned and managed	2.17	1.48	2.53	1.68	1.90	1.30

Note: Results based on Likert scale (1 = not true at all; 7 = extremely true).
Source: Author's survey; statements adapted from Redding (1995).

Redding (1995) also characterizes Chinese firms as being strong in '...strategic adaptability, due to a dominant decision maker' (64). Respondents confirm this in part with the statement, 'All decisions at our company are made by one executive,' scoring just under the mean of 4.0. Still, given the large standard deviation of 1.95, a test of means comparison was conducted; no difference with regard to where management was educated was found. The presence of non-mainland Chinese employees, however, somewhat tempers a strict decision-making hierarchy compared to firms with no non-mainland Chinese employees. For firms with non-mainland Chinese employees, the mean remains well under the cut-off of 4.0 at 3.27. For firms with only mainland Chinese employees, however, the mean jumps to a significant 4.43. As this is a weak difference in means (at the 0.10 level of significance), further input is useful here. The qualitative input regarding Chinese business gathered through open-ended questions suggests that many firms still have top-heavy management structures where teamwork is subordinate to strong, paternalistic leadership. Phrases such as, 'The leader must be effective,' 'Managers make all the decisions by themselves,' 'Family style (leadership) even interpret(ing) the subordinate's personal life,' '(The) boss makes decisions with no disagreement allowed' and 'The managers are always making all the decisions on their own; they don't care about our opinions' dominated the open-ended responses, with only one firm indicating a more participatory structure. Redding's (1995) characterization of Chinese firms as being paternalistic and centralized still apparently rings true, as do much later conclusions drawn by Ralston et al. (2008) pertaining to highly collectivist behaviour and traditional cultural traits in contemporary Chinese firms.

Of note, however, there is a negative Φ correlation (-0.482, $\Phi = .004$) between the presence of non-mainland Chinese employees and where top management were educated, indicating that firms with managers educated outside of China have more non-mainland Chinese employees. For firms with managers educated abroad, 71% have non-mainland Chinese employees compared to only 23% of firms where managers were educated locally. So, while international education does increase the number of non-mainland Chinese personnel, it does not *directly* temper more traditional paternalistic, strictly hierarchal management practice. *Indirectly*, however, the presence of foreign personnel *does* somewhat temper these practices.

Upon further analysis, the results presented in Table 6 also paint a picture of Chinese solar PV firms that are '...actively learning and using new ways of doing business' (mean = 5.69) and are spearheaded by '...very knowledgeable presidents' (mean = 5.81). These result bolster Redding's (1993, 179) observation that larger organizations are immerging in China in situations where '...the chief executive is deeply immersed and immensely knowledgeable'. Taken together with the conclusions drawn in the preceding paragraph, then, the results confirm Yeung's (2004) contention that Chinese firms engaging in wider and wider networks may still undergo fewer changes in the way they do business at home.

But what of the first half of Yeung's (2004) premise, that as Chinese firms engage global networks, they may alter the way they do business *internationally*? As presented in Table 6, there is an emphasis on business interaction with non-Chinese firms being done in a non-Chinese way. Taken together, the statements 'We do business with non-Chinese companies differently than we do business with Chinese companies' (mean = 4.89) and 'We expect non-Chinese owned foreign companies to adapt to the Chinese way of doing business' (mean = 3.92) suggest that Chinese firms have the ability (or necessity) to adapt to foreign business practices. Mann–Whitney U tests indicated no difference with regard to where managers were educated or the presence of absence of foreign employees.

There is none-the-less a propensity to sell to domestic firms of Chinese origin by firms where top management was educated in China. This appears at odds with responses to the statement, 'When possible, we try to do business with companies owned by Chinese people, either in China or abroad' (mean = 2.58). Part of this may be explained by the fact that there was no difference associated with *supplier* networks based on country of education comparisons; supplies are constrained and firms buy from where and from whom they can. Intuitively, given the large standard deviation in this category (1.50), some firms are more inclined to choose Chinese firms locally or abroad, though. This was indeed the case when *buyer* networks were examined. At least in part, this may help to explain the contradiction, although additional research would be useful to fully flush out this idiosyncrasy.

Implications for theory development

The solar PV industry is relatively new, subject to both supply and demand side shocks, and is under-researched, which raises interesting questions for theory and future research practice. In China, for example, as central and provincial level planning and investment in innovation, partnering and logistics lead to a stronger and more lucrative home solar PV market (see Chen 2014), could a multi-spatial and multi-scalar dichotomy emerge in this sector? Will solar Chinese PV firms with managers educated locally (and sourcing personnel locally) capitalize locally based on the leveraging of personal relationships and a preference for deep local buyer relationships? Internationally, will Chinese solar PV firms with internationally educated managers, sourcing personnel internationally, on the other hand, further expand their inter-firm network linkages, particularly to non-Chinese buyers abroad?

Firms in this research also indicated that they 'do business differently' with non-Chinese firms. Exactly how and why are questions for future research, in addition to whether or not supply and demand side considerations impact this behaviour. In other words, does network power impact Chinese inter-firm relationships?

Implications for practice

International cooperation remains vital to the success of China's energy infrastructure. To facilitate such cooperation, China has already agreed to reduce state support of several industries. But is it too late for solar firms seeking cooperation? After the USA imposed duties on Chinese panels, China retaliated with duties on polysilicon imports from the USA. In the case of the European solar panel dumping dispute, the international community was left with the feeling that China had simply gotten away with subsidizing and dumping. For Chinese solar PV firms, where is the 'safe ground'? Deeper international buyer–supplier relationships are potentially disturbed by these types of WTO actions, as evidenced by the difficulties that impacted Suntech Power, and supply shocks caused by these actions can wreak havoc on short- to medium-term pricing and domestic competition. Jeopardizing relationships with foreign governments, both local and national, amounts to threatening a life-line of potential funding, sales and technology transfer opportunities for all firms (Chen, 2014, makes a similar point). Perhaps it is time for governments to let international competition level the playing field in this industry.

Conclusion

The purpose of this contribution was to test the contention that interacting with global managers and increasing experience via international education are two specific modes by which Asian firms enroll in global networks, thus potentially leading to changes in the way they do business internationally yet yielding fewer changes domestically (Yeung 2000, 2004). Chinese solar PV firms were chosen largely because of their requisite participation in extra-local networks on one hand, and because of the changing spatial complexities of the local market on the other. It was also argued that this is an important, yet under researched branch of China's energy businesses, particularly considering the amount of negative attention Chinese solar firm behaviour has been receiving in the international trade arena.

Virtually, all extra-firm relationships are considered important irrespective of enrollment in global networks. Concerning inter-firm relationships, product quality and technical know-how, professional reputation and price figured most predominantly. Structurally, however, results showed that buyer location is influenced by extra-local education. At the intra-firm level, firms with managers educated outside of China have more non-mainland Chinese employees, and this somewhat tempers a more traditional strict decision-making hierarchy.

This study represents a modest effort, and the limitations should be addressed. The results should be treated with initial caution as this is a one-industry study and the data-set, while capturing a number of large firms, was limited. And while some of the results were thought provoking, the survey instrument or more in depth interviewers could have gone deeper into any number of issues under analyses.

Funding

The author wishes to gratefully acknowledge funding from Ewha Womans University.

References

Armstrong, J., and T. Overton. 1977. "Estimating Nonresponse Bias in Mail Surveys." *Journal of Marketing Research* 14 (3): 396–402.
Aylett, R. 2013. "Networked Urban Climate Governance: Neighborhood-Scale Residential Solar Energy Systems and the Example of Solarize Portland." *Environment and Planning C: Government and Policy* 31 (5): 858–875.
Bathelt, H., and N. Schuldt. 2008. "Between Luminaries and Meat Grinders: International Trade Fairs as Temporary Clusters." *Regional Studies* 42 (6): 853–868.
Bussey, J. 2013. "Learning How to Kowtow." *The Wall Street Journal*, Monday, August 5, 2010, p. 19.
Campbell, R. J. 2010. "China and the United States: A Comparison of Green Energy Programs and Policies." Congressional Research Service, Report for Members and Committees of Congress. Accessed January 3, 2014. http://www.fas.org/sgp/crs/row/R41287.pdf
Caprotti, F. 2009. "China's Cleantech Landscape: The Renewable Energy Technology Paradox." *Sustainable Development Law & Policy* 9 (3): 6–10.
Chen, M. 2004. *Asian Management Systems*. 2nd ed. London: Thompson Learning.
Chen, G. 2014. "From Mercantile Strategy to Domestic Demand Stimulation: Changes in China's Solar PV Subsidies." *Asia-Pacific Business Review*. doi:10.1080/13602381.2014.939897.
"China's Solar PV Market to Grow Bigger upon Government Support Policy." *Xinhua News Agency*, March 27, 2009. Accessed June 28, 2010. http://www.istockanalyst.com/article/viewiStockNews/articleid/3152408

Cockerill, R. 2008. "Linde Secures Access to 50% of China PV Market." *Gas World*. Accessed May 14, 2012. http://www.gasworld.com/news.php?a=3326

Coe, N., P. Dicken, and M. Hess. 2008. "Global Production Networks: Realizing the Potential." *Journal of Economic Geography* 8 (3): 271–295.

Denning, L. 2011. "China Storms into Wind, Solar: Renewable-Energy Firms, Long Reliant on Government Subsidies, Face a New Struggle." *The Wall Street Journal*, Monday, August 22, 2011. p. 34.

Dicken, P. 2011. *Global Shift: Mapping the Changing Contours of the World Economy*. 6th ed. New York: Guilford Press.

Dicken, P., P. Kelly, K. Olds, and H. W. C. Yeung. 2001. "Chains and Networks, Territories and Scales: Towards a Relational Framework for Analyzing the Global Economy." *Global Networks* 1 (2): 89–112.

Fan, Y. 2002. "Questioning Guanxi: Definition, Classification and Implications." *International Business Review* 11 (5): 543–561.

Hess, M., and H. W. C. Yeung. 2006. "Whither Global Production Networks in Economic Geography? Past, Present and Future." *Environment and Planning A* 38: 1193–1204.

Hsu, J. Y., and A. L. Saxenian. 2000. "The Limits of Guanxi Capitalism: Transnational Collaboration Between Taiwan and the USA." *Environment and Planning A* 32: 1991–2005.

Huggins, R. 1998. "Local Business Co-Operation and Training and Enterprise Councils: The Development of Inter-Firm Networks." *Regional Studies* 32: 813–826.

Jacobsson, S., and A. Johnson. 2000. "The Diffusion of Renewable Energy Technology: An Analytical Framework and Key Issues for Research." *Energy Policy* 28: 625–640.

Jansson, H., M. Johanson, and J. Ramström. 2007. "Institutions and Business Networks: A Comparative Analysis of the Chinese, Russian, and West European Markets." *Industrial Marketing Management* 36 (7): 955–996.

Kao, J. 1993. "The Worldwide Web of Chinese Business." *Harvard Business Review* 71 (2): 24–36.

Keister, L. A. 1998. "Engineering Growth: Business Group Structure and Firm Performance in China's Transition Economy." *American Journal of Sociology* 104 (2): 404–440.

Klitkou, A., and L. Coenen. 2013. "The Emergence of the Norwegian Solar Photovoltaic Industry in a Regional Perspective." *European Planning Studies* 21 (11): 1796–1819.

Koot, E. 2006. "Enormous Growth of Chinese PV Industry." *Altenergymag.com*. Accessed September 10, 2013. http://www.altenergymag.com/emagazine.php?issue_number=06.02.01&article=solarplaza

Kovalyova, S. 2012. "Asia to Overtake Europe as Global Solar Power Grows." *EOOLONGEngergy*. Accessed August 15, 2013. http://oolongenergy.com/asia-the-region-to-watch-out-for-in-solar-energytechnology/?goback=%2Egde_48640_member_119025874

Liu, W., and P. Dicken. 2006. "Transnational Corporations and 'Obligated Embeddedness': Foreign Direct Investment in China's Automobile Industry." *Environment and Planning A* 38: 1229–1247.

Ma, W. 2012. "China Says U.S. Solar Tariffs Hurt Ties." *The Wall Street Journal*, Monday, May 21, 2012, p. 4.

Marigo, N. 2007. "The Chinese Silicon Photovoltaic Industry and Market: A Critical Review of Trends and Outlook." *Progress in Photovoltaics: Research and Applications* 15: 143–162.

Marigo, N., T. J. Foxon, and P. J. Pearson. 2008. "Comparing Innovation Systems for Solar Photovoltaics in the United Kingdom and in China." Working Paper, Imperial Centre for Energy Policy and Technology.

National Renewable Energy Laboratory. 2004. "Renewable Energy in China: WB/GEF Renewable Energy Project." Accessed May 15, 2013. http://www.nrel.gov/docs/fy04osti/33067.pdf

OECD. 2009. "Eco-Innovation Policies in the People's Republic of China." Environment Directorate, OECD.

Oster, S. 2010. "China Sparks Power Play: Foreign Firms Like GE, Siements Jostle to Upgrade Electricity Network." *Asian Wall Street Journal*, May 25, p. 23.

Perry, M., and T. B. Hui. 1998. "Global Manufacturing and Local Linkage in Singapore." *Environment and Planning A* 30: 1603–1624.

Poon, J., and E. Thompson. 2003. "Development and Quiescent Subsidiaries in the Asia Pacific: Evidence from Hong Kong, Singapore, Shanghai, and Sydney." *Economic Geography* 79 (2): 195–214.

Potash, G. 2009. "China and the Future of Solar Photovoltaic Technology: CIGS Thin-Film Solar Cells Will Rock the Industry." NERAC. Accessed March 26, 2013. www.nerac.com/img/BusinessInChina.pdf.

Ralston, D., C. Egri, S. Stewart, R. Terpstra, and K. C. Yu. 1999. "Doing Business in the 21st Century with the New Generation of Chinese Managers: A Study of Generational Shifts in Work Values in China." *Journal of International Business Studies* 30 (2): 415–427.

Ralston, D., E. Holt, R. Terpstra, and Yu Kai-Cheng. 2008. "The Impact of National Culture and Economic Ideology on Managerial Work Values: A Study of the United States, Russia, Japan, and China." *Journal of International Business Studies* 39: 8–26.

Redding, S. G. 1993. *The Spirit of Chinese Capitalism*. Berlin: de Gruyter.

Redding, S. G. 1995. "Overseas Chinese Networks: Understanding the Enigma." *Long Range Planning* 28 (1): 61–69.

"Research Report on Chinese Polysilicon Industry, 2009–2010." Accessed December 17, 2013. http://www.bharatbook.com/detail.asp?id=114355&rt=Research-Report-on-Chinese-Polysilicon-Industry.html

"The Rise of Big Solar." *The Economist*, April 17th–23rd, 2010, pp. 65–66.

Sachs, J. 2009. "Economic Transition to Sustainability." *The Korea Herald*, March 24, 2009, p. 12.

Seringhaus, F. H. R., and P. J. Rosson. 1994. "International Trade Fairs and Foreign Market Involvement: Review and Research Directions." *International Business Review* 3 (3): 311–329.

Tan, C. Z., and H. W. C. Yeung. 2000. "The Regionalization of Chinese Business Networks: A Study of Singaporean Firms in Hainan, China." *The Professional Geographer* 52 (3): 437–454.

Tyfield, D., and J. Wilsdon. 2009. "Low Carbon China: Disruptive Innovation and the Role of International Collaboration." Discussion Paper 41, The University of Nottingham China Policy Institute.

US Energy Information Administration (EIA). "International Energy Statistics-Total Carbon Dioxide Emissions from the Consumption of Energy (Million Metric Tons)." Accessed May 7, 2014. http://www.eia.gov/cfapps/ipdbproject/iedindex3.cfm?tid=90&pid=44&aid=8&cid=regions,&syid=2005&eyid=2008&unit=MMTCD

van den Heuvel, S. T. A., and J. C. J. M. van den Bergh. 2009. "Multilevel Assessment of Diversity, Innovation and Selection in the Solar Photovoltaic Industry." *Structural Change and Economic Dynamics* 20: 50–60.

Whitley, R. 1994. *Business Systems in East Asia: Firms, Markets and Societies*. London: Sage Publications.

Wu, C.-Y. 2014. "Comparisons of Technological Innovation Capabilities in the Solar Photovoltaic Industries of Taiwan, China, and Korea." *Scientometrics* 98: 429–446.

Yeung, H. W. C. 1997. "Business Networks and Transnational Corporations: A Study of Hong Kong Firms in the ASEAN Region." *Economic Geography* 73: 1–25.

Yeung, H. W. C. 1998. "Transnational Economic Synergy and Business Networks: The Case of Two-Way Investment Between Malaysia and Singapore." *Regional Studies* 32 (8): 687–706.

Yeung, H. W. C. 1999. "The Internationalization of Ethnic Chinese Business Firms from Southeast Asia: Strategies, Processes and Competitive Advantage." *International Journal of Urban and Regional Research* 23: 103–127.

Yeung, H. W. C. 2000. "Economic Globalisation, Crisis, and the Emergence of Chinese Business Communities in Southeast Asia." *International Sociology* 15: 269–290.

Yeung, H. W. C. 2004. *Chinese Capitalism in a Global Era: Towards a Hybrid Capitalism*. New York: Routledge.

Yeung, H. W. C. 2006. "Change and Continuity in Southeast Asian Ethnic Chinese Business." *Asia Pacific Journal of Management* 23: 229–254.

Yeung, I., and R. Tung. 1996. "Achieving Business Success in Confucian Societies: The Importance of Guanxi (Connections)." *Organizational Dynamics* 25 (2): 54–65.

Ying, C. 2007. "Efforts of the Chinese Government for Promoting Environmental Innovation in the Fields of Energy Efficiency and Renewable Energy." Presented at the Chinese Academy for Environmental Planning, Berlin, September 20.

Zhou, Y., and T. Xin. 2003. "An Innovative Region in China: Interaction Between Multinational Corporations and Local Firms in a High-Tech Cluster in Beijing." *Economic Geography* 79: 129–153.

Regional disparity of embedded carbon footprint and its sources in China: a consumption perspective

Jin Fan[a], Yanrui Wu[b], Xiumei Guo[c], Dingtao Zhao[c] and Dora Marinova[c]

[a]School of Management, University of Science and Technology of China, Hefei, P.R. China; [b]Business School, University of Western Australia, Perth, Australia; [c]Curtin University Sustainability Policy Institute, Curtin University of Technology, Perth, Australia

Carbon emission reduction could be achieved through extensive cooperation between relevant groups such as businesses, governments and consumers. Generally, carbon emissions stem from consumer behaviour. To tackle the increasingly serious energy crisis and climate change in China, it is thus vital to control carbon emissions generated by the country's urban consumers. From a consumption perspective, we utilize a self-organizing feature map model to analyse the spatial differentiation of per capita embedded carbon footprint (ECF) in urban China. We found that the spatial differentiation is significant with the per capita ECF of the east coastal area at a high level and that per capita disposable income is the key factor affecting ECF. Based on these findings, potential business opportunities to develop low-carbon products are discussed.

Introduction

Carbon dioxide (CO_2) is one of the major contributors to climate change which is a global problem (Manne and Richels 1991). The control of carbon emissions produced via urban consumption is the most important task for China in dealing with the country's increasingly serious environmental crisis and climate change (Fan et al. 2013). At present, about 70% of carbon emissions in China are generated in the production and transportation of goods while about 30% are produced through urban consumption (NBSC 2013). The experience of developed countries shows that urbanization will lead to a sharp increase in carbon emissions. The growth rate of energy consumption in urban China has reached 8%, exceeding the country's total energy consumption growth of 7% per annum (NBSC 2013). Thus, energy saving and emission reduction in the consumption sector will play an important role in China's overall course of energy conservation and emission reduction.

Lenzen and Murray (2001) argued that the main factor driving emission growth is the increase of consumption, which may offset the reduction effect of technological improvement and industrial upgrading. Through analysing the relationship between energy consumption and lifestyle in 20,000 American families, Adua (2010) derived a similar conclusion. This effect is called the 'Jevons Paradox', that is, the improvement of energy efficiency could lead to higher energy consumption if a change of lifestyle is not achieved (Figge, Young, and Barkemeyer 2014).

We will use carbon footprint to measure carbon emissions from consumption of goods and services. The carbon footprint is a measure of the amount of CO_2 emitted through the combustion of fossil energy, which is the main source of anthropogenic emission of greenhouse gases (GHGs) for all countries in the world. China is no exception. The majority of the total carbon emissions in China is energy induced (Li et al. 2012). The carbon footprint for a consumer is the amount of CO_2 emitted either directly or indirectly as a result of the consumer's everyday activities. Therefore, it can be divided into direct carbon footprint (DCF) and embedded carbon footprint (ECF). DCF is the direct carbon emission produced by gas, coal and fuel used in the consumption process, whereas ECF refers to carbon emissions generated in the whole life cycle (development, production, circulation, and use and recycling) of goods or services that are ultimately consumed, which is not easily perceived and difficult to calculate. ECF is calculated from the perspective of lifestyle and social behaviour (LSB) (Fan et al. 2012). Compared with the physical and technical economic models, the ECF based on LSB puts more emphasis on consumption factors, which reflects the actual sources of emissions.

The rest of the study begins with a review of the related literature. This is followed by description of the main research questions. Subsequently, issues associated with research methodology are discussed. The data issues and preliminary findings are described next which is followed with more detailed discussions. Policy and business implications are then explored. The final section concludes the study.

Literature

Changing consumer behaviour is generally considered to be an option to reduce the emissions of GHGs. Since the 1990s, literatures relating to issues concerning energy and carbon emissions from a consumption perspective have emerged. For example, Vringer and Blok (1995, 2000) investigated the energy consumption structure of Dutch families from 1948 to 1996. Their results indicate that household energy requirement could be reduced if their consumption patterns were changed. Reinders, Vringer, and Blok (2003) examined the relationship between household consumption expenditure and energy consumption in 11 EU members. They found that indirect energy consumption and household expenditure are linearly correlated. Based on the theoretical framework of the environmental pressure prediction model on consumption, Rood et al. (2003) argued that the factors determining consumption patterns and corresponding environmental pressure are economic growth, changes of population and social structure, technological advance and so on. Further, through structural path analysis, Lenzen, Dey, and Foran (2004) investigated the factors that influence residential energy demand in Sydney, Australia. Druckman and Jackson (2009) analysed the relationship between household expenditure and carbon emissions in UK households, and found that while the 'dash for gas' technology occurred in the 1990s in the UK, there was no evident decoupling relationship between carbon emissions and expenditure. In addition, Weber and Matthews (2008) and Herrmann and Hauschild (2009) examined how international trade influences the household carbon footprint.

Furthermore, Benders et al. (2006) analysed the energy consumption of 300 families in Groningen, Holland, and found that behaviour intervention can reduce the direct energy consumption of the experimental groups by about 8.5% compared with the control groups, with no significant effect on indirect energy consumption. Abrahamse et al. (2007) and Abrahamse and Steg (2009) derived a similar conclusion. In addition, Steg (2008) discussed the role of information and structure strategy for family energy conservation from a psychological perspective. These studies focus on the analysis of household energy consumption or carbon footprint pertaining to different consumer behaviours and consumption patterns. However, little attention is given to the factors that influence the ECF in China. The purpose of our study is to extend the work in this area.

Research questions

Previous literature has shown that income is an important factor for household emissions (Reinders, Vringer, and Blok 2003; Druckman and Jackson 2009). Lenzen, Dey, and Foran (2004) argued that growth in per capita income and the resulting consumption of goods and services represent the main drivers for growth in the energy requirements underpinning consumption. In addition to the economic variable, other factors such as geographic location and food habits need to be considered in the analysis of emissions (Pachauri 2004). As for China, first, the economies of the east coastal area are more developed than those of the central and western regions. In 2012, the per capita disposable income in the eastern provinces is ¥29,622, which is almost 1.5 times as much as that in the central and western provinces (NBSC 2013). Second, different areas have their own dietary habits and hence consumption patterns. Third, the temperature in China's cities differs greatly during winter. It is much colder in the northern cities than in the southern cities. This factor might affect the ECF. Given these variations, we propose three hypotheses as follows:

Hypothesis 1: The spatial differentiation of urban residents' per capita ECF in China is significant.

Hypothesis 2: Per capita disposable income is the key factor affecting the ECF in urban China.

Hypothesis 3: Other factors, such as geographic location and dietary habits, might influence the ECF.

The objective of this study was to explore the regional disparity of ECF and its sources in urban China from the perspective of consumption. We focus on urban ECF for two reasons. On the one hand, the dominant position of urban residents' consumption in domestic consumption is continuously strengthened. On the other hand, data of urban consumption are available. More specifically, the main research questions addressed in our study include:

(1) What is the spatial differentiation feature of per capita ECF in urban China?
(2) What factors may influence the per capita ECF?
(3) What implications of the findings are there for relevant businesses?

Methodology

The potential factors affecting China's ECF can be investigated using conventional regression techniques. For instance, through regression analysis, we can determine the direction and level influenced by the independent variables. But, the subjectivity of variable selection is strong and may lead to the exclusion of various important variables. In addition, traditional regression analysis generally needs to meet the harsh conditions of hypothesis testing. To avoid these problems, we adopt the framework of a self-organizing feature map (SOFM) model in this study. The SOFM is a neural network model for exploring and visualizing the patterns of high dimensional input vectors in input data-set. It was first introduced to the neural network community by Kohonen (1982). The SOFM

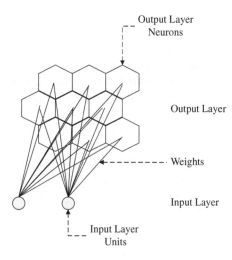

Figure 1. The SOFM architecture. *Source*: Authors' own drawing.

consists of two layers: the input layer and the output layer (Figure 1). The input layer contains one unit for each variable (such as per capita ECF and per capita disposable income) of the input vectors. The output layer consists of several neurons, each of which has an associated d-dimensional weight vector (that is, a neuron weight vector). The dimension d is the same as the dimension of the input vectors. The output layer neurons are connected to every unit in the input layer through the weight vectors (Kalteh, Hjorth, and Berndtsson 2008). In addition, the output layer neurons with similar weights are placed together.

To form a SOFM, an input vector i from the input data-set is selected randomly and an iterative procedure is executed. First, this procedure is started by calculating the distance between the input vector i and each of the output layer neuron weight vectors. The neuron with the closest distance to the input vector i is called a winner neuron. Then the weight vector of the winner neuron and its neighbouring neurons are updated in order to be moved closer to the input vector. This process is called the training procedure which is repeated until convergence, that is, until the weight vector of each output layer neuron is stable. A prominent feature of SOFM is that it not only makes the winner neurons to learn but also adjusts the weight vectors of their neighbouring neurons. In this way, neurons located close to each other in the output layer have similar input patterns (Kalteh, Hjorth, and Berndtsson 2008). By comparing the corresponding output layer neuron weights of different dimensions, we can judge the correlation among these dimensions (Mostafa 2010). Furthermore, based on the correlation analysis, factors that affect these dimensions are revealed through the analysis of anomalous characteristics of neuron weights. Therefore, the SOFM analysis can identify as many influencing factors as possible. In addition, the SOFM analysis can be conducted without the rigid assumptions of linearity or normality associated with traditional regression techniques, and it has no clear restrictions on sample capacity, which is in line with the characteristics of data for this study.

Model formulation

Weber and Matthews (2008) and Druckman and Jackson (2009) attribute ECF to functional uses that make up modern urban lifestyles such as housing, food and catering, clothing and footwear, health and hygiene, recreation and leisure, education, communications and commuting. According to Fan et al. (2012), the ECF of food and catering, and clothing and footwear can be classified as subsistence-oriented emissions, and that of health and hygiene, recreation and leisure, and education can be classified as development-oriented emissions. Other consumption categories such as housing (including residential energy) and personal transport have much higher emission intensities. Thus, ECF can be divided into and examined in four classes, namely the ECF of (1) food and clothing, (2) housing (including residential energy), (3) health, education and recreation and (4) transport (the ECF calculation technique is detailed in Fan et al. (2012)). Based on this classification, we use the proportion of ECF in each category (of the four groups), per capita ECF and per capita disposable income of the provinces as the six conceptual dimensions. Each conceptual dimension may include one or more sub-items. For instance, the housing ECF includes the ECF of electricity, heating, household articles and so on.

Model development and its application

While SOFM is usually used for clustering analysis (Moreno, Marco, and Olmeda 2006; Silver and Shmoish 2008; Mostafa 2010), it can also be used to conduct spatial differentiation and correlation analysis. In our SOFM model, provinces with six conceptual dimensions are treated as input vectors and the model will group them into different clusters. A cluster may include one or more output layer neurons. It can judge the spatial differentiation characteristics of different provinces through the study of the relationship of output layer neurons. The shading of the connecting polygons between output layer neurons refers to the topology distance. The darker the shading is, the greater the distance, and the brighter the shading, the smaller the distance. Closer physical locations of neurons have similar input patterns (Kalteh, Hjorth, and Berndtsson 2008). Therefore, through observing the shading of the connecting polygons, we can group the neurons into different clusters and analyse the characteristics of spatial differentiation for different provinces.

In SOFM, the location of the same province is fixed in different conceptual dimensions. For example, Provinces 1 and 2 are located in neuron 1, and provinces 3 and 4 are located in neuron 2 (Figure 2). According to this feature, correlation analysis can be implemented by comparing neuron weights. We use the colour of neurons for neuron weights. The brighter the neurons are, the greater the neuron weights in conceptual dimensions. If neuron weight distributions are similar in two conceptual dimensions, this demonstrates that the two dimensions are positively related (Figure 2(a)). If two conceptual dimensions are complementary, that is to say, some neurons' colour is brighter in conceptual dimension 'x', but the corresponding neurons' colour in conceptual dimension 'y' is darker, this means that the two conceptual dimensions are negatively related (Figure 2(b)).

Based on the correlation analysis, a factor analysis can be conducted. Assuming conceptual dimension 'x' is relevant to 'y', and furthermore, if the colour of two neurons is similar in dimension 'x', their colour will also be similar in dimension 'y', according to correlation analysis. If their colour is different, we can call this case as an abnormal situation. Discussing the abnormal results will help explain the influencing factors of ECF. Assuming neuron '1' is brighter than neuron '2', by comparing the corresponding sub-items in the maximum ECF province in neuron '1' and that in the minimum ECF province in neuron '2', we can provide an assessment of the influencing factors of ECF.

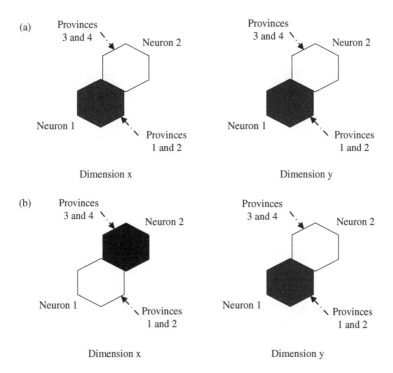

Figure 2. Feature maps. *Source*: Authors' own drawing.

For instance, if we observe that a specific sub-item in the maximum ECF province in neuron '1' is much higher than that in the minimum ECF province in neuron '2', we can examine the factors underlying this result.

Findings

Data issues

The emissions conversion factors for coal, coke, crude oil, gasoline, kerosene, diesel oil, fuel oil and natural gas are drawn from Intergovernmental Panel on Climate Change. Data for energy consumption, conversion of energy into standard coal and other conversion information are from the China Energy Statistical Yearbook (2007) (NBSC 2008a). There are no specific data for energy consumption by service sectors in China Energy Statistical Yearbook. However, the input–output table provides details of the service sectors, allowing us to identify carbon emissions from corresponding sectors according to the sectors' output shares. Urban consumption data are obtained from the China Urban Life and Price Yearbook (2007) (NBSC 2008b). In order to optimize the data interface between consumption items and producing sectors, we employ China's 2007 input–output table with 42 sectors.

Through adopting the input–output model of carbon emissions proposed by Bicknell et al. (1998) and later used by many researchers such as Ferng (2001, 2009), Turner et al. (2007), Begum et al. (2009), Fan et al. (2012) and Das and Paul (2014), we calculate urban residents' ECF for each province and use SOFM to analyse the spatial differentiation characteristics of per capita ECF. To help provide benchmark comparisons and expand our understanding of the spatial differentiation of ECF, we rank the per capita

Table 1. Per capita ECF of each province in China.

	I	II	III	IV	V	VI
Shanghai	0.26	0.32	0.19	0.23	2.69	23.62
Tianjin	0.19	0.38	0.33	0.09	2.49	16.36
Beijing	0.23	0.23	0.36	0.18	2.49	21.99
Guangdong	0.24	0.30	0.23	0.23	2.47	17.70
Zhejiang	0.26	0.33	0.25	0.17	2.23	20.57
Jilin	0.18	0.44	0.27	0.10	1.93	11.29
Liaoning	0.22	0.41	0.26	0.11	1.92	12.30
Fujian	0.30	0.40	0.17	0.13	1.83	15.51
Chongqing	0.24	0.33	0.30	0.13	1.80	12.59
Hebei	0.19	0.40	0.33	0.08	1.78	11.69
National average	0.25	0.33	0.28	0.14	1.74	13.79
Shandong	0.23	0.39	0.26	0.13	1.74	14.26
Ningxia	0.19	0.36	0.33	0.11	1.66	10.86
Inner Mongolia	0.20	0.36	0.31	0.13	1.65	12.38
Jiangsu	0.29	0.29	0.28	0.14	1.58	16.38
Heilongjiang	0.20	0.38	0.32	0.10	1.57	10.25
Shanxi	0.22	0.31	0.36	0.11	1.57	10.76
Hunan	0.25	0.31	0.32	0.13	1.56	12.29
Hainan	0.30	0.26	0.25	0.19	1.48	11.00
Gansu	0.22	0.37	0.29	0.12	1.48	10.01
Shanxi	0.21	0.39	0.31	0.10	1.47	11.56
Hubei	0.28	0.34	0.25	0.12	1.46	11.49
Sichuan	0.29	0.29	0.29	0.13	1.45	11.10
Henan	0.23	0.34	0.35	0.08	1.42	11.48
Anhui	0.28	0.30	0.29	0.12	1.42	11.47
Guangxi	0.29	0.30	0.28	0.13	1.42	12.20
Xinjiang	0.23	0.35	0.27	0.16	1.41	10.31
Qinghai	0.23	0.36	0.26	0.15	1.37	10.28
Yunnan	0.29	0.24	0.35	0.12	1.35	11.50
Jiangxi	0.31	0.36	0.24	0.09	1.27	11.45
Guizhou	0.29	0.36	0.22	0.13	1.27	10.68
Tibet	0.39	0.31	0.17	0.14	1.16	11.13

Notes: Columns I to IV present the proportion of ECF of (1) food and clothing, (2) housing (including residential energy), (3) health, education and recreation and (4) transport. Column V gives the per capita ECF (metric tons). Column VI presents per capita disposable income (¥1000).
Source: Authors' own calculation.

ECF of the 31 provinces, autonomous regions and municipalities in China. In Table 1, the per capita ECF ranges from 1.16 tons in Tibet to 2.69 tons in Shanghai. Of the 31 provinces, autonomous regions and municipalities, there are 10 with per capita ECF above the national average (1.74 tons). There are 21 others below this national average.

There are many software packages available for analysing SOFM models. We chose MATLAB R2008a as our programming tool as it offers many advantages. This software contains a variety of signal processing and statistical tools, which help users in generating a variety of signals and plotting them (Bachu et al. 2008). It applies artificial intelligence techniques to automatically identify the efficient SOFM clusters. The six indicators shown in Table 1 are treated as the six conceptual dimensions. The neurons are connected to every variable in the input layer through neuron weights (Figure 1). The number of output layer neurons is determined by the desired number of classes, which are independent of the number of the variables (Lu and Lo 2002). After developing and

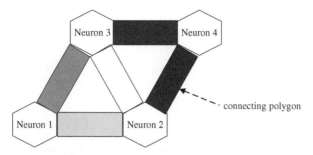

Figure 3. The distance among neurons. Notes: The numbers denote neurons 1, 2, 3 and 4, respectively. *Source*: Authors' own calculation and the weights are generated in MATLAB R 2008a.

evaluating a series of SOFMs (4, 9, 16 and 25 neurons), the model with four neurons performed reasonably well in the clustering and factor analysis and hence is selected as the preferred model.

Preliminary findings

The SOFM cluster results are shown in Figure 3. The neurons stand for the sets of the provinces. There are 18, 5, 1, and 7 provinces located in neurons 1, 2, 3 and 4, respectively. The colour of the connecting polygons between the neurons refers to the topology distance of them. The darker the colour is, the greater the distance; and the brighter the colour, the smaller the distance. In this figure, we can see that the colour of the connecting polygons between neurons 2 and 3 is brighter than others', which shows that the distances between them are closer. So, the above four neurons can be divided into three categories, namely cluster I (neuron 1), cluster II (neurons 2 and 3) and cluster III (neuron 4). The order of the clusters stands for the per capita ECF of them. Table 2 and Figure 4 show the analysis results.

The economies of Beijing, Shanghai, Zhejiang, Guangdong, Tianjin, Jiangsu and Fujian are the most developed in China. Their per capita ECF is 2.2 tons, which is almost 1.3 times the national average. This group forms cluster III. The regions in cluster III are all in the eastern coastal area. These regions account for 31% of China's urban population and 39% of the country's total ECF. This cluster is characterized with a high disposable income and a clearly above average ECF level. From the perspective of consumption, the eastern coastal area should be considered as the main regulatory target for carbon reduction.

Table 2. Classification of clusters.

Clusters	Neurons	Provinces, autonomous regions and municipalities
I	1	Heilongjiang, Jilin, Hebei, Shanxi, Henan, Anhui, Hubei, Jiangxi, Xinjiang, Qinghai, Gansu, Ningxia, Shanxi, Sichuan, Guizhou, Yunnan, Hainan, Tibet
II	2	Guangxi, Hunan, Liaoning, Inner Mongolia, Chongqing
	3	Shandong
III	4	Beijing, Shanghai, Zhejiang, Guangdong, Tianjin, Jiangsu, Fujian

Source: Authors' own work.

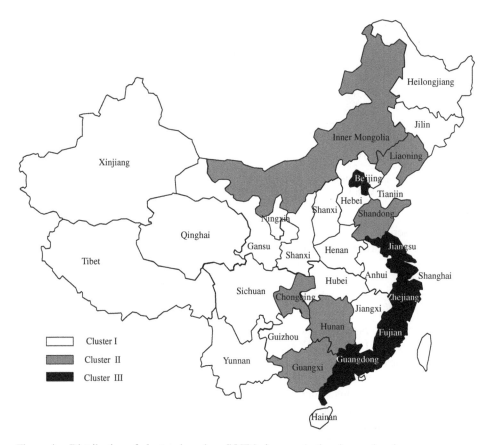

Figure 4. Distribution of clusters based on SOFM. *Source*: Authors' own drawing.

The regions in cluster II are located in the north and south of China. Their per capita ECF is 1.7 tons, which is about the national average (Table 1). However, the cultural, geographical and climatic characteristics in cluster II differ greatly. Cluster I includes the other 18 regions. The economies of these areas are less developed. Their average per capita ECF is 1.5 tons, which is below the national average (Table 1). In general, the per capita ECF in China is highly unbalanced across the provinces. For example, the per capita ECF in Shanghai is about twice as high as that in the less developed provinces. Thus, Hypothesis 1 is supported. Provincial ECF in China, however, can be expected to change in response to changes in income distribution pattern. Over time, as regional income disparity falls, poor areas will catch up with rich regions (Crompton and Wu 2005). This catch-up effect will also affect China's overall ECF in the future.

China's ECF has also been influenced by the growth in demand for energy-intensive products such as automobiles and air conditioners. In 1990, there were only 0.8 million private vehicles in China (Wang et al. 2007). However, in 2011, the total number of private vehicles reached 78.7 million (NBSC 2012). The ownership of air conditioners per 100 urban households has increased from 0.34% in 1990 to 122.00% in 2011 (NBSC 2012). These features of China's ECF imply that strong growth in ECF will continue in the future. This growth is due to the expected expansion of the Chinese economy and the strategy of stimulating economic growth through domestic demand expansion (NDRC 2011).

Discussion

In SOFM, the neurons, which share similar information, are organized in close colour proximity to each other (Mostafa 2010). In accordance with Figure 3, the neurons (hexagons) in Figure 5 represent the sets of the provinces. The brighter the neurons are, the greater the neuron weights. The weight vectors give a representation of the distribution of the input vectors in an ordered fashion (Kalteh, Hjorth, and Berndtsson 2008). Thus, Figure 5 shows the distribution of the values of the respective input components. The relationship between dimensions could be analysed by visually comparing the patterns of the neurons in each dimension. The similarity of the patterns indicates a strong monotonic relationship between the dimensions.

First, we are concerned with the relationship between per capita ECF and per capita disposable income. In Figure 5, we observe that the pattern of panels e and f is almost consistent, which means that the per capita ECF is positively related to per capita disposable income. In general, higher income will lead to higher emissions. Thus, Hypothesis 2 is supported. Subsequently, we will provide details of the ECF in the four groups, namely (1) food and clothing, (2) housing, (3) health, education and recreation and (4) transport.

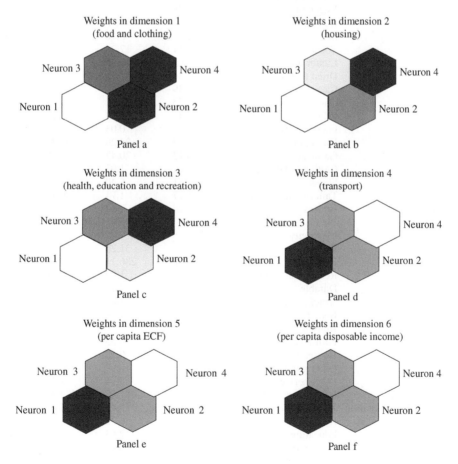

Figure 5. Neuron weight characteristics of six conceptual dimensions. *Source*: Authors' own calculation and the weights are generated in MATLAB R 2008a.

The ECF of food and clothing

Although the carbon emission intensity of food and clothing is not high, this group accounts for about 25% of total emissions (Table 1). China is still a developing country, and as a result subsistence-oriented emissions account for a large chunk. For example, food remains a very important component in the Chinese households' ECF. In contrast, the average share of food ECF in US households is only 6.9% (Shammim 2012).

Table 3. ECF per capita of each consumption item (kg).

ECF categories	Consumption items	Shandong	Inner Mongolia	Hunan	Guangxi
ECF of food	Grain	25.91	27.92	29.37	25.52
and clothing	Starches and tubers	2.82	2.23	1.65	1.74
	Beans and bean products	3.71	2.50	4.89	4.09
	Oil and fats	9.78	7.25	14.86	10.93
	Meats	43.37	44.03	54.27	67.76
	Poultries	18.91	10.67	31.21	64.07
	Eggs	21.18	9.90	10.53	10.80
	Aquatic products	43.03	9.77	28.63	39.90
	Vegetables	49.29	38.59	59.69	50.45
	Condiments	4.21	3.33	3.70	3.01
	Sugar	2.59	2.18	3.34	3.56
	Tobacco	9.11	17.25	16.77	8.60
	Liquor and Beverages	18.65	17.35	11.45	9.83
	Dried and fresh fruits	47.36	35.28	39.62	38.24
	Cake	8.49	4.17	4.93	5.61
	Dairy products	19.73	13.31	10.68	11.81
	Other foods	8.47	16.83	9.79	6.71
	Food processing services	0.04	0.03	0.03	0.05
	Dining out	30.34	34.20	32.48	34.09
	Garments	18.13	20.43	15.20	10.04
	Clothing materials	1.64	1.03	1.49	1.26
	Shoes	5.81	6.40	4.81	2.87
	Tailoring and laundering	1.27	1.74	0.70	0.41
ECF of housing	Houses	7.14	7.10	5.74	4.81
(including	Water	5.80	3.48	7.89	8.60
residential energy)	Electricity	279.48	217.77	368.90	333.23
	Fuels	69.62	31.26	53.57	44.30
	Heating	268.50	286.11	1.81	0.41
	Residential services	1.26	1.92	0.88	0.91
	Durables	11.63	8.20	7.83	7.35
	Articles for interior	1.59	1.45	0.93	0.37
	Bed articles	0.95	1.09	1.17	0.78
	Household articles	10.62	10.76	12.33	9.63
	Furniture materials	0.42	0.55	0.38	0.52
	Household services	0.49	0.52	1.05	0.62
	Other goods	12.33	16.99	10.94	9.32
	Other services	2.37	3.74	2.75	2.55
ECF of health,	Health care and medical	411.91	487.08	473.33	370.92
education and recreation	Recreation articles	5.96	5.47	4.47	4.68
	Recreation services	4.33	6.32	6.97	5.59
	Education	23.06	12.63	13.41	19.49
ECF of transport	Transport	209.94	204.06	180.66	168.34
	Communications	13.64	14.00	14.20	11.18

Source: Authors' own calculation.

As shown in Figure 5, neuron 1 in panel a is brighter. However, it is darker in panel f. Similarly, neuron 4 in panel a is darker while it is brighter in panel f. Thus, the structure of panels a and f in Figure 5 is complementary, which shows that the ECF share of food and clothing is negatively related to per capita disposable income. As the level of per capita disposable income increases, the proportion of emissions from necessity consumption such as food and clothing will gradually decrease. Consumers' disposable income is considered an important factor in shaping the structure of their consumption patterns. An increase in income is usually perceived as the major driver of changes in the volume and structure of the food consumed. According to Engel's law, richer households spend less of their budgets on food than poorer households (Égert 2011).

In panel a of Figure 5, if we regard the colour of neuron 2 as a benchmark, the colour of neuron 3 should be the same as neuron 2. However, this is not the case (shown in panel a, Figure 5). Comparing Inner Mongolia, which is the minimum (or the region with the lowest ECF share) in neuron 2, with Shandong, which is the maximum (or the region with the highest ECF share) in neuron 3, the ECF share of food and clothing in Shandong is higher than that in Inner Mongolia (Table 1). However, the disposable income of Shandong is also higher than that of Inner Mongolia, which seems to be inconsistent with the argument in the preceding paragraph. From a specific consumption item, we can find that the sum of the ECF of aquatic products, poultries and eggs in Shandong is 2.7 times as high as that in Inner Mongolia (Table 3). This is mainly due to the difference of dietary habits. Shandong cuisine is one of the Eight Cuisines of China, whereas Inner Mongolia is located in the northwest of China with different dietary habits. Thus, different dietary habits shape different demands for aquatic products and poultry causing the difference in their ECF. In summary, the above analysis shows that per capita disposable income is negatively related to the ECF share of food and clothing. In addition, dietary habit can also be regarded as a main influencing factor. Thus, Hypothesis 3 is supported.

The ECF of housing

At the national level, the ECF of housing consumption accounts for 33% of the total ECF (Table 1), which is similar to the result of Fan et al. (2012) who reported a 24–31% share of the overall ECF. For comparison, the average share of US housing ECF (including residential energy ECF) is 45.5% (Shammim 2012). In 1991, the Chinese State Council proposed changing the low rent of public houses and capitalizing gradually on housing allocation instead of welfare housing allocation as the goals of the housing system reform (Zhou 2011). As a consequence, these reforms have helped the real estate sector expand rapidly and buying a house has become an important step for improving living standards in China (Fan et al. 2012).

As shown in Figure 5, neuron 1 in panel b is brighter. However, it is darker in panel f. Similarly, neuron 4 in panel b is darker while it is brighter in panel f. According to 'Methodology' section, we can conclude that dimensions 2 and 6 are complementary, which indicates that the ECF share of housing is negatively related to per capita disposable income. The compact city theory can explain this result. The distribution densities of cities in eastern China (rich regions) and in middle China are, respectively, 13.1 times and 5.8 times as high as those in western China (Yue et al. 2005). The supporters of the compact city theory (for example, Jacobs 1961; Newman and Kenworthy 1989) believe that a compact city has the environmental and energy advantage. The main justification for the compact city is that it results in the least energy-intensive activity pattern, thereby helping us cope with the issues of global warming (Holden and Norland 2005).

In panel f of Figure 5, the colour of neurons 2 and 3 is similar. According to above correlation analysis, the colour of them will also be similar in panel b. However, this is not the case and the colour of neuron 3 is brighter than that of neuron 2 (shown in panel b, Figure 5). Comparing Shandong, which is the maximum in neurons 3, with Guangxi, which represents the minimum of neurons 2, the per capita disposable income of Shandong is higher than that of Guangxi (Tables 1 and 2). However, the ECF share of housing in Shandong is also higher than that in Guangxi (Table 1). In terms of specific consumption items, the main difference appears to be found in heating (Table 3). The ECF of family heating in Shandong (268.50 kg) is obviously higher than that in Guangxi (0.41 kg), implying that the geographic location (latitude) is closely related to per capita ECF.

In northern Chinese cities (north to the Qinling Mountains–Huai River line such as Shandong), heating is provided by the centralized heating system between 15th November and 15th March (Zheng et al. 2011). This system is highly subsidized by the government. Such a government-provided heating system does not exist in southern China. In summary, per capita disposable income shows a negative relationship with the housing ECF share. Besides disposable income, geographic location can also be regarded as the main influencing factor. Thus, Hypothesis 3 is supported.

The ECF of health, education and recreation

Cultural and recreation services including paper production require high-energy consumption (Feng, Zou, and Wei 2011). At the national level, the ECF of health, education and recreation on average accounts for 28% of the total ECF (Table 1). As shown in Figure 5, neuron 1 is the brightest in panel c while it is the darkest in panel f. Neuron 4 is the darkest in panel c. In contrast, it is the brightest in panel f. According to Section 4, we can conclude that dimensions 3 and 6 are complementary, which indicates that per capita disposable income shows a negative relationship with the ECF share of health, education and recreation. The level of social security (such as health and basic education) is much lower in western China than in eastern China (Hebei Provincial Government 2009). So, households in western China would have to spend a higher proportion of their income on health and education.

Comparing Hunan, which is the maximum in neurons 2, with Shandong which is the minimum in neurons 3, the ECF share of health, education and recreation of Hunan is higher than that of Shandong, although the per capita disposable income of Hunan is lower than that of Shandong. In terms of specific consumption items, the main difference appears in entertainment activities, which can be attributed to the leisure culture of Hunan (MCPRC 2005). In total, per capita disposable income shows a negative relationship with the ECF share. Except for disposable income, leisure culture could also be regarded as a main influencing factor.

The ECF of transport

The emission intensity of transport is the highest in all types of consumption. At the national level, transport ECF accounts for 14% of the total ECF. This share is still much lower in China than that in the USA where the share of transport alone is more than 35% of household emissions (Shammim 2012). Panel d in Figure 5 is basically consistent with panel f in Figure 5, indicating that per capita disposable income shows a positive relationship with the ECF share. This finding is in line with the results of Fan et al. (2012).

Transport is a fundamental prerequisite for a society's development and the improvement of people's life. However, the rising car ownership would increase the transport ECF. For example, despite strong control over vehicle ownership in Shanghai, emissions from the transportation sector have increased eightfold during the period 1985–2006 (Dhakal 2009). Beijing recorded almost a sevenfold increase in the same period. Hence, transport activities should be at the core of carbon-reduction policies.

Policy implications

Since the proportion of private transport ECF is positively related to per capita disposable income, the growth in transport activities may be one of the main drivers of GHGs in China. Therefore, it is essential for the personal road transport sector to share the burden of emission reduction. To achieve this goal, several policies can be devised and discussed in theory and then tested in practice. A carbon tax for fuel (mainly gasoline and diesel) could be an effective approach for carbon reduction due to its simplicity and capability to provide an immediate carbon price signal (Avi-Yonah and Uhlmann 2009). In addition to this policy, a consumption-based CO_2 emissions quota system such as the personal carbon trading (PCT) scheme could also be introduced in the personal road transport sector (Wadud 2011). Under such a system, each adult is allocated a tradable carbon allowance, which covers the carbon emitted from the fuel use of private vehicles (Fawcett 2010). People who already live low carbon lives, invest in new-energy automobiles and travel less would have surpluses to sell for profit. Those who travel a lot or use energy-inefficient vehicles would need to buy extra allowances. It could be expected that a carbon tax or a PCT system would develop a price signal for carbon that incorporates the costs of that externality and drives the market toward finding acceptable alternatives such as low-carbon fuels, renewable energy and new-energy automobiles. These changes in demand could then be viewed more as business opportunities than burdens. For instance, higher demand is anticipated by utilities that have an energy portfolio with a relatively large share of renewable energy. Furthermore many strategic opportunities could arise in new product development. For example, a vehicle manufacturer would have an incentive to develop and produce more fuel-efficient vehicles since consumers will demand more fuel-efficient and carbon efficient vehicles.

Conclusions

This research shows that the spatial differentiation of urban residents' per capita ECF in China is significant, with the per capita ECF of the east coastal area at a high level, and that per capita disposable income is the key factor affecting ECF. These imply a need for policies to encourage consumers to purchase less carbon intensive products or services, to decrease the carbon intensity of consumption and increase the utilization of cleaner energy sources (such as wind, solar and natural gas). In addition, other main factors that influence the ECF include the geographic location the dietary habit and the leisure culture. However, the per capita ECF of the underdeveloped areas is still low, and necessities such as food and clothing account for a big chunk of this. Therefore, from the perspective of consumption, there is not much space for emission reduction in these areas. To avoid an overly general 'one size fits all' policy, the east coastal areas should be considered as the main regions for carbon emission regulation.

Acknowledgements

They also thank an anonymous referee, Hongyi Lai and editor of the journal for their helpful comments and suggestions on early drafts of this contribution.

Funding

The authors acknowledge the National Natural Science Foundation of China [grant number 71301157] and the China Postdoctoral Fellowship Fund [grant number 2013M531533] for their generous financial support.

References

Abrahamse, W., and L. Steg. 2009. "How Do Socio-Demographic and Psychological Factors Relate to Households' Direct and Indirect Energy Use and Savings?" *Journal of Economic Psychology* 30: 711–720.

Abrahamse, W., L. Steg, C. Vlek, and T. Rothengatter. 2007. "The Effect of Tailored Information, Goal Setting, and Tailored Feedback on Household Energy Use, Energy-Related Behaviors, and Behavioral Antecedents." *Journal of Environmental Psychology* 27: 265–276.

Adua, L. 2010. "To Cool a Sweltering Earth: Does Energy Efficiency Improvement Offset the Climate Impacts of Lifestyle?" *Energy Policy* 39: 5717–5732.

Avi-Yonah, R. S., and D. M. Uhlmann. 2009. "Combating Global Climate Change: Why a Carbon Tax is a Better Response to Global Warming than Cap and Trade." *Stanford Environmental Law Journal* 28 (3): 3–50.

Bachu, R. G., S. Kopparthi, B. Adapa, and B. D. Barkana. 2008. *Separation of Voiced and Unvoiced Using Zero Crossing Rate and Energy of the Speech Signal.* Bridgeport, CT: Electrical Engineering Department, School of Engineering, University of Bridgeport.

Begum, R. A., J. J. Pereira, A. H. Jaafar, and A. Q. Al-Amin. 2009. "An Empirical Assessment of Ecological Footprint Calculations for Malaysia." *Resources, Conservation and Recycling* 53: 582–587.

Benders, R. M. J., R. Kok, H. C. Moll, G. Wiersma, and K. J. Noorman. 2006. "New Approaches for Household Energy Conservation – In Search of Personal Household Energy Budgets and Energy Reduction Options." *Energy Policy* 34: 3612–3622.

Bicknell, K. B., R. J. Ball, R. Cullen, and H. R. Bigsby. 1998. "New Methodology for the Ecological Footprint with an Application to the New Zealand Economy." *Ecological Economics* 27: 149–160.

Crompton, P., and Y. R. Wu. 2005. "Energy Consumption in China: Past Trends and Future Directions." *Energy Economics* 27: 195–208.

Das, A., and S. K. Paul. 2014. "CO_2 Emissions from Household Consumption in India Between 1993–94 and 2006–07: A Decomposition Analysis." *Energy Economics* 41: 90–105.

Dhakal, S. 2009. "Urban Energy Use and Carbon Emissions from Cities in China and Policy Implications." *Energy Policy* 37: 4208–4219.

Druckman, A., and T. Jackson. 2009. "The Carbon Footprint of UK Households 1990–2004: A Socio-Economically Disaggregated Quasi-Multi-Regional Input–Output Model." *Ecological Economics* 68: 2066–2077.

Égert, B. 2011. "Catching-up and Inflation in Europe: Balassa–Samuelson, Engel's Law and Other Culprits." *Economic Systems* 35: 208–229.

Fan, J., X. M. Guo, D. Marinova, Y. R. Wu, and D. T. Zhao. 2012. "Embedded Carbon Footprint of Chinese Urban Households: Structure and Changes." *Journal of Cleaner Production* 33: 50–59.

Fan, J., D. T. Zhao, Y. R. Wu, and J. C. Wei. 2013. "Carbon Pricing and Electricity Market Reforms in China." *Clean Technologies and Environmental Policy*, doi:10.1007/s10098-013-0691-6

Fawcett, T. 2010. "Personal Carbon Trading: A Policy Ahead of Its Time?" *Energy Policy* 38: 6868–6876.

Feng, Z. H., L. L. Zou, and Y. M. Wei. 2011. "The Impact of Household Consumption on Energy Use and CO_2 Emissions in China." *Energy* 36: 656–670.

Ferng, J. J. 2001. "Using Composition of Land Multiplier to Estimate Ecological Footprints Associated with Production Activity." *Ecological Economics* 37: 159–172.

Ferng, J. J. 2009. "Applying Input–Output Analysis to Scenario Analysis of Ecological Footprints." *Ecological Economics* 69: 345–354.

Figge, F., W. Young, and R. Barkemeyer. 2014. "Sufficiency or Efficiency to Achieve Lower Resource Consumption and Emissions? The Role of the Rebound Effect." *Journal of Cleaner Production* 69: 216–224.

Hebei Provincial Government. 2009. "The Existing Problems and Countermeasures of China's Social Security System." http://www.hebei.gov.cn/article/20090916/1285246.htm (In Chinese).

Herrmann, I. T., and M. Z. Hauschild. 2009. "Effects of Globalization on Carbon Footprints of Products." *CIRP Annals – Manufacturing Technology* 58: 13–16.

Holden, E., and I. Norland. 2005. "Three Challenges for the Compact City as a Sustainable Urban Form: Household Consumption of Energy and Transport in Eight Residential Areas in the Greater Oslo Region." *Urban Studies* 42: 2145–2166.

IPCC (Intergovernmental Panel on Climate Change). 2006. "IPCC Guidelines for National Greenhouse Gas Inventories." Prepared by the National Greenhouse Gas Inventories Programme. Accessed December 24, 2011. http://www.ipcc-nggip.iges.or.jp/public/2006gl/index.html

Jacobs, J. 1961. *The Death and Life of Great American Cities: The Failure of Town Planning.* New York: Random House.

Kalteh, A. M., P. Hjorth, and R. Berndtsson. 2008. "Review of the Self-Organizing Map (SOM) Approach in Water Resources: Analysis, Modeling and Application." *Environmental Modeling & Software* 23: 835–845.

Kohonen, T. 1982. "Self-Organized Formation of Topologically Correct Feature Maps." *Biological Cybernetics* 43: 59–69.

Lenzen, M., C. Dey, and B. Foran. 2004. "Energy Requirements of Sydney Households." *Ecological Economics* 49: 375–399.

Lenzen, M., and S. A. Murray. 2001. "A Modified Ecological Footprint Method and Its Application to Australia." *Ecological Economics* 37: 229–255.

Li, Q. Q., R. Guo, F. T. Li, and B. B. Xia. 2012. "Integrated Inventory-Based Carbon Accounting for Energy-Induced Emissions in Chongming Eco-Island of Shanghai, China." *Energy Policy* 10: 173–181.

Lu, R. S., and S. L. Lo. 2002. "Diagnosing Reservoir Water Quality Using Self-Organizing Maps and Fuzzy Theory." *Water Research* 36: 2265–2274.

Manne, A. S., and R. G. Richels. 1991. "Global CO_2 Emission Reductions – The Impacts of Rising Energy Costs." *The Energy Journal* 12: 87–107.

MCPRC (Ministry of Commerce of the People's Republic of China). 2005. "Changsha, Hunan: The Sudden Emergence of the Cultural Industry." http://www.mofcom.gov.cn/aarticle/difang/hunan/200512/20051201224497.html (in Chinese).

Moreno, D., P. Marco, and I. Olmeda. 2006. "Self-Organizing Maps Could Improve the Classification of Spanish Mutual Funds." *European Journal of Operational Research* 147: 1039–1054.

Mostafa, M. M. 2010. "Clustering the Ecological Footprint of Nations Using Kohonen's Self-Organizing Maps." *Expert Systems with Applications* 4: 2747–2755.

NBSC (National Bureau of Statistics of China). 2008a. *China Energy Statistical Yearbook 2007.* Beijing: China Statistics Press (in Chinese).

NBSC (National Bureau of Statistics of China). 2008b. *China Urban Life and Price Yearbook 2007.* Beijing: China Statistics Press, (in Chinese).

NBSC (National Bureau of Statistics of China). 2012. *The Statistical Bulletin of the National Economy and Social Development in 2011.* Beijing: China Statistics Press (in Chinese).

NBSC (National Bureau of Statistics of China). 2013. *China Statistical Yearbook 2013.* Beijing: China Statistics Press, (in Chinese).

NDRC (National Development and Reform Commission of China). 2011. *Outline of the 12th Five-Year Plan of National Economic and Social Development of the People's Republic of China.* Beijing: China Statistics Press (in Chinese).

Newman, P. W. G., and J. R. Kenworthy. 1989. "Gasoline Consumption and Cities: A Comparison of US Cities with a Global Survey." *Journal of the American Planning Association* 55 (1): 24–37.

Pachauri, S. 2004. "An Analysis of Cross-Sectional Variations in Total Household Energy Requirements in India Using Micro Survey Data." *Energy Policy* 32: 1723–1735.

Reinders, A. H. M. E., K. Vringer, and K. Blok. 2003. "The Direct and Indirect Energy Requirement of Households in the European Union." *Energy Policy* 31: 139–153.

Rood, G. A., J. P. M. Ros, E. Drissen, and K. Vringer. 2003. "A Structure of Models for Future Projections of Environmental Pressure Due to Consumption." *Journal of Cleaner Production* 11: 491–498.

Shammim, M. R. 2012. "The Role of US Households in Global Carbon Emissions." In *Greenhouse Gases Emission, Measurement and Management,* edited by G. Liu. In TechOpen. Chapter 8. http://cdn.intechopen.com/pdfs/32347/InTech-The_role_of_us_households_in_global_carbon_ emissions.pdf

Silver, H., and M. Shmoish. 2008. "Analysis of Cognitive Performance in Schizophrenia Patients and Healthy Individuals with Unsupervised Clustering Models." *Psychiatry Research* 159: 167–179.

Steg, L. 2008. "Promoting Household Energy Conservation." *Energy Policy* 36: 4449–4453.

Turner, K., M. Lenzen, T. Wiedmannc, and J. Barrett. 2007. "Examining the Global Environmental Impact of Regional Consumption Activities – Part 1: A Technical Note on Combining Input– Output and Ecological Footprint Analysis." *Ecological Economics* 62: 37–44.

Vringer, K., and K. Blok. 1995. "The Direct and Indirect Energy Requirements of Households in the Netherlands." *Energy Policy* 23: 893–910.

Vringer, K., and K. Blok. 2000. "Long-Term Trends in Direct and Indirect Household Energy Intensities: A Factor in Dematerialization?" *Energy Policy* 28: 713–727.

Wadud, Z. 2011. "Personal Tradable Carbon Permits for Road Transport: Why, Why Not and Who Wins?" *Transportation Research Part A* 45: 1052–1065.

Wang, C., W. Cai, X. Lu, and J. Chen. 2007. "CO_2 Mitigation Scenarios in China's Road Transport Sector." *Energy Conversion and Management* 48 (7): 2110–2118.

Weber, C. L., and H. S. Matthews. 2008. "Quantifying the Global and Distributional Aspects of American Household Carbon Footprint." *Ecological Economics* 66: 379–391.

Yue, T. X., Y. A. Wang, J. Y. Liu, S. P. Chen, D. S. Qiu, X. Z. Deng, M. L. Liu, Y. Z. Tian, and B. P. Su. 2005. "Surface Modelling of Human Population Distribution in China." *Ecological Modelling* 4: 461–478.

Zheng, S., R. Wang, M. E. Kahn, and E. L. Glaeser. 2011. "The Greenness of China: Household Carbon Dioxide Emissions and Urban Development." *Journal of Economic Geography* 11: 761–792.

Zhou, J. K. 2011. "Uncertainty and Housing Tenure Choice by Household Types: Evidence from China." *China Economic Review* 3: 408–427.

CONCLUSION

Transformation of China's energy sector: trends and challenges

Hongyi Lai[a] and Malcolm Warner[b]

[a]School of Contemporary Chinese Studies, University of Nottingham, Nottingham, UK;
[b]Judge Business School, University of Cambridge, Cambridge, UK

The conclusions presented here sum up the contributions in the *Special Issue* regarding the managing of China's energy sector, particularly regarding the demand and profile of energy as well as the marketization of the sector. Strategic, organizational and policy issues relevant to the main theme are set out. Both demand and supply scenarios for the nation's energy are seen as in flux, as the economy slackens and dependence on imports rises. Unprecedented levels of urban environmental pollution and steady growth of energy consumption in the wake of a rising living standard have brought the issue to headline-prominence as never before. China's rapidly increasing renewable energy will not change its heavy reliance on coal and a lesser extent oil in the coming decade. After decades of transformation, China's energy sector now operates in a domestic market characterized by strong governmental influence and monopolistic state firms. Abroad, China's firms are exposed to heavier market pressure and competition. While the state's policies have succeeded in ensuring energy supplies and propelling China's renewable energy manufacturers into global prominence and opening up domestic market, much room for improvement exists in the competitiveness of the domestic market and domestic energy firms, transparency of pricing and the effectiveness of regulation.

Introduction

In this concluding contribution, we will try to present an overview of the main upshot of this *Special Issue*.

As the World Bank (2014, 1) has noted:

China's *12th Five-Year Plan* (2011–2015) ... highlights the development of services and measures to address environmental and social imbalances, setting targets to reduce pollution, to increase energy efficiency, to improve access to education and healthcare, and to expand social protection. Its annual growth target of 7 percent signals the intention to focus on quality of life, rather than pace of growth.

With the news that China will pass a new environmental law, it is clear that the pressure of public opinion has had its effect on the Chinese legislature to deal with the above issues. According to *Xinhua* – 'Senior Chinese lawmakers on Wednesday expressed concerns over the country's low energy efficiency and high emissions, as a recent report suggested that China is lagging behind its energy conservation and emission reduction targets' (*Xinhua* 2014, 1). China has set tight targets for emission cuts and energy saving in its *12th Five-Year Plan* (2011–2015), by which consumption of energy per unit of GDP should be cut by 16% and carbon dioxide emissions should fall by 17% by 2015 from the levels of 2010.

China's recent economic slowdown has also focused attention of the demand and supply for energy. But the percentage of imports in China's energy-mix is rising. Among its worries are the strategic ones relating to movement of oil-tankers which come from the Gulf as they pass through the Malacca Straits. There is even talk of building an access-port on the Burmese coast and moving oil by pipeline straight to the Chinese mainland. Its imports of oil projected to surpass those of the USA as the world's largest importer by 2015 and to become its largest oil consumer, say, by 2030.

On the demand side, the utilization of energy has slackened. Economists have long looked at energy consumption as a proxy for economic growth and no less in the Chinese case (see Rawski 2001, 347). A falling rate of growth may mean less energy is consumed if the official statistics can be trusted (see Sinton 2001, 373). Domestic coal demand is down and prices have fallen. On the supply side, it is clear that national resources are under constraint – China already produces almost a quarter of the world's coal – but domestic supplies are feeling the brunt. China's coal boom is coming to an end as high labour costs add to its woes. The government is threatening to close high-cost coal-fired power stations. Nevertheless, this slowdown in energy demand may be a development in the short or intermediate term. In the long run, as urbanization is almost sure to progress and the people's living standard to increase energy consumption may well be on the upward trend.

However, China has allegedly embarked on a 'green revolution'; it has abundant alternative energy resources:

> China has abundant clean energy resources. Hydroelectricity has the potential of 600 million kilowatts, wind and solar power generation can reach 2.5 billion kilowatts and 2.7 billion kilowatts respectively. If all these resources can be converted into electricity effectively, 50% of China's energy consumption can come from non-fossil fuel sources. (see *Wall Street Journal*, 2014, 1)

On the other hand, talk of a 'green revolution' may not only be glib, but even premature given the extent of China's energy dilemmas. China is now estimated to be the world's top emitter of greenhouse gases, having overtaken the USA in 2007. The degree of pollution in Beijing is already almost unprecedented by WHO standards. In late Winter 2014, the concentration of PM 2.5 particles – those which go deep into the lungs and into the bloodstream – rose to 505 micrograms per cubic metre, where the international agency recommends a safe level of around 25. Scientists talk of it resembling a 'nuclear winter'. According to a 2012 *Asian Development Bank* report, less than 1% of China's 500 biggest cities would satisfy the WHO's air quality standards. The possible effects on health and life expectations are dire. Environmental damage, in total, may be costing up to 10% of the nation's growth annually. Yet a pro-active reduction of GDP expansion is not really on the agenda.

In light of the severity and colossal implications of energy in China, it is imperative that a rigorous and timely understanding of this topic be generated. This *Special Issue* has delivered a robust attempt to address issues related to this topic. These topics include the current and projected conditions of energy demand and energy mix, the role of and governmental policies towards renewable energy, the reform, regulation and corporate governance of gigantic state-energy firms, the internationalization of the largest state oil and gas firms, and the rise and transformation of the solar PV industry and market.

Findings

The main themes of the contributions to this *Special Issue* are listed in Table 1.

The *common threads* linking the above contributions to this Symposium are threefold. The first is the economic importance of energy in general and of coal as an energy source, as well as the phenomenal rise of renewable energy. The second is the international significance of China's energy firms, especially those related to oil and gas and solar PV manufacturers. The third is the omnipresent influence of the state in the transformation of the conventional and renewable energy sectors in China.

The *distinctive threads* differentiating the contributions to this *Special Issue* may be found to relate to Thomson and Boey (forthcoming), Lai, O'hara, and Wysoczanska (forthcoming), Gress (forthcoming) and Fan et al. (Wu et al. forthcoming). Thomson and Boey (forthcoming) suggest that China's energy consumption will continue to grow, and while China's dependence on coal, and to a lesser extent on oil, will continue, the contribution from nuclear, gas and renewable energy will rise. They also suggest a growing role for nuclear and gas energy. Lai, O'hara and Wysoczanska (forthcoming) highlight the growing international investment profile of Sinopec and CNPC and the relative prominence of strategic assets and sectoral specialization in the overseas deals of both giants. Gress (forthcoming) uncovers the importance of commercial and cultural factors in the Chinese solar PV firms. He finds that firms place critical importance on product, price and competency when choosing suppliers and buyers, somewhat typical of high-tech firms, but that there is none the less a lingering influence of culture, location and personal relationships on these decisions, particularly for firms less firmly ensconced in global networks. Wu et al. (forthcoming) devote their attention to the factors underlying embedded carbon footprint (ECF) across provinces in China. They find that the coastal provinces have the highest per-capita ECF and that per-capita disposable income determines the per-capita ECF. They also find that a higher level of per-capita income

Table 1.   The main themes of the contributions.

- Development and diversification of energy profile
  STRATEGIC

- Development and pattern of China's renewable energy
  STRATEGIC

- Reform of national state-owned energy enterprises (SOEs) and SOEs–state relations
  ORGANIZATIONAL

- Reform and corporate governance of SOEs
  GOVERNANCE

- Pattern and rationale of overseas investment of China's major energy firms
  ECONOMIC

- State subsidies and domestic and international markets of China's Solar PV industry
  POLICY

- Global networks and expansion of China's solar PV industry
  ORGANIZATIONAL

- Spatial differentiation of per capita embedded carbon footprint (ECF) in urban China and key determinants
  GEOGRAPHICAL

in a province is associated with lower consumption and ECF of food, housing, as well as health, education and recreation, but a higher level of transport and related ECF.

Many of these deal with a range of policy issues related to energy and the energy business. Thomson and Boey (forthcoming) caution against the excessive optimism over renewable energy in China and point to the continuous dominance of coal as an energy source in the coming decades. They do see greater room for policies promoting diversification of energy sources, such as nuclear, gas, wind and solar power. Dent (forthcoming) gives credit to the state-directed expansion of renewable energy in China. He sees the state's policy of mixing regulatory mandates, financial support and market-based tools as a key to China's rapid rise as the leader in renewable energy generation capacity in the world. Through public investment and state-energy firms, the state acts as a supplier of public goods in jump-starting the growth of renewable energy and making them gradually commercially viable. The only exception to public investment is in the solar PV industry, which has remained largely private. Seconding Dent's thesis is Chen's (forthcoming) argument that the state's subsidies have helped the solar PV and wind power manufacturers in China to conquer the global market at the early stage of their development. Chen (forthcoming) also argues that at a later stage, the state's subsidies are helping the solar PV and wind turbine manufacturers to expand the still premature domestic market and reduce their reliance on the saturated international market. The reform of state-energy firms also relates closely to policies. Liao (forthcoming) argues that the Chinese government has only embraced half-hearted restructuring and allows colossal state-energy firms to continue to exercise a massive influence on price setting and the disposal of their profits. Rooker (forthcoming) sheds light on the limits of reform of state-energy firms and deficiency of corporate governance, which is reflected in the absence of growth in market-based financing for these firms.

Discussion

Our aforementioned findings can be summarized as two 'betweens' – between conventional and renewable energy and between the market and the state. There are three main points to make here. The first following point relates to the first between, whereas the second and third following points concern the second between.

First, a range of energy sources will coexist and expand in China. These sources include coal and oil, renewable energy – chiefly hydro, wind and solar power, as well as cleaner or advanced conventional energy such as gas and nuclear. While China will continue to expand and reply on coal and oil, the country will expand its use of nuclear and gas power, which has thus far been severely underutilized. In May 2014, Russian state-controlled entities Gazprom and China National Petroleum Corp (CNPC) signed a $400-billion and 30-year gas supply deal in Shanghai. Under this biggest energy contract that it has ever signed Russia will begin delivering gas from 2018, gradually increasing to 38 billion cubic metres a year and totalling over 1 trillion cubic metres for a whole contractual period (BBC 2014). More importantly, renewable energy in China will grow even much faster than coal and oil, consolidating China's status as the leader in power-generation capacity of renewable energy. We will thus expect to see explosive expansion of China's firms specialized in renewable energy especially wind and solar, and to a lesser extent, hydro. Also, a surge in the use of energy sources such as nuclear and gas is likely. We should also expect steady growth of firms specialized in conventional energy such as coal and oil.

Second, the state has been and will remain a major player in the development and transformation of the energy sector in China. As Dent (forthcoming), Chen (forthcoming) and Gress (forthcoming) document, the state plays an instrumental role in strategically grooming the infant industry of solar PV and wind power manufacturers in the international market and then in the domestic Chinese market. No wonder in a survey conducted by Gress (forthcoming), solar PV firms in China attached high importance to their ties with national and local governments. On the downside, the state is reluctant to decisively turn the largest energy firms into truly market-based corporate players. It allows them to enjoy near-monopoly positions in their own sectors, wield strong leverage on energy policies, and enjoy and use internal financing as a way to escape the disciplining of market-based financing.

Third, the market exercises its influence directly in sectors with pervasive global linkages (such as the solar PV manufacturing and state firms listed in the international market), but less so in sectors which have less international exposure (such as coal and oil production and electricity generation). Gress (forthcoming), for example, finds that Chinese solar PV firms are highly cognizant of the importance of both national and local governments abroad to their business success, and that they engage international trade shows to build corporate and brand recognition globally. Interestingly, he also finds that enrolling in global networks impacts the depth and breadth of Chinese solar PV firm supplier and buyer networks abroad. In addition, Rooker (forthcoming) finds that major Chinese oil and petrochemical firms (especially firms other than CNPC and Sinopec) have relied more on related party transactions and internal financing, and that they have resorted less to market-based financing which implies corporate oversights and market disciplines. When dealing with international corporate players and in making overseas investment, Lai, O'hara, and Wysoczanska (forthcoming) find that market-based factors such as sectoral specialization and strategic assets have been granted prominent consideration.

Conclusions

Our conclusions point to the strides and limits in the transformation of the energy sector in China. As highlighted above, the state has successfully overseen and funded the rise of renewable energy firms as global players of manufactures. It has also allowed the largely oil and gas firms to expand aggressively around the world. Yet there is much to desire for in terms of marketization of state-energy firms especially inside China and of the transparency of energy policies. Viewed in this light, the transformation of the energy sector in China is incomplete, stuck between the state and the market. Limits are apparent in areas concerning institutions and regulations, such as corporate governance, corporate financing and competitive pricing to the advantage of consumers. Nevertheless, the Chinese policy-makers might have seen the situation very differently – they have come to abhor the free market whose vice has been shown in its ugly full form via the economic rampage caused by the financial crisis in 2008. They may accept the hybrid of a state-directed market as a 'virtuous model' for economic and corporate development in China.

Turning to the issue of energy mixture, the continuous prominence of energy sources such as coal and oil in China can have dire implications for the world. Combustion of per unit of coal and oil generates far higher carbon emission than other energy sources such as gas and renewable energy sources. Furthermore, as Wu et al. (forthcoming) suggest, per-capita ECF will inevitably grow when per-capita disposable income rises across provinces in China. China is certainly heading towards this direction with continuous, albeit slowing, economic growth. The Chinese may also view increasing energy consumption as their natural right similar to that enjoyed by residents in developed economies. This downside of expanding energy demand is mitigated partially by the explosive growth of renewable energy in China.

As *The Economist* (2013, 1) has put it:

Yet China also has advantages in addressing its – and the world's – environmental problems. Its leaders understand the challenge of climate change better than their predecessors and perhaps their international peers, too. They are good at taking action on high-priority issues. Because the country is a late developer, it should be able to learn from the mistakes of others – and not build energy-guzzling cities. China has a huge domestic market, cheap capital and sunny, windy deserts: the ideal environment to build a zero-carbon energy system. It is the silver lining of a very dark cloud. If China cannot do it, no one can.

References

(All contributions to the *Special Issue* mentioned above are not specifically noted in the references below, the reader is asked to refer to the Contents for these).

BBC. 2014. "Russia Signs 30-year Gas Deal with China." Accessed 21 May 2014. http://www.bbc.co.uk/news/business-27503017

Chen, G. Forthcoming. "From Mercantile Strategy to Domestic Demand Stimulation: Changes in China's Solar PV Subsidies." *Asia-Pacific Business Review*. doi:10.1080/13602381.2014.939897

The Economist. 2013. "China and the Environment: The East is Grey." *The Economist*, 10 August 2013. Accessed 1 May 2014. http://www.economist.com/news/briefing/21583245-china-worlds-worst-polluter-largest-investor-green-energy-its-rise-will-have

Dent, C. Forthcoming. "China's Renewable Energy Development: Policy, Industry and Business Perspectives." *Asia-Pacific Business Review*. doi:10.1080/13602381.2014.939892

Fan, J., Y. Wu, X. Guo, D. Zhao, and D. Marinova. Forthcoming. "Regional Disparity of Embedded Carbon Footprint and Its Sources in China: A Consumption Perspective." *Asia-Pacific Business Review*. doi:10.1080/13602381.2014.939899

Gress, D. Forthcoming. "Enrolling in Global Networks and Contingencies for China's Solar PV Industry." *Asia-Pacific Business Review*. doi:10.1080/13602381.2014.939898

Lai, H., S. O'Hara, and K. Wysoczanska. Forthcoming. "Rationale of Internationalization of China's NOCs: Seeking Natural Resources, Strategic Assets, or Sectoral Specialization?" *Asia-Pacific Business Review*. doi:10.1080/13602381.2014.939896

Liao, J. X. Forthcoming. "The Chinese Government and the National Oil Companies (NOCs): Who Is the Principal?" *Asia-Pacific Business Review*. doi:10.1080/13602381.2014.939893

Rawski, T. G. 2001. "What's Happening to China's GDP Statistics?" *China Economic Review* 12 (4): 347–354.

Rooker, T. Forthcoming. "Corporate Governance or Governance by Corporates? Testing Governmentality in the Context of China's National Oil and Petrochemical Business Groups." *Asia-Pacific Business Review*. doi:10.1080/13602381.2014.939895

Sinton, J. E. 2001. "Accuracy and Reliability of China's Energy Statistics." *China Economic Review* 12 (4): 373–383.

Thomson, E., and A. Boey. Forthcoming. "The Role of Oil and Gas in China's Energy Strategy: An Overview." *Asia-Pacific Business Review*. doi:10.1080/13602381.2014.939890

Wall Street Journal. 2014. "The Smart Way to Power China." *Wall Street Journal*, 24 April 2014. Accessed 27 April 2014. http://online.wsj.com/news/articles/SB1000142405270230451870457 9521082841768734

World Bank. 2014. *Overview*. Washington, DC: World Bank. Accessed 1 May 2014. http://www.worldbank.org/en/country/china/overview

Xinhua. 2014. "Report, Chinese Lawmakers Worried Over Energy Efficiency and Emissions." Accessed 25 April 2014. http://news.xinhuanet.com/english/china/2014-04/23/c_126426250.htm

Index

Note: Page numbers in *italics* represent tables
Page numbers in **bold** represent figures
Page numbers followed by 'n' refer to notes

INDEX